RETAILING MANAGEMENT

Retailing Management

Analysis, Planning and Control

David Walters
Marketing Subject Leader, European Business School

First published 1994 by
THE MACMILLAN PRESS LTD
Houndmills, Basingstoke, Hampshire RG21 2XS
and London
Companies and representatives
throughout the world

ISBN 0–333–60805–4 hardcover
ISBN 0–333–60806–2 paperback

A catalogue record for this book
is available from the British Library.

Printed in Great Britain by

Antony Rowe Ltd
Chippenham, Wiltshire

This book was written during a period of personal difficulties and it is time to say that without the moral support of Lynda, of my family and the Wrights, it may never have been completed. It is dedicated to them all with thanks. They are owed much more than I can ever repay.

Contents

List of Tables and Figures

Tables

Figures

Acknowledgements

Experience over the years suggests that writing books is a much easier task than typing the manuscripts, producing diagrams and listening patiently to numerous ideas. Two people undertook this task. Suzannah, my daughter, spent many hours at the word processor producing the manuscript. In the process her four children were clearly neglected and I can only hope that 'Garr' will not always be seen as the 'Demon' responsible. Lynda, my partner, and her son Christopher, put up with a house that often resembled the aftermath of a paperchase, long periods of uncooperative silence as well as long spells on the word processor.

I am convinced that I had much the easier time.

DAVID WALTERS

1 Understanding How the Business Makes Decisions: Corporate Strategy, Critical Success Factors and Strategy Implementation

INTRODUCTION

The purpose of this book is to explore the implementation issues of strategy decisions and to do this requires an understanding of how the business functions. In this first chapter we discuss these functions within the context of revenue generation, margin and management and cashflow management. Our interests are much more concerned with the management of these business functions rather than the accounting procedures that they present managers.

Given that the focus of interest is concerned with implementation rather than the development of strategy some brief reference is to be made to strategic options facing retailing businesses. The reference is made in order that the subsequent activities may then be placed in context. It is necessary to do this if we are to consider the usefulness of critical success factor appraisal, and the resultant strategy implementation issues and actions.

The concept of added value is important in this discussion. Customer expectations and customer satisfaction are typically equated by offering an additional component to the transaction, this component is added value. Added value may be seen as core product benefits, tangible product characteristics or product augmentation; product in this context is of course the retail offer, i.e. merchandise, customer service, store environment and communication/information.

Creating added value requires management to commit resources to specific purposes and this requires them to take decisions concerning the allocation of resources. The resources, fixed and current assets, are essentially scarce in that financial constraints limit the access of the firm to an inexhaustible asset base.

Consequently, for management to implement strategy they must be aware of the major performance components of the business and how those relate with each other internally and how they are coordinated to achieve successful performance externally. The task of utilising assets to create competitive

1

advantage is as much a result of skilful implementation of strategic response as is the strategic response decision.

1.1   UNDERSTANDING THE BUSINESS AND ITS CUSTOMERS' RESPONSES

Retailing management is concerned with four primary functions: it must generate sales; it must generate adequate gross margins. It must manage operations such that all expenses and transactions are paid and an acceptable return on shareholder investment is achieved. It must also generate cash for both the operational activities and strategic development of the business.

To do this effectively requires a detailed understanding of the business, and of how retailing businesses operate. In Figure 1.1 a basic model of a retailing company is represented. The model illustrates the primary functions quoted in the previous paragraph. It identifies the four functions and the activities associated with each of them. Sales volumes are maximised when the company has a clear target customer group to aim for. This not only requires a clear understanding of the expectations of the customer group, it also requires an understanding of the additional 'offer' characteristics that if presented to the customer would result in increased sales and loyalty. The issue can be simply described:

If customer perceptions > customer expectations:
customer satisfaction is achieved.

Clearly:

If customer perceptions < customer expectations:
customer satisfaction is not achieved.

And:

If customer perceptions + added value > customer expectations:
customer satisfaction + competitive advantage is achieved.

It follows that efforts made to identify target customer groups' specific expectations can be very rewarding for the retail company. We shall return to this topic in detail.

Effective merchandise selection is essential if both customer satisfaction and competitive advantage is to be realised. There is another aspect to this activity. Effective merchandise selection, through relevant buying and merchandising decisions create the gross margins from which, provided sales volumes are sufficiently large, sufficient funds are generated to meet operational expenses and to provide cash to expand the business results. We

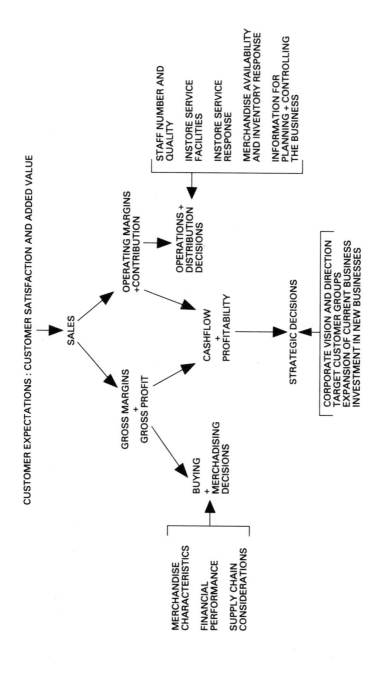

Figure 1.1   Retail business activities and decision areas

shall explore the detail of effective merchandise selection in Chapter 3. Here it is sufficient to suggest that there are three concerns: merchandise characteristics (these should meet customer expectations of choice, quality, exclusivity, etc.) ; financial performance (the margins to be achieved in quantitative terms) and; the supply chain considerations (the service performance levels to be achieved, by whom, when and where).

Operations and distribution decisions are another important component in the   model of the retailing business. Cost-effective management of these activities results in customer satisfaction, enhances added value, and of course has an important influence on cashflow and profitability. The activities which influence the size of the resulting operation margins will be discussed later, but from Figure 1.1 they can be seen to be concerned with the management of staff, merchandise, space and services. Effective control is achieved by timely and accurate information flows.

Retailing businesses are ongoing activities. If they are to be expanded such that the rewards to the owners continue (i.e. an increase in both dividend and share value) and if the other stakeholders' interests are to be satisfied (e.g. continuous employment for the staff with personal growth and development opportunities; expanding business for suppliers, etc.) it follows that strong cashflows and profit streams are required. It also follows that both can only be achieved if the business is managed efficiently and effectively. The strategic decisions suggested by Figure 1.1 can only be considered if the management has identified a target customer group opportunity that is capable of generating a sufficiently large sales volume. It is also necessary that the buying and merchandise decisions that are taken achieve both customer expectations *and* also company expectations for gross margin and stockturn performances. Further, the cost-effective management of the operations and distributions activities is essential if there is to be a financial capacity and capability to enable strategic options to be pursued. It follows that without a healthy business, the strategic development of the business becomes more difficult, particularly if funds have to be borrowed from the money markets or if further share capital is issued (and, as a consequence, control is diminished).

Effective retail management is achieved when the decision making is coordinated throughout the business. The impact of decisions taken in one area of the business can have serious implications for other functions. For example, a decision to expand the merchandise range by adding related product groups will create demands for space in retail branches, may require specialist sales activities, will require distribution service and create an extra demand for working capital. In the medium and long term there may well be an impact on fixed capital requirements, due to a demand for an expansion of fixed assets and capital equipment. An example of how management decisions can create unforeseen problems occurred some years ago. In the late 1970s Tesco decided to focus on a price offer (Operation Checkout) rather than the existing trading stamp incentive. The sales increases were very large due to the success of the decision, so large in fact that the distribution system was put under immense pressure as the customer demands increased and as the Company strived to maintain availability service in their outlets. Subsequently a review of depot needs was undertaken and building programmes accelerated. Effective management is coordinated management and coordinated management can only be achieved when the management understands the inter-related nature of its business. Part III of this text is devoted to exploring this topic.

1.2   STRATEGY: DEVELOPMENT AND IMPLEMENTATION

In any discussion concerning the management of a business we have to place the decisions to be implemented within the context of the strategic decisions that have been taken. The examples given in Figure 1.1 (Corporate vision and direction, identification of target customer groups, expansion of the current business and, investment in new businesses) can only be implemented if a clear view of corporate expectations accompanies these intentions. Clearly it requires more than this. The board (or management group responsible for the decisions) will have considered the external business environment (and the opportunities their appraisal suggests are available) together with a review of the internal (company) capabilities and capacities which may operate to enhance or constrain their strategic initiatives.

They are influenced in their decisions by not only their appraisal of the business opportunities offered by the external environment and the internal characteristics but also by past performance and, more importantly, the reasons for that performance. Figure 1.2 suggests a structure of this process. It portrays a situation in which the company's performance during the past five years has been compared with those of competitors and the economy. From this appraisal a number of strategic directional options have been identified (i.e. consolidation and productivity, repositioning, growth and diversification). The basis of the selection of strategies from these options is the result of the external and internal review of the business in its environment. Thus given an objective view of the future of the business environment and the extent of the opportunities it offers, together with an equally objective view of the company's capabilities and capacities, the strategic options to be pursued to meet specific objectives can be determined. The outcome is a realistic view of how the planning gap may be filled together with an assessment of the risk involved. The task of the 'executive' is to determine the precise requirements for the *revised objectives* together with a view of the levels of risk they consider the company capable of assuming.

Clearly there is an interesting balance to be decided between risk and

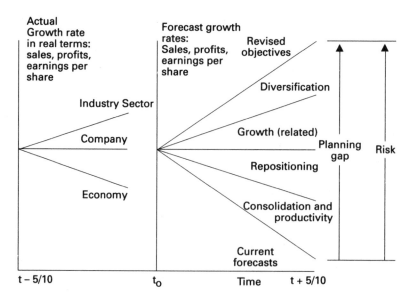

Figure 1.2   Strategic options are conditioned by past performance

return. For example, if the company pursues a *consolidation and productivity strategy* (increased performance from the existing resource base to provide margin, volume, and asset utilisation improvements) the risk is low but so too is the expected rate of return. A *repositioning strategy* (meeting the changing needs of existing customers and related customer segments) increases both risk and return, however, the increase in risk should not be very large because the business is operating within a familiar environment and the resource allocation requirements are not large. A *growth strategy* (expansion into related merchandise areas or trading environments) is accompanied with increasing risk as resources are allocated in an increasingly unfamiliar environment: any decision to pursue growth should be justified by higher returns to the business. *Diversification* (expansion into new merchandise areas, new trading/delivery formats, customer services or service products; conglomerate and international activities) requires considerable returns for the resources allocated, risk is high and clearly if opportunity costs are considered the cost of failure can be considerable.

1.3   EVALUATING STRATEGIC OPTIONS

The selection of an appropriate strategy will be influenced by a number of considerations. The issues of strategic fit and of organisational structure are major issues. There are others. Rumelt (1988) proposes four criteria that should be applied to a business strategy:

- *Consistency*: the strategy must not present mutually inconsistent goals and policies.
- *Consonance*: the strategy must represent an adaptive response to the external environment and to the critical changes occurring within it.
- *Advantage*: the strategy must provide for the creation and/or maintenance of competitive advantage in the selected area.
- *Feasibility*: the strategy must neither overtax available resources nor create unsolvable sub-problems.

He suggests that a strategy which fails to meet one or more of these criteria is strongly suspect. He suggests further that '... Experience within a particular industry or other setting will permit the analyst to sharpen these criteria and add others that are appropriate to the situation at hand.'

It is possible to add to Rumelt's criteria and to consider their use as evaluation criteria during the formulation and implementation of strategy. Clearly the influence of each criterion will vary according to the strategic change considered. The evaluation process will review corporate, functional and support strategies. The criteria we shall use, together with a description of their applications are:

Consistency

The strategy should be consistent throughout the range of components within the strategic planning process. The consistency should be both longitudinal and temporal. Longitudinal consistency is concerned with decisions taken throughout the hierarchy of strategies, i.e. corporate, functional and support strategies. For example, a *corporate strategy* decision to reposition the company should be reflected through the *functional strategies* by changes in merchandise characteristics; customer service facilities [such as an emphasis on determining services (those elements of customer service additional to the expected levels of service known as qualifying services)]. See Walters (1988), Cook and Walters (1991). The consistency of trading format and store environment should be reflected in a relevant approach to visual merchandising and in customer communications by the increased use of customer store selection and purchasing behaviour information in promotional activities.

Within the *support strategies* consistency is maintained by ensuring that marketing services for research and development activities are co-ordinated to facilitate the decisions taken in positioning and functional strategies. Finance can be seen to have numerous influences. Not only must funds be available to ensure adequate investment in both fixed and working capital at an acceptable cost but also that in arranging the availability of capital there will not be unexpected demands for unusually (inconsistently) high levels of performance for profitability. The implications for operations concerns the management of store personnel and facilities such that the expectations of customers are met and are consistent with the changes that the positioning has brought about. Distribution's task will be to ensure that merchandise allocation and availability levels are established and maintained. Human resources strategy should consider the number and quality of staff required to meet the new positioning, together with a review and the restructuring of development and training programmes. Finally the systems strategy should be concerned with changes in decision support systems and to identify changes in the patterns of information content and flows that will be necessary if systems consistency is to be maintained.

There are issues concerning other components of the 'management system structure'. Clearly a major concern is consistency between strategy changes and the values of the management, 'owners' and employee groups. If the strategy formulation process has been managed effectively then inconsistencies should not occur, however, it is here where the temporal aspect of consistency is important. If the future direction of growth is likely to create conflict with the groups' values it is possible that their interests may well be affected. For example, job specifications and power structures may shift (particularly if the strategy is divergent over the planning horizon). Structure is another component of the management structure system that may change over time. Consider the impact of repositioning, leading to the development of specialist formats on a business with a simple configuration and organisation structure. A move towards a divisionalised structure can create major inconsistency for resource allocation. Similarly there are implications for style and skills. Patterns of decision making and delegation will change and may be inconsistent with the existing business. A repositioning strategy may also result in a change in the effectiveness of basic skills as elements of distinctive competence. (The notion of a management structure system is based upon the work of Waterman, Peters and Phillips [1980].)

Consonance

This was described earlier as an adaptive response to the external environment and to the critical changes occurring within it. There are three elements of change to which the business must adapt. The first is the environment itself. Business history is replete with case histories of companies failing to monitor change and then to consider the implications of those changes for its corporate direction.

The second concerns the competitive environment. Not only are existing competitors attempting to change and to 'fit' into the new environment but new competitors appear as new opportunities are identified, or perhaps as technology offers more cost-effective delivery methods in existing product-markets. The third element of change concerns the business itself. Major elements of the management structure system are likely to change with changes in senior managerial personnel. A new chief executive may bring with him a radically different view of major issues comprising the company's values set. It is almost certain that he will bring a different view of corporate direction and this may involve changes in senior managerial roles.

The issue of consonance also has longitudinal aspects in as much as changes in the business environment should be met and matched with a change in corporate direction that has identified, and responds to the changes with a logic that is indeed consonant with the changes perceived.

The competitive issues of consonance require the company to focus upon what Rumelt describes as the difference across firms at a given time. He makes a comparison between what he describes as 'generic' and 'competitive' strategies. The generic strategy of the firm is the basic pattern of economic relationships that characterise the business and determine whether or not sufficient value is being created to sustain the corporate direction (this assumes the corporate direction to be a valid response to the current business environment). The competitive response is essentially a switch of emphasis. The analysis is comparative and external, for example the competitive view of return to the firm is concerned with return on investment and the measure of success is market share rather than sales growth. The issue of consonance in this context is to ensure that the view of competition and competitive comparative measures are similar to those of competitors; if they are not, the result may be that the company distances itself from the market place.

The third aspect of consonance concerns the company itself. Here the concern is that the management structure system reflects the attitudes, perceptions, expectations (as well as the structure, style, systems, etc.) that are shared by businesses that are in their sector and indeed by those who are not directly in contact. The point we make is simply that if this consonance does not exist on both an intra- and inter-business basis the company will find itself confronted with difficulties in recruiting key personnel as well as problems in such aspects of its business as sourcing, etc.

An interesting aspect of consonance in this context is that of structure. Many businesses develop and expand around a broad specialisation. This specialisation broadens over time and diversification opportunities begin to be appraised against increasingly broader criteria. There comes a point at which the management structure system becomes stressed. For example, structure requirements for a business only operating a chain of news, stationery, books and music outlets changes considerably when DIY is added. The other elements also experience change. Systems for planning and control differ as do the management information requirements – to meet structure and, therefore, decision making differences. Management style may differ markedly (certainly between the base business and the new business in this example) with management behaviour being much more 'aggressive' in the new business with more centralised control. Staff requirements together with methods of recruitment, training, etc. may differ markedly as may the motivation and incentives required to match different job specifications. Differentiation and distinctive competences are very likely to occur. In the example given, the base business may well find that providing customer choice (merchandise led differentiation) supported by a satisfactory (to the customer) level of service is necessary to provide the company with a sustainable level of competitive advantage. The new business may well find that it is customer service that provides it with differentiation. Values also differ. Many businesses find that recently acquired businesses have quite different attitudes, and approaches to staff, suppliers and possibly customers. Given these issues it makes good business sense to reconsider the structure of the business. Companies facing such problems have divisionalised and have opted for a conglomerate structure within which the components operate as entities with their own management system structures (and objectives). Their task is to meet the performance requirements of the 'centre'.

'The key to evaluating consonance is an understanding of why the business, as it currently stands, exists at all and how it assumed its current pattern', (Rumelt). Once this is understood, together with an understanding of the economic model of the business, the impact of changes can be assessed.

Continuity

If strategy is to be successful, then as a long run initiative, it should be developed with continuity in mind. Gilbert and Strebel (1988) (in a discussion on competitive advantage) consider the importance of the industry life cycle (see Figure 1.3). During the emergence stage, innovation and development are important issues. Standardisation marks the first important transition whereby the product (or offer) or the manufacturing/distribution process becomes an industry and rapid growth takes place. The few (but large) industry competitors seek to rejuvenate the product/offer.

Multiple food retailing and DIY have demonstrated this life cycle effect. Asda in the late 1960s and early 1970s developed the superstore concept. Large units with wide choice for customers, located out of town or on the edge of town provided the convenience of easier car parking. This was the emergent stage of the cycle. Industry views concerning standardisation were 'agreed' as Sainsbury, Tesco and others developed similar formats and rapid growth took place. Maturity comprised a situation of fierce local competition; initially for sites and once developed, for customers. Rejuvenation comprises elements of merchandise-led and/or customer service-led differentiation. Wider and deeper ranges have been introduced and customer services and service facilities have also been added.

The issue of continuity concerns the impact of the industry life cycle on the management system structure. There will undoubtedly be significant impact on some elements such as systems, style, staff and skills with considerable

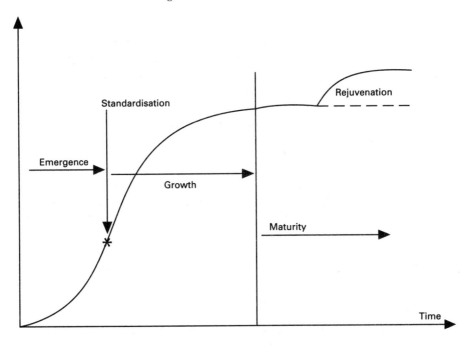

Figure 1.3   The industry life cycle

Source: Gilbert, X. and Strebel, P., 'Developing Competitive Advantage', in Quinn,
J.B., Mintzberg, H. and James, R.M., *The Strategy Process* (New Jersey:
Prentice Hall)

impact on structure and values. Clearly it is not always possible to forecast
the development of specific life cycles. However, often it is possible to
reach conclusions on how the industry may develop given similar situations in other industry activity chains. An example of similar, even parallel
development has been that of the large scale DIY format which is (like
food retailing) dominated by few competitors operating large off-centre retail
units. Forecasting such patterns of development enable the participants to
develop the necessary continuity characteristics for competitive advantage.

It follows that continuity may well be disrupted by future developments
within the company's business sector. The impact of these discontinuities
should be considered during the strategy evaluation process. At best they
may be provided for within the context of the strategy but failing this they
will have been identified and can be expected and their impact minimised.

Creativity

The extent to which a strategy is creative will vary. It could be assumed
that there is more scope for creative thinking when the corporate direction

proposes a strategy which is new to the company and some 'distance' from its current activities. However, if we consider the problems created by the recession of the early 1990s, it is likely that the creative strategies were those aimed at improving performance through consolidation and productivity rather than diversification. Similarly in periods of growth the successful companies are those who identify opportunities in adjacent product-markets or who offer specialist formats with specific focussing in a sector in which they are established.

It is suggested then that creativity is a way of looking at strategic problems rather than offering new and different approaches to the corporate direction. The creative strategy is that which uses the existing management system structure to develop competitive advantage together with a higher competitive performance profile than its major competitors. Consider an example.

The 'Next phenomena' was initially successful because it capitalised on an opportunity to respond to a particular 'need' for a targeted merchandise and trading format in a period of economic boom. Consumer spending was at a high level and the creative approach by Next received a dramatic response. With hindsight what we see is a management system structure being created in which the strategy element was clearly dominant and prescribed the characteristics of the other elements. Thus the skills, structure, systems, style, staff and most importantly the values were developed around a retailing innovation. The problems arose when it was necessary for retrenchment (consolidation and productivity). The company had, up to this time, thought only in terms of growth and diversification around a successful format: when faced with declining volumes it was unable to redirect its 'creativity'.

Creativity is an important component of the evaluation process. It is a reflection of the ability of the management system structure to respond to quite different external business environment situations. It is rooted in the values of the company and reflects a combination of attitudes towards both internal and external satisfaction requirements and the ability to respond to changes in them as and when the business environment itself changes.

Competitive Advantage

Differentiation and competitive advantage will be discussed in detail later in this chapter. Here it is necessary to make the point concerning the reasons why they are seen as important.

Competitive strategy focusses on the performance differences among firms rather than what it is they have in common. The issues are not so much 'how can this activity be performed?' but rather 'how can we perform it better than our rivals?', and indeed this can be extended to 'what else can we add to it that our rivals either do not have – or could not offer?'.

Thus competitive advantage, and the ways and means it can be created

and sustained becomes a philosophy of the business. At all times throughout the business structure, staff at all levels should be encouraged to think
in terms of how value can be added to the customer offer and to appraise
competitors' offers in the same context. Clearly this is an important feature
within the set of values the company has established and operates within.
However, it will not become a permanent feature unless it is built into the
other elements of the management system structure. Rumelt suggests that
competitive advantage can normally be traced to one of three roots: superior resources, superior skills, or superior position. Resources and skills
reflect the ability of the business to perform better than or at lower cost
than competitors. Positioning advantage implies that it offers at least adequate return on investment and, moreover, can offer the company security
in that often the costs of competition for rivals would be prohibitive. However,
it must be remembered that to be sustainable the basic environmental factors that underlie the decision to adopt the positioning posture remain stable.
Examples of stable and unstable environmental factors can be seen in food
and apparel markets. In food distribution the factors have changed, but have
done so slowly, thus enabling the multiples to maintain their respective
positioning with minimal adjustments. Clothing markets have been dramatically different. The Next format was rapidly imitated and even Marks &
Spencer reacted to what, presumably, they saw as significant shifts in the
environment and the responses of their competitors.

Rumelt comments on the role of size and economies of scale in maintaining positioning. The argument is that volume operations increase
contribution margins and that volume activities are able to amortise the
costs of research and 'offer' development over larger revenue and profit
returns. The additional margins earned can therefore be channelled into increasing differentiation and competitive advantage. There is also an argument which proposes that large volumes and high market shares can lead to
product-market dominance which facilitates a 'leadership' role. In this
way a retailing company can influence the characteristics of competition
towards areas favourable to their skills and resources, which also enhances
credibility.

Capacity Utilisation

The proposed strategy should be evaluated within the context of the utilisation of fixed and current assets. Thus it should be examined with this in
mind. The analysis should consider:

- The utilisation of sales area;
- The utilisation of service area;
- The utilisation of personnel;
- Stocks, flows and the distribution system;

- The return on investment to:
    stockholding;
    customer service facilities;
    customer credit;
- The utilisation of systems.

The utilisation of existing capacities (and of those planned) is an important consideration when strategy is evaluated. Clearly maximum use of both fixed and current assets is essential, but their alternative uses should also be considered. Resources are scarce and opportunities numerous and the decision for managers is *which* opportunity to pursue such that total profits are maximised. Thus it follows that the utilisation of *all* assets is an important consideration.

The model proposed by Figure 1.4 identifies the main components of a retailer's asset base and suggest that it is important to consider the impact of volume throughput in both quantitative and qualitative terms. The quantitative effects are identified by estimating the likely activity levels to be achieved by alternative strategy options. For example stockturn, accounts receivable periods, cash generation; together with measures of contribution (or gross) margin return on investment in each area would suffice as quantitative measures of net current assets. The qualitative measures are based upon customer responses. Customer expectations for variety and choice, together with high levels of availability can be measured in both attitudes and visit and purchasing behaviour. Thus the utilisation and productivity measures should reflect the expectations of the customer base and the activity ratios should reflect both internal and external expectations.

Other qualitative issues concern operating philosophies and methods. Often it is found that to compete successfully (or to launch a new format) a company requires to restructure its 'delivery system'; elements of customer service can shift their priorities from seemingly unimportant roles to become vitally important in the customers' store selection and product purchasing process. Therefore while the capacity may exist, its focus may differ.

Capacity adjustments are also considered in the evaluation. Clearly the fixed and variable cost issues are very important, but equally so too are the effects of time. Fixed assets cannot be expanded rapidly and with this in mind (together with an allowance of time for delays, etc.) the evaluation should consider the implications of such delays.

Capacity

The ability of the company to attempt the strategy within the physical and financial resources available (or reasonably obtainable) has been discussed above. During that discussion we inferred that there are important qualitative issues to be addressed and in this section we will extend the discussion.

15

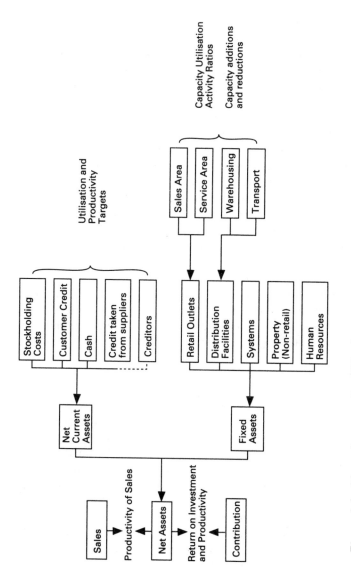

Figure 1.4 Measuring capacity utilisation

Essentially these are the limitations (or more positively, the facilitating characteristics) that are available. Rumelt suggests three basic questions which we consider against the context of the management system structure:

• Has the organisation the problem-solving abilities and competences required to implement the strategy? Given that a strategy provides structure to the general issue of the business goals and approaches to coping with its environment, it follows that it is the role of management to carry out the detailed tasks defined by the strategy. Do the *skills* exist or are they easily obtained? If not the capability of the management system structure must be questioned.

• Does the management system structure have the degree of 'coordinative and integrative skill' necessary to carry out the strategy? The point here is that often new strategies require management to integrate hitherto disparate activities. Flexibility in the *structure* element of the management system structure can facilitate such integration.

• Does the strategy challenge and motivate key managerial personnel and will it gain their acceptance? Here we are considering elements of the management system structure such as *values, style, staff* as well as skills. Without support, skills and other characteristics become unimportant as they cannot be brought into focus.

In many respects these questions reinforce the qualitative issues raised in the previous section. There can be little doubt that they are of prime importance to the process of strategy implementation. Without positive answers to these questions it is arguable whether the strategy would be pursued.

Credibility

Earlier reference was made to the credibility of a strategy decision in the context of expansion into a product category. The suggestion made was that by expanding volume in a particular area the company could influence the customers' expectations and in so doing become the 'market leader'. In other words this would create credibility with the target customer group.

There are five other aspects of credibility that should be considered when evaluating a strategy. These concern the internal credibility of the strategy to the management of its implementation. Another aspect of credibility is that of suppliers, a third concerns the 'owners' of the business and the City, a fourth is the reaction and response of competitors and finally the company should aim to be seen as credible by the community at large.

Customers are the most important of the company's assets. Their continued patronage is the guarantee of continuity for the business. It follows that at all times the company's activities should be seen as logical (and therefore credible) to the target customer group specifically and equally to peripheral, infrequent customers. This requires consistency within the range of positioning decisions; merchandise selection should be within a specified range of criteria, as should the other positioning elements.

Customer service decisions should equally be consistent within the customer service strategy and the store environment (through the role of visual merchandising and service facilities) be integrated into a 'complete offer'. The role of communications is to inform and to persuade and to do so credibly. A poorly directed mailing (wrong target customer and inappropriate offer) will damage the credibility of the company. Hence the positioning strategy statement is a vitally important element of overall strategy. It should tell customers clearly how their expectations are being responded to.

We have referred to the requirement of any strategy to be able to challenge and motivate managerial personnel. To do this effectively requires the management group to accept the strategy as credible. If they believe in the efficacy of the strategy then it will be accepted and they will work towards its implementation. The process by which the management group accepts the strategy as credible will undoubtedly use past experiences and the values and style of the management system to determine its credibility.

Suppliers will appraise their customers' strategy and make their own decisions concerning credibility. Some may seek congruence between their customers' offers and their own products. Their appraisal may be based upon empathy between the product within the customers' assortment or possibly between the product and the store environment. Alternatively, or possibly additionally, the congruence they seek may be the level of customer service offered to purchasers of their products.

Credibility and the shareholder (and the City) is crucial. It is widely accepted (albeit reluctantly) that sector analysts have a powerful influence in the decision whether or not to 'buy, sell or hold'. Clearly this aspect of credibility has more or less significance depending upon whether or not the company is seeking to expand the business. For example, if a rights issue is contemplated, it follows that the company should prepare the 'owners' by demonstrating sound planning for future developments that will increase the returns to the shareholder.

Competitors' attitudes are also very important. A strong market position is difficult to attack if it is supported by customer loyalty which is reflected by high customer traffic flows with high average transactions for each visit. Such a situation may persuade a competitor to pursue an alternative strategy to that of confronting a company which is well supported by its customers.

Finally there is the question of credibility with the community. It is very important that the company develops empathy with the community across the issues that are of current importance. Furthermore, it should take a lead in developing community attitudes towards future issues. Examples of such credibility issues would include recycling of paper and glass, unleaded petrol, youth employment and trade with countries whose internal politics are internationally found to be undesirable.

Corporate Performance

The topic of performance will be dealt with in detail in subsequent chapters. However, it is an important criterion in the overall process of strategy evaluation and is discussed broadly at this point.

The strategy should be capable of producing both marketing and financial performance to satisfy the critical success factors and objectives (discussed next). During the evaluation, forecast revenue and profit streams should therefore be examined with a view to performance across a number of parameters. The 'marketing element' of the strategy should be focused on its achievements to obtain customer performance. We are particularly interested in their activities (which can of course be quantified) and these relate to:

- Frequency of purchasing visits;
- Average transaction value;
- Range of purchases made;
- Repeat visits.

These data for target and peripheral customer groups enable a profile to be constructed of how the business will appear from a traffic flow and revenue aspect. The important feature of the review should be to establish viability of the strategy. For example, it is possible to compare current and forecast customer performance activities: a large disparity should be questioned and examined in detail.

The qualitative aspects of the 'marketing element' are more difficult to evaluate. They consider customer attitudes, their perceptions and expectations of the retail offer. Again we should compare current attitudes with those we expect to obtain in the future. To obtain some measure of future perceptions research should explore the expectations of both target and peripheral customer groups against a background of social change. An example of this type of 'macro-information' is the 'Planning for Social Change' work offered by the Henley Centre and the more specific shopping focussed research of Target Group Index (TGI), etc.

Financial performance should be evaluated at two levels. The first level is a review of the strategic issues of sales, profits and cashflow and their interrelationships. The second level pertains to operating activities and is concerned with productivity measures achieved from space, employees, stockholding and service facilities. Again the concern of the evaluator should be with the viability of projected performance levels. For both levels the issue is: can the strategy proposed produce the performance necessary to meet satisfactory levels of return on existing and proposed investment over the planning horizon without demanding performances from the management system structure which are obviously not possible?   .

1.4 IMPLEMENTING STRATEGY: IDENTIFYING OPTIONS

If the proposed strategy meets these criteria the issue of implementation remains. The use of critical success factors is helpful in the integration as well as the identification of strategic options.

The use of the concept of critical success factors as an aid in business planning is not new. More recently the information management literature has featured the application of critical success factors as part of the process of developing corporate strategy, an information strategy and subsequently an information technology strategy.

The use proposed here is as a means for identifying options for implementing strategy. The examination of the company's business environment will have identified its distinctive competence(s) (its strengths and weaknesses) and will have identified the customer based opportunities and broader environmental based threats that are likely during its planning horizon. From an appraisal of these opportunities and threats together with consideration of past performance and distinctive competence, the performance expectations of the shareholders and other influential groups, and a view of the level of risk seen as acceptable to the business, a quantified objective will be established for the business. This may be a single objective expressed as sales volume, net profit or earnings per share. The outcome of the appraisal will also include broad directions for the corporate strategy options discussed earlier (see Figure 1.2).

Thus given the performance expectations, and the implied level of acceptable risk, expressed in both the objectives and corporate strategy direction, the task of implementation can be commenced.

Figure 1.5 proposes a simple model which describes the options available to management responsible for the implementation task. With the objectives established and a risk profile determined we can use the critical success factors established through customer research to identify and evaluate the corporate strategy options available for implementing strategy decisions of the board.

The first step is to quantify the objectives, i.e. establish rates of increase or perhaps target levels of achievement, for sales volume, gross margin, operating margin, cashflow and productivity performance and to establish qualitative goals for customer added value. With this done critical success factors should be identified, those which have significant influence on the specific objectives being considered. Often critical success factors can be seen to have an influence on more than one objective in which instance it is considered in the context of the objective upon which it has the greater

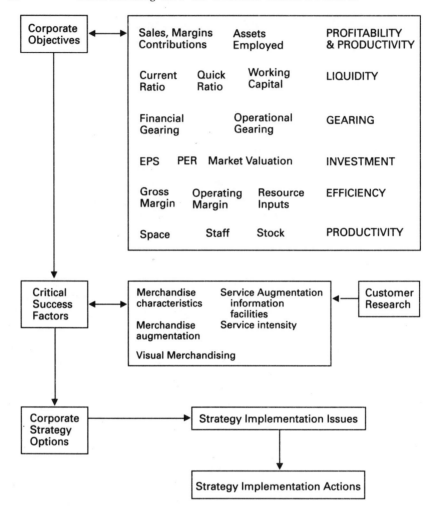

Figure 1.5   Using critical success factors to develop corporate strategy options

impact with a view to making decisions that are not sub-optimal as far as other decisions may be concerned.

1.5   CRITICAL SUCCESS FACTORS: A FORMAT FOR DETERMINING COMPETITIVE ADVANTAGE

Critical success factors (CSFs) are helpful in identifying corporate strategy options by first identifying competitive advantage requirements. These are the issues to be considered if a specific CSF is to be totally effective in its role in contributing towards successfully achieving the target set for the objectives. With both CSFs, strategy options and strategy implementations issues agreed, the process of implementing the strategy should then be clear and can be initiated.

To ensure success in maintaining customer satisfaction all businesses should identify those characteristics or features that are essential to the business: the key issues that the company must accomplish if it is to be successful. Leidecker *et al.* (1984) suggest:

> Critical success factors (CSFs) are those characteristics, conditions or variables that when properly sustained, maintained or managed can have a significant impact on the success of a firm competing in a particular industry. A CSF can be a characteristic such as price advantage, it can also be a condition such as capital structure or advantageous customer mix; or an industry structural characteristics such as vertical integration.

The authors give examples of critical success factors in four industries:

- *Automobile Industry*
  Styling
  Strong dealer network
  Manufacturing cost control
  Ability to meet EPA standards

- *Semi-conductor Industry*
  Manufacturing process: cost efficient, innovative, cumulative experience
  Capital availability
  Technological competence
  Product development

- *Food Processing*
  New product development
  Good distribution
  Effective advertising

- *Life Insurance*
  Development of agency personnel
  Effective control of clerical personnel
  Innovation in policy (product) development
  Innovative advertising
  Marketing strategy

They also discuss the Hofer and Schendel (1978) application of the concept of critical success factors to strategic analysis. Hofer and Schendel suggest that critical success factors are important at three levels of analysis:

specific to the firm, the industry and the economic, social and political environment. Analysis at each level can identify a source of potential critical success factors. At the macro level (the economic, social and political environment) the analysis of opportunities and threats may indicate CSFs that will enable the firm to avoid threats and capitalise on opportunities. An industry analysis focuses the CSFs upon competitive advantage through the valuation of competitors. At the level of the firm the analysis should be aimed at identifying what *has* made the business successful and the factors *necessary* for future success.

Critical success factors identify the requirements for making a successful response to customer expectations and the options for cost-effective 'production' of the attributes which comprise the product–service–delivery offer. Given the CSFs necessary for success (and therefore to create sustainable competitive advantage) the asset structure of the business may be decided. For example, a product–service–delivery offer with little differentiation but with high volume potential may suggest a capital intensive high volume 'production plant' installation. The reverse may obtain an offer which is specialist (and differentiated) requiring changes to be made to meet individual customer specifications. Here the opportunity to use a high volume/low cost approach is clearly limited.

It follows that asset structures and cost structures can vary by industry sector and by market segment. It is necessary, therefore, to identify the CSFs necessary to compete successfully. Not to do so may result in an inappropriate 'offer' to undertake the task of maximising customer satisfaction which in turn may (and almost certainly will) leave the firm in an uncompetitive situation.

The critical success factors we might expect a retailing business to adopt would be developed using the basic elements of its business, i.e. merchandise characteristics, customer service, store environment features and customer communications. Figure 1.5 illustrates how critical success factors may be used to direct linkage between corporate objectives (which are essentially financial in their nature of prescribing expectations) and the strategic options available to the firm.

An essential feature of the 'model' is the customer research activity which identifies the important components of customers' expectations which should be considered in the formulation of the company's critical success factors. It is likely that critical success factors will emerge that link the basic elements. An example of this is visual merchandising. Here, the use of both merchandise and store environment resources to create informative and persuasive displays which are seen as important by customers during their store selection and product purchasing decisions' may assume a dominant role and if this is so, will likely be a critical success factor in its own right.

There are other features that may be important in this respect and while we will be discussing them in detail in subsequent chapters they are intro-

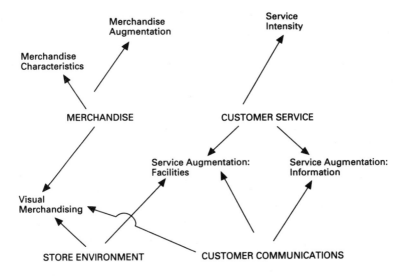

Figure 1.6   Component factors of critical success factors

duced briefly during this discussion. Figure 1.6 proposes that the four basic elements identified earlier can be broken down into more specific components or attributes and can be linked together to describe features which are of importance to customer expectations. Brief descriptions, which will be amplified subsequently, are:

- *Merchandise characteristics* features such as variety, quality, availability, style and exclusivity are usually rank ordered by customers when determining store preferences.

- *Merchandise augmentation* additional but related product features, such as accessories, which are not typically part of the usual merchandise offer, e.g. venting kits on appliances, leather belts (rather than imitation leather) on apparel products are features of merchandise augmentation.

- *Visual merchandising* the use of both merchandise and space to create persuasive and informative displays which reflect consumer buying habits or expectations for advice e.g., coordination (ladies wear, furniture) end use (appliances, DIY, tools and equipment). The level of merchandise density (stockholding/space) reflects the extent of visual merchandising.

- *Service augmentation facilities* additional, related service features that add service characteristics to the product/service merchandise offer which are not typically part of the usual offer, e.g. interior design, colour advice, 'wardrobe' services, credit plans and other financial services as well as changing room areas, cloakrooms, childcare and crèche areas.

• *Service augmentation/information* all aspects of information advising customers of product/service characteristics and availability instore and through promotional and other communication media.

• *Service intensity* the number of customer service dedicated store personnel as a proportion of the total.

The relative importance of critical success factors will depend very much upon the positioning of the offer. A service-led retailer will emphasise both merchandise and service augmentation characteristics supported by variety and exclusivity merchandise characteristics. By contrast a price-led offer will focus on price, restricted choice, high merchandise density with minimal services.

To return to the proposal made earlier that the critical success factors, once identified, can be used to determine strategic direction. Figure 1.7 proposes a number of strategic implementation issues and actions that could well be derived from customer research. We shall be discussing critical success factors within the context of attribute research and development from a perspective of resource allocation in subsequent chapters. At this juncture it is useful to demonstrate how the process may be used and to suggests (hypothetical) linkages. In Figure 1.7a the merchandise based characteristics suggested can be used to identify specific features (within the area of consideration) that are a response to customer researched expectations and which will result in a situation with the targeted customer group whereby customer perceptions are equal to (or ideally exceed) their expectations. Ideally if the result is a situation whereby the combination of customer perceptions together with added value can be achieved, the company can develop a position whereby sustainable competitive advantage results and the ideal situation in which the retail company becomes a 'first choice' store (or destination purchase store) will occur.

Other examples are suggested in Figures 1.7b, c, d and e. Clearly there will be quite different implications for different types of retailing offers. The use of critical success factors in the decision making process identifies at an early stage where the strategic (or operational) emphasis should be developed and identifies the major issues that confront the company in the implementation of strategic and operational decisions based upon the critical success factors. The analysis also identifies the extent of the strategic move necessary for success. An analysis resulting in minor changes to the business plan if its objectives are to be met (see Figure 1.5) for profitability, efficiency and productivity may simply require a corporate strategy based upon *consolidation and productivity*. Some changes to merchandise or customer

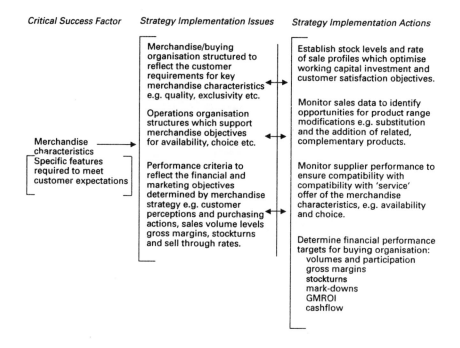

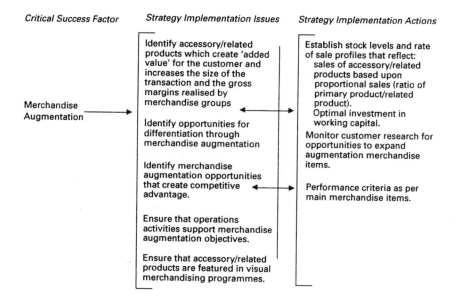

Figure 1.7(a–e)   Using critical success factors to direct strategy decisions

Fig. 1.7   cont.

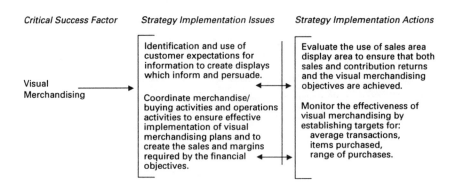

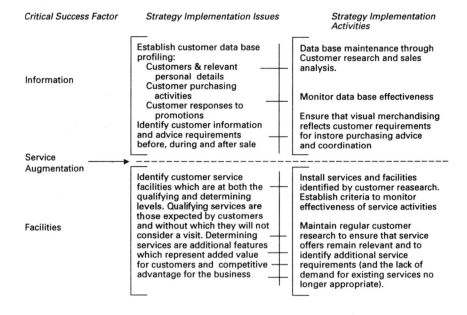

Fig. 1.7 cont.

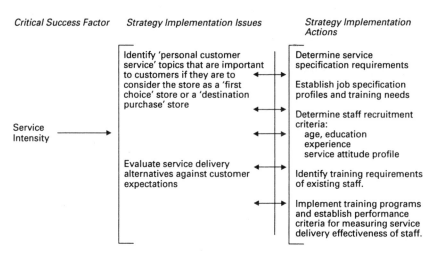

Critical Success Factor   Strategy Implementation Issues   Strategy Implementation Actions

service characteristics may suggest *repositioning. Growth* strategies would be confirmed by research which confirms the continued importance of existing critical success factor features in maximising customer satisfaction together with research which identifies product-market development potential. Research which identifies that significantly different critical success factors are to be the basis for future corporate success suggests that the existing 'offer' and its positioning is unlikely to met customer expectations in the medium or long term and that some form of diversification strategy should be seriously considered by the company.

SUMMARY

This chapter has identified the important issues to be considered when implementing strategic and operational decisions. It has also suggested a structure for reviewing strategy prior to undertaking the management activities necessary to initiate the task of implementation. This review should ensure that the process of implementing the strategy will flow easily.

We also considered a framework for identifying the important implementation activities that will be crucial to the success of the tasks. Within the defined performance requirements of a prescribed corporate strategy (the result of an evaluation of the business environment, its opportunities and threats, and a realistic evaluation of what the business can expect to do) its objectives can be specified. From these targets critical success factors and strategic issues can then be identified and evaluated.

The chapter also discussed the relationship between customer satisfaction, customer expectations and added value. The conclusion reached was that to ensure successful implementation of a decision to change the business direction the requirements are for customer perceptions plus added value to be greater than customer expectations. If this is realised both customer satisfaction and competitive advantage are achieved.

Part I

Understanding the Business

INTRODUCTION

Part I comprising Chapters 2 to 9, considers in detail the issues confronting effective and integrated retailing management. The topics discussed are described by Figure P2.1 in which the model developed in Chapter 1 is expanded to consider specific topics of interest to management. In Chapter 2 we consider how sales volume can be increased by looking at the opportunities available to the company to achieve sales increases through existing loyal customers and from an expanded customer base.

Chapter 3 examines issues involved in successful gross margin management, the three components of which are merchandise selection, financial considerations and supply chain considerations. Within each area there are specific topics identified that can, and do, influence gross margin performance. The initial point is made that successful gross margin performance is imperative to the long-term success of the business.

Operating margin management considers the successful management of staff, stock and space to achieve customer satisfaction at an acceptable level of profitability. In Chapter 4 the topics discussed are: branch operations, distribution operations and field management activities.

Chapter 5 deals with the vital topic of cash generation. This is discussed at two levels. Operational cash flow is generated from the management of buying and selling activities. Strategic cash flow considers long-term factors such as depreciation and other sources available to the business.

In Chapter 6 the rather large topic of management economics in retailing is discussed. This chapter considers the specific economics of operational and strategic decisions and discusses how they can have an impact on decision-making and implementation.

Chapter 7 returns to supply chain considerations. Supply chain management is seen as an increasingly vital activity in the overall process of managing margin performance. The components of the supply chain and their activities are examined in detail.

Overseas activities by retailers have had mixed success. Chapter 8 discusses recent developments by some larger companies within the context of changing patterns of trade on a global basis.

Chapter 9 considers the issues raised by the earlier chapters in Part I. It reviews the implications of the decisions that management make within the context of the financial structure and management of the business. It also considers the topic of organisational structure as a factor in decision making responsibility. The chapter introduces the topic of performance measurement and the influence of management groups.

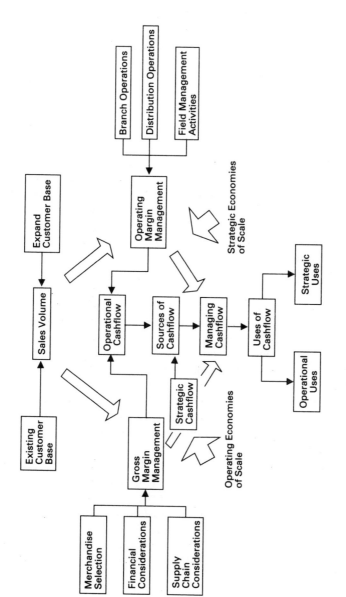

Figure P2.1

2 Customer Expectations, Retail Response: the Components of Sales Volume

INTRODUCTION

Without sales there is no business. This is the first and most obvious reason for the emphasis on sales generation in a retail business. There are other reasons. A minimum volume of sales is necessary if an optimal utilisation of fixed assets is to be realised. If the sales fail to materialise, it is likely that diseconomies will occur which will result in a decrease in the operating margins of the business. Both economies and diseconomies of scale are discussed in Chapter 6.

Sales volume is also important within the context of market share. Commanding levels of market share can be useful in enabling the market leader to create, and exert influence over market characteristics and competition (such as price levels, quality of product and service, trading style and store environment. Often territorial presence (and therefore volume and market share) can have an influence on competitors' expansion plans, acting as a possible barrier to entry. Strong regional sales can also be helpful in making focused advertising cost-effective.

It follows that generating sales volume is an important feature of strategy implementation. It will be shown in Chapter 7 that decisions affecting the productivity of current and fixed assets are an important consideration in developing sustainable economies of scale. The impact of sales volume on asset productivity and margin performance also has an important influence on the financial structure and performance of the business.

We can assume that by now the principle of customer perceptions exceeding customer expectations resulting in customer satisfaction is established. Furthermore, so too is the earlier discussion concerning objectives and critical success factors and the role of sales in these. The components of this role is a useful place to start. It will be remembered that sales have five component factors:

- An increase in browsing visits
- An increase in purchasing visits
- An increase in the size of transactions
- An increase in the usage of purchases
- An increase in the items purchased

Any implementation activity should have one or more of these as its task. This chapter continues by identifying the issues involved in pursuing an increase in sales. We are considering two aspects of sales increases; those from existing customers and those obtained by expanding the customer base (see Figure 2.1).

2.1 INCREASING SALES FROM THE EXISTING CUSTOMER BASE

It is generally accepted that it is less difficult to increase sales obtained from existing customers. It is not difficult to understand why this should be so. Existing customers are aware of the nature of the offer and support it to a greater or lesser degree. There are a number of possible ways in which sales of existing customers may be increased.

Increase the Spend of Core Customers

Every business has core customers, customers who visit and purchase both regularly and frequently. It is a relatively easy task to identify these customers and to ascertain their purchasing activities and to establish their preferences. By understanding their preferences (and their dislikes) it should be possible to increase the frequency of their visits, to increase the proportion of purchasing to browsing visits and to expand the size of their purchases.

Not only is this a low risk activity (these customers usually are very willing to give their views and opinions) but they are also willing to demonstrate increased loyalty by responding with their purchasing when they consider they have been consulted. Clearly the very first activity to be considered is to research the preferences and relative perceptions of the company's regular and loyal customer base to ascertain:
How can we improve the existing retail offer by making appropriate changes to:

- merchandise characteristics
- the range and levels of customer service
- the store environment
- customer communications programmes

What these core customers perceive as more attractive in competitors' offers.

If the core customer has changed selection and purchasing activities recently.

Given that the company can accommodate the changing needs that it has identified, small incremental changes within the offer may result in a significant increase in the core customer visit and spend frequency. It follows

34

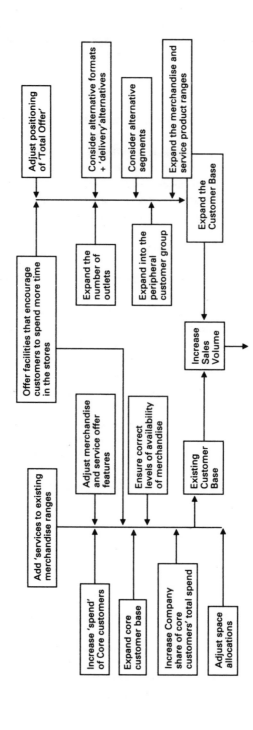

Figure 2.1 Options for increasing sales volume

that these customer changes should be monitored and responded to as a matter of course. To do so will ensure that the most obvious and effective means of increasing sales is not overlooked.

Expand the Core Customer Base

Assuming that the retail offer is well supported by the existing core customers, it follows that there should be an effort to identify other consumers sharing core customer characteristics. Given a target customer profile, store catchment areas should be 'searched' for consumers with the same or similar profiles.

It is very likely that the efficient company has established an effective research activity for this purpose. Similarly, customer communications programmes are likely to be in place. However, this possibility may be overlooked, often because the 'core customer' is shared by a strong competitor.

Increase Company Share of Core Customers' Total Spend

There are a number of factors to be considered. The first is to ascertain the share of customer spend the company regularly receives and in what merchandise categories. Low shares may suggest that a competitor is favoured as the first choice store and the company is used as a 'top up' source. However, it could reflect competitors' promotional activities, whereby price offers are made across staple item ranges encouraging customers to purchase more than their immediate use requirements during incentive offers.

Another issue may concern customer perceptions of specific elements of the merchandise range. For example, a competitor's offer comprising more variety by the inclusion of manufacturer brands compared with retailer brands may influence customer choice. Similarly the addition of support services in specific merchandise categories may influence customer purchasing preferences. It follows that quality and exclusivity perceptions will have similar effects.

In making evaluations (and subsequently) decisions concerning share of customer spend other factors should be considered. Is the merchandise category large enough to bear the costs of competition? Are there characteristics, such as a combination of product perishability and distance from the store, that influence customer purchasing decisions? Is the merchandise category one which is considered to be a core merchandise group, and therefore one in which the company should demonstrate dominance?

Adjust Space Allocation

A regular review of rate-of-sale per unit of space can be helpful in maintaining an optimal level of sales. This is particularly necessary across the core merchandise range categories where adjustment of category and individual product space allocation can increase overall sales and space productivity.

The combination of electronic point of sale (EPOS) data together with space management programmes offer the merchandise manager a powerful planning facility. Increasingly important is the facility to respond to local demand and it is in this role that the sensitivity between space and rate-of-sale of merchandise offers a competitive benefit.

Add Services to Existing Merchandise Ranges

By adding services to existing merchandise ranges, there is the opportunity to offer added value to the customer and establish differentiation at one and the same time.

There are a number of examples of successful activities. Wardrobe services in ladieswear retailing are often used as an example, but others exist. Increasingly, advice and information services are offered by furniture and home improvement retailers. The cosmetic and fragrance houses also offer (through their larger customers) a 'consultancy service' which extends well beyond the use of their products and into colour co-ordination and health concern.

Adjust Merchandise and Service Offer Features

Customers are both dynamic and discerning and are known regularly to visit competitors' outlets to monitor merchandise and service characteristics. There have been significant (and major) changes in the circumstances of many consumers and the alert retailer reflects these in the offer.

Currently a major impact has been the prolonged period of recession from from 1989 to the early 1990s which has brought about a major change in consumer confidence and in their perception of future employment prospects and therefore expenditure patterns. Given that many home owners have found that their mortgage value exceeds the real value of their property significant changes in spending patterns have been noticeable. Severely hit are durables, whilst furniture in the home and the apparel markets have lost considerable volume.

The response that might have been expected would have been to reduce choice (and pass the margin benefit on to the customer) and to reduce some aspects of service. It is interesting to note the response of Littlewoods with their 'happy hour' and other promotional activities, aimed at the lower income groups. However, little sensitivity has been demonstrated towards the once affluent groups, whose personal gearing has severely reduced their disposable income and whose view of their prospects has created doubts concerning perceived disposable income.

It follows that while there may be a competitive requirement to consider how differentiation may be accomplished by adding to the combined merchandise and service offer, there can be an equally powerful argument that can be made for selective reductions to these offers and in so doing demonstrating sensitivity towards the customers' changed circumstances.

Ensure Correct Levels of Availability of Merchandise

Many companies fail to achieve maximum sales volume because they neglect to maintain an in-stock position across the merchandise assortment. Clearly the maintenance of unnecessarily high levels of availability is expensive and can be punitive.

The optimal situation would appear to be one whereby high levels of availability are offered selectively. Current best practice suggests that a 'Pareto analysis' of the merchandise assortment will identify a core range for which high levels of availability should be offered if sales are to be maximised. Variations around this should be considered to meet competitive necessity.

There are a number of logistics solutions to maintaining acceptable cost levels and, at the same time, offering acceptable availability to customers. Recent developments in just-in-time and rapid-response inventory systems help with optimising the cost of providing this inventory service.

Offering Facilities that Encourage Customers to Spend More Time In-Store

As suggested by Figure 2.1, this topic is common to both increasing sales through the existing customer base and by expanding the customer base, i.e. finding new customers.

The length of time customers spend in stores is a function of their shopping intentions. We shall discuss the issue of shopping mission types in later chapters, at this juncture it is sufficient to make the point that consumers have a range of different purchasing motives which are influenced by their needs on any specific occasion and by their experience with the specific retailer offers. These result in six possible types of shopping mission:

- Destination purchases; where a *specific* purchase is planned;

- Planned regular purchasing visits; which may or not be store specific but, during which a planned regular purchase occurs (e.g. a weekly food shopping visit);

- Planned comparison shopping visits; during which information is sought but a purchase is not necessarily made;

- Planned browsing visits; which are part of a consumer's leisure activities, which, in turn, are social activities;

- Distress purchases; made for forgotten items or for items for which there is an immediate requirement;

- Impulse purchases; which may, but not necessarily, occur during a planned shopping visit.

Thus, if the consumer's perceptions (based on experience) of a specific retail company are that the offer is limited to their making a series of regular but short visits to purchase a few items the reasons for this view should be explored. It is likely that the customer considers either the merchandise or the service (or both) lacking appeal in specific ways and, if these issues were addressed, may well become a more frequent customer, with a higher level of expenditure.

It follows that regular research aimed at identifying the fit between customer expectations and perceptions, and the subsequent management action to redress the differences, the result may be a shift from one mission type to another, more profitable mission.

2.2   INCREASE SALES BY EXPANDING THE CUSTOMER BASE

Given that the suggested options for expanding sales from existing customers have been evaluated, and where cost-effective implemented, the focus should then be directed towards the potential offered from new customers. Again there are a number of options.

Expand the Number of Outlets

Provided that the existing offer formula has the appropriate appeal and that other conditions are met then new customers will be attracted by increasing the number of outlets traded from.

However, to be both successful and profitable, we must be sure that there is likely to be a sufficient sales volume generated. Furthermore, it should be established prior to making a commitment on expansion that there is sufficient distribution and operations management capacity available to continue to provide the level of service that has proved successful with the business as it exists. This is particularly relevant for large multiples, whose purposes in expanding their outlet base, include competitive motives as well as the increase in sales.

Often, as a large company expands its sales outlets it may begin to take sales from its own neighbouring stores as well as from competitors, or simply by offering a service to an area where no similar retail offer has been available. There are indications that this has occurred for some companies. As the business expands, ideally the increase in sales per unit of sales area indicates a commensurate increase. If the selected area is under-shopped then it may expect the incremental sale increase per unit of space to be greater than the company average per unit of sales area. If this does not occur then reasons for the shortfall should be identified. Clearly there is little point in expanding a business if the increased volume provides excessive increases in costs, reducing both productivity and profitability.

Expand into the Peripheral Customer Group

The concept of market segmentation is well established and the notion that customers differ is understood and accepted. Often the differences are such that the customers within each segment have no common denominator because the segments are discrete.

However, it is possible that at the areas of overlap between closely related segments (which remain separate) there exist potential customers who may be attracted to the offer if an incentive, or perhaps a promotional thrust is made. For example, customers separated by preferences for quality differ from those seeking quantity. However, those for whom exclusivity is paramount may be attracted by the design or style attributes that are the preference characteristic of an adjacent segment. Thus it may be possible to make an offer to an adjacent segment without compromising the offer being made to the existing core group of customers.

Adjust the Positioning of the 'Total Offer'

This option is similar to the previous topic. It follows that often, because of external influences, customer preferences shift away from the offer the company has made successful. The difference here is that it is the target customer group, the core customers, that have begun to demonstrate a change in preferences.

Provided the shifts are detected sufficiently early, then changes may be made. These may (ideally) be very small and as a consequence result in no significant changes in merchandise characteristics (certainly none that require re-sourcing) or changes in customer services that require major changes to staff levels or quality or perhaps service facilities.

One way of ensuring that changes are kept to a minimum is to use ongoing customer research. Tracking studies monitor customer perceptions of both the company and its closest competitors. The result is a regular review of customer preferences and responses to changes made in the retail offer.

Consider Alternative Formats and 'Delivery' Alternatives

Many retail formulae are based upon a structure of fixed assets that require high levels of sales to ensure that not only are the fixed costs recovered but that a targeted return on capital employed is retrieved. If both the format and the return on capital employed is rigid then there is little scope for the company to expand into low volume areas.

However, if the company takes a more flexible view of its business it may find alternatives that enable expansion to be undertaken. For example, it may decide to reduce the width of the merchandise offer made in low volume locations. By operating out of smaller outlets the level of sales to be achieved will be lower and the economics of the business unit will become more attractive. It may be that they make immediately available only the core merchandise range and expand the offer by an instore (or home used) catalogue and ordering facility. Equally they may franchise the business in areas where, because of the volume/cost relationship to overhead, they would operate unprofitably but others without the fixed overhead could make acceptable profits.

It may also be profitable for the company to consider totally different delivery media. A common example is that of companies using mail order. More recently electronic media are being introduced in an expansion of home-shopping. The successful use of MINITEL (in France) by a wide range of products and services is evidence of the options available using this format.

Customer Alternative Segments

An increase in sales is possible if the company is prepared to consider operating in other segments. This may be necessary if the size of their existing customer segment has been decreased to the extent that it is no longer economically viable or, more likely, that competitive activity is increasing and is threatening profitability.

Care should be taken to ensure that the offer made to the alternative segment is relevant to customer expectations. The offer should be specific to that customer group and not the existing offer with a number of superficial changes. The company should also be prepared to accept quite different levels of margins, i.e. those in the existing business may not be achievable for all sorts of reasons. Furthermore, they should also be prepared to accept different retailer/customer relationships. For example customers using convenience food stores typically do so for distress purchases and would not consider making large weekly purchases: thus the frequency of customer visits would be low as would the average transaction. These differences would appear very large to a food multiple retailer considering a move into the convenience segment of the market sector. However, there would be compensating differences in both capital and operating costs and clearly it is the overall result that must be evaluated.

Expand the Merchandise and Service–Product Ranges

Finally, sales increases may be achieved by expanding the merchandise and service assortments. Again customer research is useful in identifying opportunities to expand both the customer base and the merchandise and service offer. The growth of the food multiples during the 1970s and 1980s was achieved largely by attracting customers who, hitherto, had used specialist butchers, bakers, produce and other specialist outlets. More recently they have added pharmacies and post office services to their portfolios, these having had a similar effect.

There are a number of issues to be addressed. First, there should be a level of existing customer confidence that facilitates the move into new activities. This is clearly important when sensitive areas such as financial services are concerned. With hindsight it would appear that the Marks & Spencer move into financial services was facilitated by the high level of consumer confidence they enjoy. Their move may also have been difficult without demonstrable expertise. This often requires an investment in human resources, together with systems and other facilities, if an efficient and competitive offer is to be made. There are other examples, some of successful additions, some not so successful. The John Lewis Partnership has been successful in the expansion of its business by using an incremental approach, furniture and home furnishings developed from an acknowledged expertise in fabrics. However, for some retailers, customer confidence in related areas did not result in successful entry into areas such as computers and office equipment.

SUMMARY

This chapter has suggested that the business should be concerned to make sales generation a major area of activity. As we discussed in the first chapter, sales are the important element of success of any retail business. Without an acceptable level of sales the volume of profit generated will be insufficient to attract and retain shareholders and the cashflow will be insufficient to meet operating expenses and to expand the business. Margin percentages are one thing, actual amounts may be something different.

This chapter has also discussed the options available to the retail firm to expand sales. The point was clearly made that it is easier to expand sales volume by making the business more attractive to existing customers, such that they increase their purchasing visits and the size of their transactions. Expanding the customer base is more difficult, and is accompanied with higher levels of risk and lower profitability. Chapter 14 will expand this topic.

3 Managing Gross Margins

INTRODUCTION

It is essential that if the retail business is to be successful then gross margin management is one key to the success. We have established (in Chapter 1) the importance of gross margins and in this chapter expand the discussion by considering some of the important facets of gross margin management.

Buying and merchandising activities are central to the business and if these activities fail to respond to customer expectations the result will be seen in the failure of the business to achieve the desired customer response of frequent high spending visits. Poor margin achievement is typified by ineffective merchandise selection, poor availability and failure to support merchandise selection decisions with promotional activities.

If gross margin objectives fail to be met then it follows that contribution and cashflow objectives will also fail to reach their targets. The consequences of this situation will be felt throughout the business: for example, it may be necessary that in order to meet a contribution objective economies will be made by reducing expenditure elsewhere such as staffing levels. It is illogical, but not unusual, for management to attempt to resolve problems in one area of the business by taking action elsewhere, in a totally unrelated area.

This chapter is concerned with three areas of managerial consideration: meeting customer expectations through effective merchandise selection; the working capital issues (financial considerations) and supply chain management. (See Figure 3.1.)

3.1 MERCHANDISE SELECTION: MEETING CUSTOMER EXPECTATION

Merchandise Characteristics

The merchandise selection and procurement activity is a major use of working capital. If the planned rate of customer purchasing visits and transaction values are to be achieved and margins maximised then it follows that the customer expectations for, and of, the merchandise offer should be met as closely as possible.

Typically the merchandise characteristics required by customers have a major input into the merchandise strategy. There are a number of key issues of concern both to customer satisfaction and profitability. Furthermore, they should be reviewed on any occasion that strategic direction is changed or implemented.

42

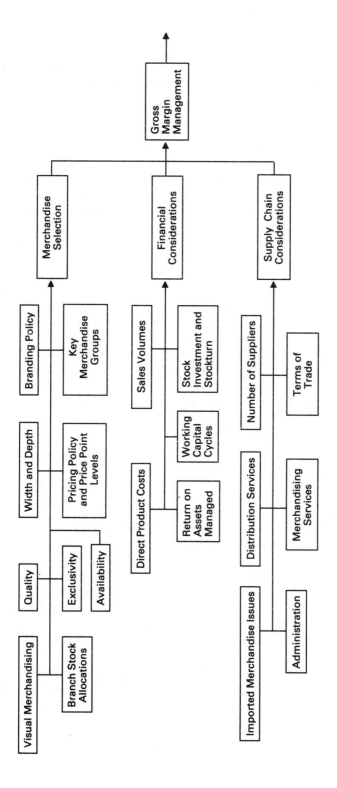

Figure 3.1 Managing gross margins

Branding Policy

The role of both manufacturer and retailer brands in the customers' store selection and product purchasing decisions have significant implications for profit planning. It is well known that retailer own brand products have a margin advantage over manufacturer brands. However, the role of the retail brand has changed significantly in recent years. From being a lower priced/ slightly lower quality alternative of the manufacturer's brand it became a bench-mark for quality matching but still with a price advantage. Currently the view of the retail brand is that it also has a significant role in the positioning strategy of the business as well as carrying a profit yielding role. It is essential not to lose sight of the role of the manufacturers' brands. For a number of retail offers form a key role. For example, price-led retailing often relies upon the ability to offer customers a wide range of nationally known products, usually promoted nationally by the manufacturer, at lower prices than those of competitors. Examples of sectors where this applies can be seen in food, appliances and the electrical ranges of the DIY sector.

Clearly the role of the brand in the consumer decision matrix is important and it follows that strategy implementation activities should consider this as important input. Options open to decision makers have expanded to include the possibility of 'buying' suppliers production capacity and in this way developing an interesting form of exclusivity. Quality is clearly linked with branding. Both manufacturer and retailer brands enjoy strong quality images. Whereas product exclusivity can be negotiated between large retailers and suppliers, no manufacturer (or retailer for that matter) can negotiate differential levels of quality.

Key Merchandise Groups

Key merchandise groups form a significant role in a retailer's merchandise strategy. Typically they are a statement of the retail offer, determining the nature of the business, i.e., whether the retailer is a specialist or a mass merchandise business and within these categories the precise nature of the specialisation. An example may be helpful. Furniture retailing is a specialist retail activity, however, the offers differ widely varying by price, quality, style and by customer services. Similarly, DIY retailers are specialists but a close look at their offers discloses a range of offer differences: some focus upon home improvement (kitchens, bathrooms, etc.), others on home maintenance, and yet others on fashion in home decor.

One other aspect of key merchandise groups concerns the company's concern with those elements of the merchandise range that are responsible for providing volume sales and thus a large proportion of company profit and cashflow objectives. They are usually structured to offer high availability levels across a range of pre-selected size, colour, style and other dimensions. Often the allocation of additional distribution resources are made to ensure the maintenance of high-in-stock targets.

Pricing Policy and Price Point Levels

Competitive and stable prices are an important feature of customer expectations and their store selection and product purchasing activities. Price is an important consideration in merchandise planning because familiarity with the sales activity between price points can provide useful information for stock holding. For example, if it can be ascertained that by far the largest proportion of sales occurs between two specific price points, it follows that these should form the basis for offering maximum choice features and availability to ensure that overall sales objectives are met.

Price is often used by consumers as a surrogate for quality and occasionally exclusivity. It often occurs where no other comparison exists such as a major manufacturer's brand or that of a retailer with a strong reputation.

It is essential that the role of price be identified during strategy formulation process. If it is ignored (or misunderstood) the implications for sales, profit and cashflow will only become clear after implementation.

Width and Depth

Width and Depth decisions are important elements of the merchandise strategy. They are a response to customer expectations of variety and choice. Extensive width and depth are essential if credibility with the customer is to be established in a specific merchandise group. There are many merchandise groups for which it is necessary for the retailer to establish a 'critical mass', (high levels of width and depth) before the business is considered to be an automatic first choice for that particular merchandise group.

The implications for working capital commitment are obvious, so too are the implications for risk. Clearly, as width and depth are increased, so too is the amount of working capital commitment. (The working capital issues will be discussed below – see financial considerations.)

The risk issues, while concerned with financial considerations, also have customer implications. Very wide and deep ranges should also demonstrate concern for customer satisfaction. It follows that while the customer may well be offered choice and variety the offer should be relevant to their needs, for example a large range of size alternatives, or an inappropriate selection can result in antagonised customers who fail to find what they want from what at first appears to be an extensive offer. It can also result in a loss of confidence by customers who consider company personnel to lack an understanding of the market and its characteristics. These factors should be considered when attempting to implement a change of strategic direction particularly involving new customers.

Quality

Quality decisions interrelate with customer perceptions of other merchandise characteristics. An obvious link is that between quality and price whereby customer perceptions and expectations are positively correlated. Quality and exclusivity share a similar relationship in that quality may be used to differentiate merchandise offers from those of competitors and in so doing is seen as having a measure of exclusivity. Often the quality offered by a market leader is used by customers and competitors as a sector standard.

Quality has cost implications. Not only does a superior product specification add cost through higher quality materials and labour content, but it is expensive to monitor and maintain. Quality control costs can be a significant element of total product costs, particularly for products sourced from overseas suppliers. It follows that any changes of strategy involving quality require close examination from two points of view: both customer expectations of quality and quality service maintenance may have considerable cost implications; quality control costs to maintain levels of customer expectations can involve investment in fixed and valuable costs such that anticipated levels of profitability may be difficult to meet.

Exclusivity

Exclusivity can be a significant feature within the consumer's decision matrix. Equally it can form a major element of a retailer's offer. For both it has cost implications. Customers who respond to exclusive merchandise are prepared to pay extra for this benefit. However, typically their expectations are for exclusivity across the 'offer' and in a larger context exclusivity may thus become expensive. Maintaining a standard of exclusivity does have far reaching cost consequences, not the least being the very high costs of sourcing exclusive merchandise ranges and the in-store commitments (the location and amount of space) to maintain the exclusivity. Once again it suggests the need for careful examination before strategy implementation is contemplated.

Availability

Availability is a basic element of consumer expectations. However, it is also an expensive factor, one which can increase costs markedly. The costs are not simply related to stockholding, which in themselves can be prohibitive, but concern space at the point-of-sale and within the distribution system. For these reasons most retailers are selective and attempt only to offer high levels of availability for competitive purposes. Thus we see a careful selection from among fast moving merchandise ranges for specific treatment, for which a lack of availability will undoubtedly result in the loss of a sale. From a strategic point of view there is clearly a need to examine any issues that are likely to create cause for concern if higher than expected availability expectations by customers are anticipated.

Visual Merchandising

Visual merchandising has two roles: persuasion and information. Both roles have significance for gross margin achievement. Both can encourage the customer to increase the size of a purchase. Information does this by identifying colours and styles that co-ordinate to create a 'personal image' for the customer, and in so doing persuades the customer to purchase a range or a collection of items. Well constructed visual merchandising should co-ordinate merchandise into 'situational' or 'usage' displays thereby identifying totally with customer utility requirements.

Visual merchandising requires the allocation of capital and labour resources. Capital is required in the form of space, fixtures and service facilities. In addition there is a requirement for working capital application (merchandise) and often some duplication can occur. This suggests a need for a co-ordinated and programmed approach to visual merchandising with the objective of reinforcing the positioning strategy. This raises an interesting issue. The importance of visual merchandising varies both across market sectors and by segment within sectors. The ladieswear sector is a prime example of this issue. The exclusive, high quality, classic styled segment relies heavily on visual merchandising to inform and persuade; whereas the variety chains with much less exclusive offers use visual merchandising to a much lesser extent.

Clearly visual merchandising is an important issue during any consideration concerning shifts in positioning. It can involve considerable expenditure in store layout and fixturing.

Branch Stock Allocations

Gross margins can be increased by increasing the purchase volumes. Clearly one view on this is for all branches to carry representative stockholding of the merchandise range. Often this is impracticable due to the size of their sales areas. However, possibly more important is the need to recognise the differences in items of regional demand. Apparel retailers are very aware of the very significant differences in physical attributes, colour and style preferences that occur throughout a country of the size of the United Kingdom. Given that retailing is becoming international, it follows that these differences are likely to become even more significant.

The implications for gross margin management are quite clear: there are a significant number of products for which consumer preferences and requirements differ. These may occur over short distances or across international or semi-international territories. It is important therefore that the temptation to increase gross margins through broadcast distribution be thoroughly evaluated. Failure to do so could result in an unacceptable level of markdowns.

Once again the significance for strategy decisions is important. The results of repositioning, growth and diversification can be seriously affected by an erroneous assumption that such strategy shifts will be rewarded by greatly improved gross margins through increased volumes.

3.2   FINANCIAL CONSIDERATIONS

The success of the profit plan depends very much upon the management of working capital deployed during merchandise selection and procurement. Unless relevant control information is available the short and long term viability of the business will be at risk. A change in strategic direction is likely to be important in this respect and clearly the financial implications of such a change should be thoroughly investigated. The issues of concern should include:

Sales Volumes

Sales volumes have a very large impact on gross margin achievements. The typical relationship is one for which buying terms increase as volumes purchased are increased. There are two aspects to be considered. First, as identified above as volumes are increased so the buying discounts from suppliers increase accordingly, but so too does the risk of markdowns if the selection is poor or if the 'shelf-life' of the merchandise is very short. Fashion products are in this category and it should be noted that fashion product life cycles for both menswear and ladieswear vary by market segment. Thus classical styling will have a longer life cycle than high-fashion products and consequently having less risk may be purchased in greater volumes.

  Margins may also be increased if merchandise ranges offer less variety. The issue to be resolved relates to the customers' preferences and expectations. If customers prefer choice and variety then the merchandise should reflect this in its width and depth: the implications being that the company should focus on limited purchase volumes. Conversely, if the customer prefers low prices and limited choice the buying may be much deeper with the increased margins being used as part of the customer offer.

Stock Investment and Stockturn

An essential feature of working capital management concerns the management of stock levels. There are a number of aspects to this topic. By maintaining stock levels at a level consonant with the requirements of customer expectations for choice and availability cost benefits accrue. Stockholding costs are optimised and so too are financial requirements. However, less storage space is required and it follows that less fixed capital resource is consumed, thereby releasing capital for use elsewhere in the business. Well managed distribution systems (increasingly using information technology) can determine stockholding requirements very accurately and are able to analyse demand and replenishment stock flows to ensure that stock levels and locations are such that customer service aspects of inventory management are maintained at the lowest possible costs. Quick response systems are used selectively to ensure that distribution service is applied differently across the merchandise assortment.

An aspect of stock investment and stockturn that is important is the facility to generate negative working capital. It follows that if customer preferences favour low price and minimum choice the width of the range is narrow and the number of suppliers used can be lower than that required for a wide ranged offer. It also follows that buying administration can be simplified and costs reduced. Clearly with fewer suppliers for any given volume of purchases (assuming economic viability) the buying margins will be increased. Add to this the characteristics of fast moving merchandise (such as perishable good products, e.g. milk, bread, etc.) then the stockturns generated can exceed the payment cycles for the merchandise. As a result merchandise may be sold a number of times before the retailer receives a request for payment. This characteristic, negative working capital, enables the retailer to use suppliers working capital in developing the business, thereby reducing their own financing requirements and costs.

A number of issues emerge as important within the context of strategy formulation and implementation. Any change should consider the issues arising in terms of fixed and working capital commitments. These considerations should not be restricted to storage and transportation aspects of distribution service but also consider systems requirements. As intimated earlier, the response systems of businesses within the same market sectors can and do differ markedly between segments.

Working Capital Cycles

Working capital cycles are obviously closely related to stock investment and stockturn characteristics. The working capital cycle is also influenced by the structure of the distribution service system and by the credit taken by customers. The length of the working capital is the amount of time taken from payment of suppliers to the receipt of payment from customers. It is a measure of the company's efficiency in converting stocks into sales. Identification of the location of inventory and the number of days sales cover that exists at each location reveals the time period for which the company must finance inventory in the cycle. In a business making a profit, the cash received at the end should exceed the total cash amounts paid out during the working capital cycle. This is essential in order that taxes, interest, dividends and capital replenishment and acquisition be paid without resort to external funds.

The impact of working capital cycles can have a major impact upon strategy decisions. Consider a repositioning example in which a company re-locates its offer in a segment of the same market sector but within which customer service expectations, specifically for credit, are greater than those experienced in its existing segment. The following changes in the working capital cycle could occur:

	Current segment	*Proposed segment*
Depot Stocks	17	28
Outlet Stocks	3	7
Credit Customers Payments	10	42
	30	77
Less Suppliers Credit	30	42
Days to Finance	0	35

While this is an hypothetical example, it illustrates operating differences that can occur. Stockholding is expanded to improve customer choice and the use of a service card as opposed to being a cash and credit card business creates a working capital cycle that requires funding. Clearly the costs are met either from enhanced margins or from increased borrowing. If the requirements are met from increased borrowing care should be taken as there may be significant issues to be dealt with if volume forecasts do not materialise. See Chapter 9 (pp. 136–7) for a fuller discussion.

Direct Product Costs (DPC)

Direct Product Costs (DPC) have an influence on both gross margin management and operating/contribution margin management. Accuracy and time relevance are essential as is their need to represent a sufficiently large proportion of the costs for which the retailer is responsible or can influence, if they are to be useful. Often company accounting systems are based upon absorption principles rather than direct or marginal costing systems and as a result many of the costs become absorbed into an operating overhead.

The usefulness of comprehensive direct product costs relates to the facility of being able to substitute a lower cost option for a product towards which the customer is indifferent. Of particular interest to gross margin management is the incremental impact upon overall margins from a specific supplier and how this changes the overall gross margin achievement. Certainly this aspect of direct product costing should be considered in strategy changes which will result in volume shifts from suppliers and the impact on profitability from a reformulated merchandise offer.

Return on Assets Managed (ROAM)

Return on Assets Managed (ROAM) is a control concept being introduced by large multiple retailers. The Dupont concept of profitability and asset management, i.e. gross margin multiplied by asset turnover is the basis of ROAM. It has application in multiple retailing, particularly in management situations where buying and merchandise managers have investment responsi-

bilities for very large stock values. In sophisticated installations, the use of
negative working capital is included by calculating the effect of managing
stock turns *and* payment cycles. ROAM has been found effective in del-
egating investment decisions and motivating managers.

3.3 SUPPLY CHAIN CONSIDERATIONS

The selection and management of suppliers can have a considerable impact
upon gross margin management. Increasingly, retailers are becoming aware
of the benefits of supply chain management; the total system of inventory
stocks and flows between point of manufacture and point-of-sale. It is interesting to note that whereas the interest of physical distribution managers
of the late 1960s and 1970s was focussed upon manufacturing and finished
goods storage towards the point-of-sale the reverse is now the case: the
focus is upon consumer satisfaction, with the objectives of supply chain
management set to do this effectively at an optimum cost. There are a number
of issues of interest to this discussion:

Number of Suppliers

There is an optimum number of suppliers for any retailer. There are a number
of criteria which influence the numerical total and this will be governed by:

- The expectations of customers for choice, quality, exclusivity and
  availability. As these increase so too is the probability that the number
  of suppliers to ensure that 'service' is obtained and therefore maintained.

- The share of the total sales of the business held by suppliers. It is unwise
  to permit any one supplier to increase its share to a level at which a
  measure of control is lost to that supplier.

- It follows that circumstances may exist where a supplier may be the only
  one available for certain 'exclusive' merchandise. If the retailer's positioning
  is strong enough (e.g. Harrods or perhaps Marks & Spencer) two options
  may exist: identify and jointly promote a substitute product or, alternatively, develop an own-brand. However, it must be said that a strong customer franchise is required. Such a situation may occur in a highly
  concentrated supplier industry.

Clearly these issues will have an impact on the realised margin. The retailer
will need to consider both the quantitative and qualitative issues (i.e. margins and supplier influence) in developing a supply strategy. A shift of
strategic direction may require a complete review of supply markets and

relationships with suppliers: these may require the retail company to accept a reversal of supplier/distributor relationships, with control shifting towards suppliers (or the reverse). Either way, the buying and merchandising activity will need to identify and accommodate such differences.

Terms of Trade

The amounts and structure of discounts vary by sector as do the settlement terms. These may have serious implications for company strategy shifts. The effect of settlement terms on working capital cycles was discussed earlier. Overseas sourcing may introduce the retailer to an unfamiliar business relationship.

Distribution Services

Distribution services are important from two points of view. Clearly the more services that are provided by suppliers the lower the costs of the retailer and consequently the higher the resultant gross and contribution margins. Possibly more significant are the considerations of reliability and quality of the service. Many retailers develop a dependence upon their suppliers for distribution reliability which they too reflect in their merchandise and customer service offer. Thus supplier selection should establish the ability of potential suppliers to meet the level of service required and the ability to sustain that service. This decision has implications for other resourcing decisions. If a substantial amount of the distribution activity is to be delegated to the suppliers then the company owned distribution facilities will be less than if they undertook the total distribution task. Accordingly the investment in fixed assets dedicated to distribution will be less. It has two implications: the first is that control is also being delegated to the supplier, thereby making changes more difficult, and secondly there is also the issue of dependency, which is increased. The decision for the retailer concerns how much control should be delegated in order that resources may be used elsewhere – what is the opportunity cost? Will the profile change over time? Will a shift in the retail company's strategic direction require a change in its strategy? Examples do exist. Many furniture retailers now hold only floor stock as samples. Sales are completed from their suppliers' stocks in suppliers' vehicles.

Merchandising Services

Similar issues exist. However, the growth of retail brands and, in particular, the increased emphasis on the role of merchandise and customer service in positioning implementation has led to a decrease in the level of suppliers' activities within the store. Nevertheless for a discounted/manufacturer brand-led business the contribution made by manufacturers merchandising services can be significant in cost savings and therefore can enhance gross and contribution margins. Again a shift in strategic direction may require the situation to be reviewed: this would require significant changes in buying and merchandising organisation structures.

Imported Merchandise Issues

The longer the supply chain the more difficult it is to manage and therefore management time and costs are higher. Quality is equally difficult to control and can be erratic. Thus what may have been an attractive offer from an overseas supplier may not, when these additional costs are considered, realise the same margins. Research suggests that both costs and quality of overseas produced merchandise have improved in recent years. This changes the benefits offered, away from low cost alternatives towards exclusivity. However, there remains the need to allocate management and buyers' time to travel etc. and thus costs remain high. Shifts in strategic direction may be accompanied with a change in customer expectations. For example, increased quality, availability and a desire for product continuity may require sourcing policy changes. The issues of margins and customer satisfaction become important factors.

Administration

The costs of supply chain management vary with the number of suppliers and with the level of their involvement in the supply chain. We have discussed some of the issues involved earlier in the context of delivery and merchandising service. Other aspects of this topic include the administration of order processing and order progressing. Increased application of IT systems reduces the cost of order transmission and, in particular, of stockholding costs. However, these benefits must be considered in the context of the implication of integrating the supply chain an increase of which suggests an increase in the dependency on selected suppliers. The long term issues must be balanced against short term cost benefits. So too must the possibility of a change in strategic direction. It is possible that other segments operate in a totally different manner. A low volume segment (in the same market section) may not have a viable throughput to justify the investment in systems which link supplier and retailer.

SUMMARY

This chapter has discussed the issues of concern to management when considering the implications of strategy implementation upon gross margins.

Three broad areas of gross margin management were considered; effective merchandise selection, financial issues (particularly working capital management) and supply chain considerations. Clearly the topics discussed within each of these broad areas will have different issues and implications for individual retailers and perhaps may be shared by retailers within the same market sector or segment.

The overall issue to emerge from this chapter is that *effective* gross margin management requires a clear understanding of customer expectations. With this the task of *effective* merchandise selection is made easier and the management of the supply chain also becomes much clearer in terms of merchandise and service requirements of suppliers.

Effective gross margin management provides a sound marketing and financial base from which the business can operate. With a relevant merchandise offer customer transactions can be increased, mark-downs minimised and both profitability and cash generation optimised. We shall return to this topic in Chapter 14.

4 Managing Operating Margins

INTRODUCTION

In recent years the most successful retail businesses have been those which have increased their operating margins. Given low growth in most retail sector markets, it has been a focus on improving productivity of both human and physical assets that has provided a growth in profitability.

Notable in the sector have been the food multiples. They have operated in a low growth market for some time and have been well aware that there has been little potential for increased profitability other than from efficiencies in the business.

Given that the gross margins achieved by an effective buying and merchandising activity are finite, it follows that to achieve a maximum operating contribution, the operational activities of the business must be well managed and meet the objectives set by management.

This chapter considers three areas of operations management; branch operations, distribution and field operations. It also discusses, briefly, some of the issues involved in branch development. The issues are shown in Figure 4.1.

4.1 BRANCH OPERATIONS

A considerable proportion of a retail company's costs occur operating the business. There has been significant activity in the application of technology which has had a number of influences. Clearly the most significant has been in the context of information: EPOS has provided timely and accurate data which has enabled stockholding costs at branch levels to be lowered and staff scheduling to become more cost-effective. EFTPOS has provided the facility for increasing margins (by reducing transaction charges) and increasing cash available to the business (by decreasing the time taken to obtain cash from customer transactions). Technology has also been used by multiple retailing to substitute technology for labour. Specifically the use of technology to rationalise stockholding and manpower has made a major contribution towards a continued improvement in contribution margins. There are a number of aspects that should be considered within the overall topic of branch operations.

Market Rent

The move by many companies to charge realistic market based rents to their branch outlets has resulted in equally realistic book performances from the

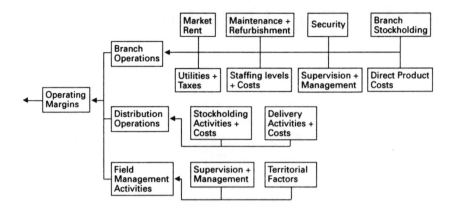

Figure 4.1 Managing operating margins: components factors and activities

branches. So much so that when the adjusted performance levels were reviewed there was concern expressed as to the 'real' profitability of many businesses. While it may be argued that initially this is an accounting adjustment the significance of market based rents become considerably more important when strategic implementation issues are evaluated, particularly involving the redeployment of property or the acquisition of more sites.

Another related topic concerns the payment and motivation of branch management and staff. If incentive payments have been based upon branch contribution performance achievements, it follows that an adjustment of branch operations costs by the adoption of market, rather than notional rents may result in some dissatisfaction.

The high level of activity during the latter half of the 1980s resulted in large increases in property freeholds, leaseholds and rent payments. Many of the increases were considerably larger than were budgeted, resulting in under-performance achievement for many companies. This led to most companies undertaking vigorous evaluation of both existing and proposed locations. The result was a withdrawal by many of the multiples from a large number of branches creating a surplus of property, and a downward trend in prices. It follows that strategy implementation activities should consider the significance of recent events carefully. While the availability of low rented property may be attractive the surplus may soon become a shortage and further expansion expensive.

Utilities and Taxes

Utilities costs have received constant attention by retailers since the large increases in energy costs experienced during the 1970s. The expansion strategy of the 1980s and the move towards larger units has resulted in the development of computer based energy management systems. However, energy costs remain high and the impact of the privatisation of gas and electricity should be monitored closely to identify changes in pricing practices of the new businesses.

The revision of the local rating system has been the subject of considerable debate. It will have a significant impact on branch operating costs, particularly for companies whose strategic development has included the move into large retail units. For others who maintain a high street presence, increases in tax may result in large increases in operating costs and subsequent rationalisation.

Maintenance and Refurbishment Costs

Typically new developments are designed with low maintenance costs as a design requirement. However, there is a large amount of retail property that was built without the advantage of recent low maintenance systems and the costs may be becoming excessive. Of particular concern should be the impact of increasing sales activities in these outlets which may result in large increases in customer traffic flows and, as a consequence, large increases in maintenance costs.

Refurbishment costs should also feature in the implementation decision. Outlets designed for specific retailing applications may require very expensive remodelling and refurbishment. We have only to look back over the past ten years to see how retailing has changed. It is a dynamic activity and retailer response to consumer change may require extensive property alteration costs: a factor to be considered when developing implementation plans. Of particular importance is the fact that the life cycles of speciality retail formats are decreasing suggesting that alteration/refurbishment costs be carefully considered within the context of life cycle span and revenue, cash and profit generation expectation.

Staffing Costs

Here the issues are: number of staff, their quality and skills. Staff costs are a major element of operating costs and these have risen in recent years. The high overall levels of employment during the 1980s added to operating costs and the depressed levels of sales resulted in the review of staff numbers during the early 1990s. Wage rate increases were often greater than sales increases and accordingly margins were depressed.

Other issues now require consideration. The role of customer service has added training and development costs, necessary for the development of the levels of service now required. Add to this the longer operating hours now a feature of multiple retailers, offers and staffing costs become a large issue when strategy implementation is considered.

Stock Investment at Branch Level

Stockholding costs were considered during the discussion on gross margin management. Some points for consideration within the context of operating margins are of particular interest when management is considering strategic changes.

The first concerns critical mass. To obtain credibility within the target customer group, there is a minimum amount of choice and availability (i.e., width and depth) within a merchandise category that is acceptable. Clearly this may amount to a considerable investment for a business of any size.

A second issue concerns the nature of the way in which stockholding costs increase. As the number of stockholding points increases (together with adjustments to improve availability within selected core product groups) the level of stockholding increases exponentially.

It becomes clear that the increase in working capital requirements can be significant and should be included as a major issue when strategy implementation is considered. The implications for fixed costs will be discussed subsequently.

Direct Product Costs

The issues of customer choice and gross margin yield were discussed in the previous chapter. Here it should be emphasised that unless there is an adequate accounting system, capable of allocating activity costs to merchandise categories, DPC offers little benefit.

For operations management purposes the specific cost data required concerns the handling and storage activities of merchandise, with particular emphasis on excessive cost items. With these identified, their impact may be evaluated in the context of the revenue benefits that accrue to the inclusion of the merchandise within the assortment. For evaluation purposes the interest is upon incremental differences at an operational level.

Decisions relating to strategic choices may require considerably more information than is currently available from DPP/DPC systems. Of particular interest in many situations is the incremental impact of change and of the impact on both gross and operating margins of changes in the merchandise mix. To be effective this requires that customer response and perceptions be considered.

Supervision and Management

The size of many retail outlet types has expanded as the nature of these businesses has changed. For example, the rapid rate of change of the DIY sector has been accompanied by a complete restructuring of the activity. From a high street based, fragmented retail sector comprising specialist activities (i.e. paint and wallpaper outlets, hardware, timber stockists and plumbing specialists) there is now a highly concentrated sector. As it grew it has changed dramatically, operating out of very large off-centre units, often with multi-million pound turnover and large numbers of staff.

The managerial skills required to manage the outlets (and the specialist activities within them) require highly trained and motivated personnel. It should also be noted that in many instances the apparent 'transferability' of managerial skills is, when examined closely, only superficial. It follows that before implementing a diversification proposal that involves large retailing units there should be a rigorous examination of the nature of the operating tasks to identify what synergy might exist but also the additional 'plant', systems and personnel development requirements.

Security

There are three aspects of security to be considered. The first concerns the security of the merchandise. Theft by customers and by internal methods is increasing. The cost of security is increasing as the sophistication of security systems increases. Similarly, there is a security issue for the premises and here too the costs are increasing for the same reasons. There is also an increasing problem of personal security for personnel at all levels in the business and at all times of the day, not only during operating hours.

Security should be included as a factor when strategy implementation is planned. There are likely to be important considerations for high value merchandise (audio-visual equipment) and security issues differ markedly by geographical location, even between locations in neighbourhoods. The impact of security measures upon customer service activities should be evaluated prior to firm decisions being taken.

4.2 DISTRIBUTION OPERATIONS

Branch distribution activities and service requirements can, and do have totally different cost profiles. The implementation process should consider the customer service requirements of target customer groups together with the likely service which will be available from suppliers. Both aspects of service influence the two major cost components; stockholding and delivery.

The majority of retailing companies optimise distribution operations thereby ensuring that service and costs are at levels acceptable to both customers and their operating budgets. It follows that the distribution system evolving from this process has characteristics and cost profiles that are specific to: the size of the business; the customer service offered; the geographical characteristics that may have an influence on distribution, the characteristics of the merchandise offer, and the trading format, i.e. size and location of the retail outlets. It should not be surprising to find that distribution systems are exclusive to the company's business philosophy and activities and that very little (similar to the nature of the management of the outlets) can be transferred without modification.

Stockholding Activities

Some aspects of stockholding costs were discussed in an earlier section. There are some remaining issues. The first concerns the decision that is made on the extent of the need to be able to control the level of availability within the service offer to customers. If there is a strong competitive need to ensure high levels of availability then often the decision to control stock *within* the company follows. Core product stocks are held in company distribution facilities in order that the retailer can exercise control. Clearly the costs and benefits should be evaluated because the costs of such a decision extend well beyond the stock investment. They include the size of the facilities, staff and supervision, systems and transport decisions.

A second issue concerns the delivery to customers of large, difficult to handle products such as furniture. If this aspect of customer service is significant, then it follows that it too requires to be evaluated: the activities identified in the previous paragraph become more significant in terms of the size of cost elements.

Delivery Activities

Delivery costs are clearly closely related to stockholding cost issues with the additional consideration of time and distance. Expansion strategies are based on expanding the sizes of existing outlets or increasing the number of the outlets. In both situations there are cost implications. Expanded outlets will require more deliveries and these may be 'specialist' if the merchandise range assortment is expanded. An increase in the number of outlets will also involve an increase in costs. Furthermore these may not be incremental increases. They are more likely to include fixed costs, i.e. additional vehicles and equipment together with staff.

Both stockholding costs and delivery costs are influenced by supplier/ retailer relationships. Large retailers have had a dominant position with suppliers in recent years, however, this may change as the EC standardisation of tariffs has encouraged some centralisation and concentration of manufacturing and distribution from locations in continental Europe. Some commentators are suggesting that this may redress the balance of power within the supplier/distribution set. Should this situation occur, it suggests that service concessions will be available from large suppliers only on the basis of volume of business placed.

4.3   FIELD MANAGEMENT ACTIVITIES

There has been a move towards reducing the numbers of field management and service activities within the larger multiple retailers. This has occurred in an attempt to reduce costs but more important has been the influence of the application of information technology for planning, communication and control of the stores' routine activities.

Of particular interest when planning strategy implementation is the impact that any fundamental change might have upon field operations costs. For example, a shift towards a market position in which the target customer group is more responsive to service would require some considered thought on the extent of the implications this move could impose upon the business. This would require a completely new approach to performance criteria, to staff numbers, quality and training and field supervision and management activities.

Supervision and Management

Management styles differ markedly between sectors: it is not difficult to find major differences between businesses in the same sector. It should not, therefore, be assumed that a successful operations management approach will be equally successful when it is applied to a strategic alternative.

One of the first tasks facing management when implementing a strategy option should be, having considered operations issues, how the retail offer differs within the context of the major positioning elements (i.e. merchandise characteristics, customer service, trading format and store environment and customer communications) and further, how these differences will affect the management of operations.

The concerns should not be confined simply to new business ventures. Quite often the expansion of the merchandise assortment to include products requiring quite different visual merchandising methods can involve hitherto unnecessary operations methods. These can be costly. The cost may be due to errors of omission (e.g. poor response to customer instore expectations) resulting in lost sales or possibly the costs of introducing methods and systems that (because of low volumes) do not earn a return on their investment.

Territorial Factors

Typically growth strategies seek to expand the business incrementally. An existing formula is 'rolled out' into territories which were often seen as less attractive or, more likely, were some distance from the central administration activity.

There should not be a field management problem if there is simply an expansion of the existing business. For example, in businesses which are centrally controlled and for which it is important that a uniform 'image' be presented to customers and standard merchandise offers are made with tightly controlled stock levels, field operations costs may be high. The food and DIY multiples are examples of centrally controlled businesses. By contrast the department store sector, which often has quite different customer profiles for each of its locations, has a more open approach. Geography can influence the nature of the control requirements: in France the Carrefour company, operating nationally, clearly found that operations and some buying decisions are handled much more effectively if done so locally.

Information Technology has facilitated centralised control. The transfer of branch performance data for management purposes can be achieved rapidly, accurately and at low cost. The application of computer aided design (CAD) packages permit visual merchandising and space allocation decisions to be implemented and monitored. Consequently, field management activities can be made more cost-effective.

SUMMARY

This chapter has identified the major issues and activities that should be examined by management responsible for implementing management decisions. The operating margins of the business are responsible for generating contribution to the overhead recovery and profitability of the business. Three areas have been suggested as important and they should be examined closely prior to any irreversible decision made. It is important to remember that as the business moves away from its main core theme its expertise becomes less and time is required to develop an approach which ensures that maximum productivity from operations management is achieved.

We have discussed the need to relate decisions to customer expectation factors. Again it must be remembered that as the business moves into new customer segments not only do customer expectations change but so too do competitors and they too should be evaluated. We shall consider this topic further in Chapter 14.

5 Managing the Cash Generation Activity

INTRODUCTION

Cash and profit are two of the main concerns of the business. They are both important but they are different. Cash is an asset of the business which can be used to purchase goods or services. Profit is the surplus resulting from a period of trading, having deducted all business expenses from sales revenue. Profit is an accounting measurement not an asset owned by a business.

Clearly the business is interested in both cash and profit. Cash is needed to pay suppliers and employees and to expand the business, while profit is needed to provide a return to the owners of the business and to maintain the confidence of investors, financial markets and commentators.

The importance of cash to the business can be seen in Figure 5.1. The business generates cash from sales to customers and from funds borrowed (for short periods, e.g. bank overdrafts or long periods, e.g. long term loans from specialist lending facilities in banks). They may also obtain cash by selling shares in the business. Lenders and owners receive interest payments and dividends from businesses as payment for the loss of the use of their funds. Cash is used to buy merchandise for resale (at a profit), to pay employees' wages and to pay the operating expenses of the business. Cash is also used to replace assets used in running the existing business and to purchase assets to expand the business. The business may also be expanded by acquiring other businesses. Cash may be used to do this but usually it is financed by borrowing (long term funds) and/or by issuing shares in the acquirer's business or the 'new' business formed after the acquisition.

In this chapter we are concerned with managing cashflow. We have established the importance of cash to the operational running of the business and for the strategic growth of the business. We shall continue by considering the sources of cash and the factors to be considered when making decisions concerning the alternative sources. If cash is generated it is for a purpose and again we consider operational and strategic aspects of cashflow uses. Both cash generation and cash use have aspects of risk that must be considered. While we shall discuss this issue in detail in a subsequent chapter, some aspects of risk will be mentioned briefly.

5.1 USES FOR CASHFLOW

Firms generate cash for a number of reasons, which may be considered as operational uses and strategic uses. Both share the same objective; the

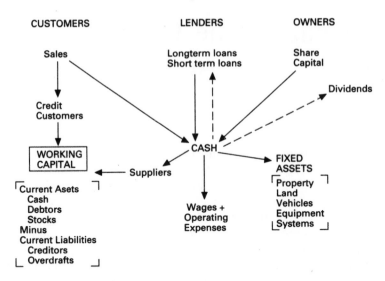

Figure 5.1   The role of cash in the flow of funds through the business

maximisation of the wealth of the shareholders of the business and this is
equal to the discounted value of the expected future net cashflows into the
business. This objective requires the firm to consider both strategic investment decisions, i.e. the size and capacity of the business and operational
short term investment decisions upon the most profitable use of the firm's
capacity. Having decided upon strategic direction the implementation of
management decisions concerns the most profitable use of the capacity
generated. The rate of return expected from various projects will influence
the sourcing decision for the funds. However, many applications of funds
are often for non-profit making facilities, to implement health and safety
regulations. Clearly, for such applications, high rate of interest sources will
be avoided. For other purposes, such as to fund an acquisition the company
may have little choice but to accept a rate of interest imposed by the sources
and upon which investment decisions must be based. Figure 5.2 illustrates
the sources and uses of cash.

Operational Uses of Cash

There are a number of reasons why companies may require cash. Some of
these are aimed at improving the short term financial structure of the business, some may be an operational necessity, while others are aimed at simply
improving facilities for employees.

Losses from Operations
These can occur for a number of reasons. Mark-downs often occur because
of poor trading conditions or perhaps because of inefficient buying. Typically the problem can be relieved by accepting lower margins from an in-

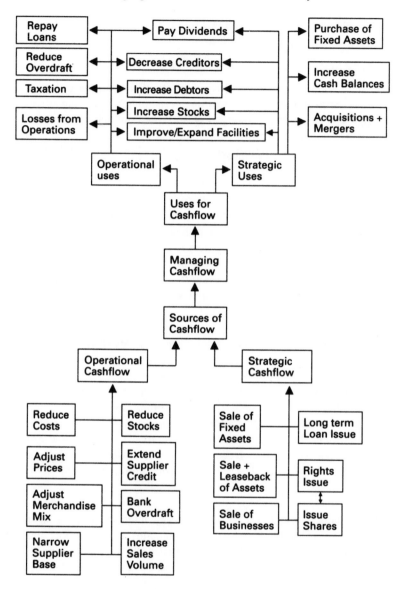

Figure 5.2 Managing cashflow: sources

creased sales volume, failure to do so will require the company to obtain the necessary funds from other sources.

Pay Tax
The payment of tax is a legal obligation and one for which provision should be made from the profit and loss account. There are different forms of tax, some having quite different impact upon operating and strategic decisions.

While tax accounting is a complicated and specialist activity, the necessity to generate funds to pay tax is quite simple.

Reduce Overdraft

Interest rates fluctuate and with them the cost of debt to the business. Typically, short term debt is subject to more frequent changes and often, if the rates move upward over a prolonged period, the company may prefer to use its own funds generated from operations to finance the business during the time period it considers interest rates to be too high for its type of business.

Repay Loans

Loans may be both short and long term. Usually both are for a specified period and consequently their repayment requires scheduling. Clearly there is a demand for cash to meet these obligations. Poor trading performance may lead to the company seeking external sources of cash to repay the loan or perhaps to the renegotiation of the loan. A difference in interest rates can influence this decision. Indeed, a view that suggests a prolonged period of low interest rates and encourage businesses to renegotiate loans.

Facilities Improvements

As suggested earlier in this Chapter not all projects are directly profit earning. Some projects require cash in order to meet obligations, either imposed by legislation or to make improvements to facilities that will in turn improve employee/company relationships. Quite often such expenditure can be helpful during a strategy implementation programme. For example, a consolidation and productivity strategy requiring job restructuring and rationalisation may be facilitated by expenditure of this nature. It requires low cost cash.

Some features of the use of cash have implications for both operational and strategic uses of cash. The following four topics share this feature.

Pay Dividends

Paying dividends is essential if the shareholders' interests are to be maintained. Often the level of dividends expected (and paid) do not reflect the actual performance of the business. As a consequence the payments cannot be met from the profit generated and are supported by cash either from retained earnings or from external sources.

There are other reasons why dividend payments in excess of expectations are made. A company expecting to make a significant strategic move such as an acquisition may wish to make a positive statement to the shareholders of the target company.

Decrease Creditors

Again both operational and strategic factors are to be found. An operational factor could be based upon a move by suppliers to encourage a faster turn round of accounts in order to improve their own cashflow situation. Hence a retailer may find an increase in buying discounts an acceptable trade-off for prompter payment of the supplier's account. If the supplier accounts for a large proportion of the retailer's business the cash differentials may be quite large.

A significant strategic factor may be the need for the retailer to improve its payment profile and credit rating prior to undertaking expansion. The planned growth may be in the same (or in an adjacent) product-market. If it plans to use existing suppliers and increase its business with them, it may consider that is in its best interests to improve its payment performance prior to negotiating new business terms.

The implementation of a strategy change may well require a different approach to trade creditors. For example, a highly concentrated supply market is able to apply strict controls on credit allowed to distributors and the opportunity for retailer customers to 'extend' payment cycles and terms may not be available. Consequently, the cash requirements for prompt settlement of suppliers' accounts will be greater.

Increase Debtors

There are both operational and strategic aspects to this topic. An operational factor may occur during periods of recession when sales may be achieved, only if credit facilities are made attractive. For example, the consumer durable and motor vehicle retailers were badly affected by the recession during the early 1990s and in an attempt to maintain sales volumes were offering zero rate credit, delayed payments and other incentives. There was an increase in cash requirements for this purpose.

A strategic aspect that may require serious consideration because of its cashflow implications would concern expansion into a segment in which customers are highly sensitive to service. For example, a positioning shift into the 'international label boutique' segment by a ladieswear retailer or department store is likely to increase customer credit expectations levels. These may be 'factored' by using credit card company facilities, however, the benefits of customer contact through a customer data base driven by a store card may be more attractive: choice of the latter option will require an increase in cash resources.

Increase Stocks

The operational implications of an increase in stock levels occur for a number of reasons. The most common cause is the need to offer improved availability in core merchandise groups. A similar situation may occur for competitive reasons: rather than compete on price alone, some segments such as specialist high priced apparel retailers, may find customer expectations for choice are more important than availability for customer satisfaction.

Strategic considerations of stock increases are concerned with the 'permanent' requirement for both availability and choice in target segments. High levels of stock may require additional sourcing as well as increased levels of merchandise for service purposes. The additional sourcing may require overseas supplies and the lead time increases will require an increase in cash requirements. There will also be an impact on fixed assets, we will discuss this below.

Strategic Uses of Cash

The strategic uses of cash are typically for expansion and growth purposes. They may be for expanding the existing business or undertaking new ventures.

Purchase of Fixed Assets

A major use for cash is the purchase of fixed assets. This may be to expand the existing business or as fixed assets for a diversification programme. Expanding the existing business is accompanied with less risk than acquiring fixed assets for a new venture. The type of location and its size are 'known factors', and there is sufficient experience within the business to be able to estimate the anticipated price, its 'performance' and thereby an estimate of the return on investment.

However, acquiring assets for new ventures requires considerable analysis to establish a profile of the performance requirements of the asset, e.g. sales/contribution per unit of space, capacity for growth and expansion, vulnerability to competition from nearby competition. In addition the cost characteristics and nature of ownership arrangements (e.g. freehold, leasehold, length of lease, rent reviews, flexibility on uses) adjacent businesses, and, most important the customer profile. Given this information, it is possible to derive revenue and cost forecasts, apply a sensitivity analysis package and from this estimate a return on investment.

It should be remembered that whereas cash is a liquid asset with very high flexibility, fixed assets do not share this facility and typically can only be liquidated after having accepted a penalty. Furthermore, there is always the possibility that an alternative may offer a higher return.

Increase Cash Balances

Prior to making a strategy change it may be useful to increase the negotiating flexibility of the business by building strong cash balances. It is possible that an acquisition can be agreed quickly, and with less disruption to the company, if cash is the basis of the bid. Consequently for some companies, it is important to manage cash balances in line with the implementation requirements of the strategic direction. Equally strong cash balances also offer flexibility when negotiating for fixed assets.

Acquisitions and Mergers

The previous paragraph suggested that one of the motives for increasing cash levels is to facilitate acquisitions. An important feature of a cash based acquisition is that, whereas a share based takeover can dilute the price of both companies' shares (and may also have an impact on the control of the new business), the cash based acquisition does not. However, it is important to consider how the cash is raised since borrowing also presents problems.

5.2 SOURCES OF CASH

Cash can be generated from two sources. It may result from operating decisions which are taken with a number of objectives in mind, one of which is to generate cash for use elsewhere in the business. Typically the decisions taken affect short term activities. Cash may also result from long term, structural decisions which affect the financial and asset structures of the business. Clearly current practices may not be operable in new segments or sectors.

Operational Cashflow Considerations

Retail management does not have the means to make changes to its operations which can have prompt influences on the use of cash in many of its activities. To reduce the need for cash is in effect to increase the operational cashflow within the business.

Increase Sales Volume

If we return to Chapter 1, Figure 1.1, the basic model of the firm, we can see that sales are an important feature of successful businesses. As we shall see from a subsequent Chapter, the impact of an increase in sales on a business can be very significant on its performance characteristics. If a sales increase can be achieved without an increase in the fixed costs and fixed assets of the business, the increased return on investment (capital employed) may be significant.

Equally it can be seen that the increase in cash available to the business will be large if margins are maintained, more so if productivity increases can work through the operational activities to improve operating/contribution margins. Economies of scale throughout the business increase as the business maximises its throughput on an optimal asset base. When faced with implementing strategy, these relationships should be identified, understood and utilised.

Reduce Costs

By reducing costs the business uses less cash and thus makes it available for use elsewhere in the business, or more likely, reduces the need to borrow cash on overdraft. This latter aspect also has the duplicate effect of also reducing financing costs. The recession period of the late 1980s and early 1990s, was a period during which many companies undertook large rationalisation actions which resulted in considerable reductions of overall costs and reduced cash requirements.

While the benefits of lower cost businesses are obvious, the impact on customer service was for many detrimental. Not only were staff numbers reduced but often so too was quality, service became slow and service quality reduced. It follows that businesses should attempt to evaluate the impact of cost reductions upon customer perceptions (and actions) as well as on cashflow.

Adjust Prices

A review of the price competitiveness of the merchandise offer is likely to reveal areas of strength and of weakness. Areas of weakness are sections of the range where no major added value to customers can be seen relative to competitors and it follows that prices among competitors are likely to be similar offering little competitive flexibility.

However, it is also likely that some parts of the merchandise assortment do have added value advantages and these should be considered in the context of offering a monopoly benefit. For example, there are merchandise items for which differentiation is relatively easy and this characteristic together with the offer of choice to customers reduces their price sensitivity. In these situations prices may be increased with little adverse response from customers.

Price reductions on price sensitive merchandise categories may also result in improved revenues and cashflow. Care should be taken to ensure that sales of merchandise for which prices are reduced actually result in increased profitability as well as increased revenue and cashflow. An arbitrary reduction of prices may result in an increase in operations and distribution costs, thereby decreasing profit and increasing the demand for cash. A consolidation and productivity strategy may benefit from such an approach.

However, it should be said that a market based approach to pricing will ensure sales at acceptable margins and will avoid the need for sales at marked down prices.

Adjust Merchandise Mix

Cash generation can be significantly influenced by merchandise decisions. A narrow range of merchandise will restrict customer choice but will, if sales volumes are maintained, increase stock turn. Assuming that suppliers are paid with the same frequency the result will be an increase of cash available to the business. This policy has been used with considerable success in businesses which are characterised by high average stock turns. Skilful merchandise management and selection can result in minimal impact to customer expectations for choice but can maximise the benefits of negative working capital, i.e. the amount of suppliers' cash used within the business. The impact of negative working capital can be very significant. An increase in stock turn from once every six weeks (stock turn 8.6) to one every two weeks (stock turn 26) is feasible in commodity merchandise groups with stable demand, particularly if an EPOS system is used to capture sales data and generate orders. The result is that payments to suppliers lag behind sales thereby generating a large amount of cash for use within the business. It should, however, be an integral part of the company strategy.

Narrow the Supplier Base

The effect of rationalising the number of suppliers also reduces cash tied up in the business. For each supplier there is a level of safety stock in the business, together with a number of activities (such as order placement, progressing, checking, receiving and quality control checks) each of which generate costs and a requirement for cash.

Selective rationalisation which reduces costs without significantly affecting customer responses clearly offers benefits. However, there may be hidden costs. Most retailers operate with multiple suppliers in order to ensure cover should one or more supplier be unable to supply all, or some, of the needs of the business. A reduction in the number of suppliers may increase the risk of stock-outs and lost sales. This has both short term and long term implications for the business resulting in, initially, lost sales but ultimately in lost customers. This approach should clearly be used cautiously.

Reduce Stocks

Similar costs and benefits are likely to accrue if stocks are reduced. However, if viewed selectively there can be low risk cost benefits. Clearly stocks of core products or core ranges would only be reduced following a carefully considered review of sales patterns. Items that are slow moving may be reduced once no adverse impact on customer satisfaction has been ascertained as likely.

An effective alternative is to consider a reduction in stockholding locations. This suggests that rather than eliminate some items from the range, they are held centrally with a given delivery period such that customer service is only marginally reduced. This has other benefits. At the store level of operations, it releases space to more profitable merchandise or service uses, thereby increasing overall profitability of sales capacity. It will also improve the utilisation of the distribution facilities by optimising rate of sale and rate of delivery costs. The result is that cash can be released throughout the business.

Extend Supplier Credit

Extending the payment terms by delaying paying suppliers' invoices has a similar effect on cashflow as adjusting the merchandise mix (see above).

However, there are disadvantages. Often suppliers will take the cost of delays into account when entering subsequent negotiations. Secondly, should the supplier be in a position in which capacity is restricted, those retail customers with a history of slow payment are usually the first to receive partial orders.

This practice should preferably be used in consultation with suppliers who may well offer alternatives such as sale or return or additional discounts for concessions, e.g. instore merchandising access, exclusivity (or spatial preference).

When considering strategy development and implementation, industry sector practices should be ascertained and their implications for cashflow management evaluated. Failure to do so may result in future difficulty.

Bank Overdraft

A common operational source of cash is a bank overdraft. Overdrafts can be expensive and may be difficult to obtain. To ensure that costs are minimised and also to convince the bank that the business is in control of its cashflow, a cashflow schedule for an appropriate trading period should be prepared. A cashflow schedule identifies variations in sales activity throughout the trading period; the lead and lag periods of ordering and payment of suppliers; and variations in operating expenses which may correlate with the sales activity. In this way the surpluses and shortfalls in cashflow are identified and overdraft requirements better managed.

Clearly there are implications for strategy implementation. Changes proposed to the core business strategy and/or structure may have implications for cashflow management. New business ventures may have quite different 'seasons' and therefore different cashflow schedules. There is also the possibility of identifying a business with complementary cash use and cash generation profiles which, when combined, may significantly reduce the external cash requirements of the overall business.

Strategic Cashflow Considerations

Cash may be generated by decisions which have a long term impact on the business. These may change its financial structure, its asset base or both.

Sale of Fixed Assets

By disposing of fixed assets large amounts of cash can be generated. There are a number of issues that should be considered. Once the asset has been sold (particularly land and buildings) it may be expensive, if subsequently it is found that market opportunities, hitherto unrealised, materialise and the company wishes to exploit them. This was a significant feature of the 1980s but the recession of the 1990s resulted in a depression of property and land prices and consequently both assume more realistic prices.

Secondly, there is a 'once only' effect. Once the cash is released and used elsewhere, it obviously cannot feature in the company in any future capacity. The significance of this point is that a number of retail businesses improved both cashflow and profitability by selling underutilised land and property assets to bolster profits (and dividends) during periods of poor trading performance. Thus a short, or at best medium, term benefit was gained but for some it may have long term 'costs'.

Sale and Lease Back of Assets

This offers a compromise to the situation described above. The ownership of the asset is relinquished, however use of it continues. Sale and lease back releases cash for use elsewhere in the business but because the asset no longer features on the balance sheet, its subsequent sale to increase profits is no longer an option.

Both the sale of fixed assets and sale and lease back have strategy implementation significance. A number of acquisitions and mergers have been undertaken because of the potential to realise cash and profit from the sale of fixed assets (and the sale and lease back if the asset has strategic significance). Quite often post-acquisition the new, larger, company has too many outlets. The growth of the British Shoe Corporation is an example of how serial acquisitions can result in an excess of sales capacity. Similarly, the growth of Sears has resulted in subsidiary companies competing with each other, or at best, 'overlapping' very similar retail offers. It follows that growth strategies should be evaluated for opportunities to rationalise outlet representation provided that sales and profits (and most importantly customer service) are not compromised. Sale and lease back is often referred to as 'off balance sheet' financing.

Sale of Businesses

Just as assets can be sold so too can businesses or subsidiaries. This usually occurs in two ways. Often when one business acquires another, it may dispose of parts of the acquired business. This may be because it planned to do so in order to finance the acquisition or, alternatively, it may do so because it recognises that it lacks the expertise to manage the business successfully and that the use of its managerial expertise would be more profitable if it reduced the size and scope of the business to match its perceived strengths.

A second reason for selling a subsidiary business may be to release cash to meet the expense of managing the remainder of the business. A number of examples of this aspect occurred during the early 1990s. Retailers, such as Burton and Ratner, undertook large amounts of debt financing in order to expand. The debt required servicing (see next topic) but because sales volumes declined, the cash was not available to maintain interest payments. Initially the debt may be 'restructured' but if the funding sources become concerned about the future repayment of the loans, they will insist on the sale of viable parts of the business which will provide cash and reduce the level of the outstanding borrowings. Often the businesses themselves reach this conclusion and themselves decide upon the sale of parts of the business which may have appeal to other companies, often competitors.

Long Term Debt

Some of the characteristics and issues associated with long term debt have been mentioned in the previous paragraph. Long term debt (debentures, etc.) has the major advantage of offering the company the benefit of deducting the interest paid as an expense of the business, thereby reducing tax and increasing the return to the shareholder. As we saw above, the major disadvantage occurs when the business encounters trading difficulties: the interest payments remain but often the profitability of the company is low.

Debt financing was popular during the 1980s and many companies used it to expand the size of their businesses through acquisition. The interest payment commitment does, however, require businesses to generate high levels of income and, as discussed earlier, if this cannot be achieved in the market-place, assets (or businesses) are sold.

Debt also changes the financial structure of a business. Ideally there is a combination between debt and equity (shareholders' capital) with which the 'financial community' is happy. If the debt proportion increases to too high a proportion of the long term financial structure further borrowing is more expensive (i.e. the interest rate charged is raised to reflect the perceived risk) or may be refused altogether.

Clearly this topic can be a major issue for successful implementation of a growth based strategy requiring finance. Management should consider the strategy from the financier's viewpoint and attempt to assess the risk that they perceive.

Issue Shares

Another option the company has to fund long term projects is to issue more equity shares. While this does not have the tax advantage of debt financing, it does not have the major disadvantage of an ongoing commitment to pay interest to bondholders. The company issuing shares does not necessarily have the commitment to pay dividends unless they are preference shares (for which there is a fixed rate of dividend [usually cumulative] if declared).

The issue of shares may take one or more of a number of forms. The equity base of the business may be expanded by offering shares of ordinary capital. More often, if it is to raise cash, a rights issue (an offer of shares to existing shareholders) is undertaken.

The major issue concerns control of the company and the company issuing shares is mindful of the fact that if too many shares (with voting rights) are issued, the control of the company could shift into the hands of a group whose interests are not congruent with the former major shareholders.

It follows that, if cash is to be raised by a share issue, care should be taken to ensure that the control of the company remains much the same. Failure to do so could result in the company raising the required cash to implement a strategic directive but with a new board of directors who may reverse the decision.

SUMMARY

This chapter has identified the major sources and uses of cash of typical retailing businesses. During the discussion, the major advantages and disadvantages have been identified and discussed.

The final point to be made concerns the need for management to identify *all* of the issues involved when undertaking either short term or long term sourcing and use decisions. Recent history (the late 1980s and early 1990s) suggests that a number of problems that beset some very large retailing companies could have been avoided if they had considered all of the likely events of the external business environment. Operational cashflow and strategic cashflow will be considered in Chapter 14.

6 Strategic and Operating Economics of the Business

INTRODUCTION

When implementing strategy it is useful to consider the impact of decisions that are about to be taken above the strategic and operating economics of the business. It is also worthwhile to consider how the economics of the business can influence implementation decisions. For example, the decision to increase shopping facilities by opening branches for business on Sundays and on public holidays may enhance the utilisation of the assets or indeed may require additional expenditures that lower the returns to the business. The business should question the motives of such moves. Is the move seen as a strategic initiative to add value to the customer offer or is it a competitive reaction? Furthermore, what can the business expect of its sales volume profile: will it increase or perhaps will it merely be spread across the increased hours of opening?

The answers to such questions are important issues particularly as far as the performance of the fixed assets are concerned. The distribution function should be structured to offer a service response to planned volume throughputs, the nature of these will vary with the pattern of business. Clearly any change in the business which may result in changes in the timing and volume of throughputs may have significant implications for the size of the distribution facilities and the scheduling of order assembly and deliveries. The economics of the distribution function could possibly change significantly with a demand from the branches for smaller, more frequent deliveries.

Clearly the existence of assets with high costs and the need for high volume throughput to achieve planned utilisation and cost recovery can also influence the strategy decision. Obvious examples are those of investment in distribution facilities, information technology and include 'intangibles' such as national advertising campaigns. For each there can be a substantial impact on economies of scale when volume is increased.

We shall discuss the characteristics of economies of scale and the various sources of economies of scale in this chapter. We shall also consider the types of diseconomies of scale that firms may be confronting beyond certain levels of output or size.

6.1 SOURCES OF ECONOMIES OF SCALE

Managerial economics offers an interesting literature based upon the theoretical analysis of business cost structures. It suggests that costs of production, distribution, managing and controlling the business should be considered when considering options which involve varying the levels of volume of the business activity. These concerns are similar for manufacturing and distribution businesses and are based upon the debate surrounding the characteristics of the long-run cost curve.

There are a number of sources of economies of scale that are both internal and external to the firm. Here we shall consider: firm economies of scale (these include production/capacity economies, procurement, promotional, technological, funding, property, replication and managerial economies of scale); specialisation; economies of scale due to indivisibilities, stochastic economies of scale, and economies of scope.

Production/Capacity Economies

These are often the basis for considering the basic mathematics of many examples of economies of scale. It is a basic concept in physics that in an industrial process requiring a mixing activity the surface area of the container increases much less rapidly than does the volume of output as the size of the activity is expanded. Thus it follows that the productive capacity of capital equipment rises faster than does its purchase price: a warehouse capable of twice the throughput of a smaller one will typically be built and commissioned for less than half its cost. Maintenance and repair costs are likely to be similarly disproportionate.

This relationship raises some interesting issues concerning the expansion of various elements of the business. It explains the move towards centrally managed and located distribution activities. Clearly the impact on margins can be significant if the investment/cost per unit relationship can be managed to ensure that high levels of throughput will be realised. Similarly the expansion of outlet numbers will have a similar impact. It follows that provided the cost of the activity which responds in this way represents a significant proportion of total costs then expansion of the business to take advantage of the economies of scale (all other things being equal) makes sound sense.

Procurement Economies

In large businesses, such as multiple retailers, high volume sales result in higher gross margins.The relationship is one in which the percentage increase in buying terms or margins is related to the percentage increase in volume. In addition there are often additional benefits and services which have a favourable impact on operating costs.

This effect can also accrue to buying organisation costs. The increase in variable costs necessary to service large increases in purchase volumes, serviced by the same fixed cost infrastructure, is relatively low and therefore can create an opportunity to increase margins and possibly make pricing more competitive. This is of particular interest to multiple retailers whose merchandise offer includes a significant proportion of non-differentiated commodity products or products with a number of similar characteristics as those offered by competitors. Examples of commodity products include non-fashion apparel, many food product ranges, and hardware DIY ranges. All have sufficiently similar characteristics for them to be added to the range of an existing buyer. Thus fixed costs are not increased and the range extension offers an opportunity to increase profits incrementally.

Promotional Economies

Promotional economies occur in two ways. There is the effect due to the size of volume of purchases of media space and time, for which discounts and preferential times or journal space locations are given, thereby lowering the overall cost of promotion and possibly increasing the effectiveness.

There is also the benefit that multiple retailers obtain when they operate a concentration of stores within a television or other media region. This will achieve greater effectiveness than a retailer with the same number of outlets dispersed across a larger geographical territory. The economies are likely to be wider in their nature than simply due to promotional effectiveness. Concentrated promotions typically generate high sales volumes and these will benefit the retail company from a buying margin and distribution cost advantage. Often these benefits can be significant when a range of products is promoted in a large area, such as the South East and London, where the volumes realised are high.

Technological Economies

Again we see the benefits of economies of scale for large companies who are able to invest in technological applications. Size is a benefit because it enables the business to make extensive use of technology in functions and activities (and at various levels) of the business which smaller and medium size businesses could not make viable.

An obvious example concerns the use of electronic point of sale (EPOS) equipment. There are numerous applications, for all sizes of business but the benefits are only maximised when the EPOS system is used to link in with suppliers' production and distribution activities and thereby manage the supply chain. The smaller business can achieve operating economies from more efficient stock control (and therefore lower stock investment) but the major benefits accrue to size and wider applications of the system.

Similarly for CAD (computer aided design) packages, there are enormous strategic and operating economies that can be created by the large company. For example, store layout and design projects can be completed for a chain of stores, and the design project implemented in a few weeks. Previously (without CAD packages) this would have taken months possibly a year or more, for a chain of 150 stores. Clearly the small/medium size retail business could not begin to contemplate such investment.

Distribution technology in order transmission, assembly and progressing, vehicle and warehousing activity scheduling (to mention but a few activities) is also a function of size. Here the smaller firm can obtain indirect benefit by either belonging to a group activity (e.g. a symbol group, such as SPAR) or by bulk purchasing from a large wholesaler who is using these technological applications effectively and sharing the cost savings with customers.

Funding Economies

It has been suggested (in the financial management literature) that there are benefits from size when funds are required. It is suggested that sources are wider and costs of funds (i.e. interest rates) are lower, the cost of the activity necessary is also probably lower. Clearly the view of risk to the lender is based upon the size of a borrower together with a record of successful trading. Furthermore, the large P.L.C. has many more options. Funds can be raised by expanding the equity base as well as by short and long term borrowing: increasingly the use of overseas sources is occurring, particularly the use of EC funds markets.

It is arguable that obtaining funds is too easy for large companies. Many of the leveraged acquisitions of the late 1980s were eventually seen as high risk investments as the companies involved struggled to service the interest payments from declining revenues.

Property Economies

This is also a size based topic. Larger companies benefit by establishing property functions within the firm to locate and negotiate (and dispose of) property requirements. They are staffed by architects and surveyors so that not only is there considerable expertise within the firm but this expertise is used to lower the costs of transactions and development of new locations.

Size is also of benefit when dealing with developers and property agents. The trading formats (and therefore property requirements) of the large multiples are well known. It follows that the property agents will approach the large retail companies with locations that 'fit' their format requirements. Similarly the contractors used by large multiple retailers benefit from previous experience in developing and constructing outlets for specific clients.

Economies of Replication

Economies of replication occur when a business expands by reproducing its format. Multiple retailers who expand by increasing the number of outlets, all of which use a similar design and operating method, benefit from economies of replication.

Clearly they also benefit from other scale effects (discussed above) as the overall size of the business is increased. The benefits may be quite large due to the fact that the increase in business is likely only to carry variable costs as the recovery of most of the fixed costs has largely been achieved. Furthermore they also benefit from the 'experience effect' (a phenomena based upon repeated activities and actions the more often they are undertaken).

Stochastic Economies of Scale

This scale effect is associated with inventory levels held to provide 'assurance' against a distribution failure. The safety stock level carried reduces, as the size of the business increases, when expressed as an amount per outlet or as an overall percentage of stockholding. Levels of safety stock carried depend upon a number of factors which include; the number of suppliers for a product category, the reliability of suppliers' deliveries, the importance of the product to the customer, product value, product storage characteristics (such as perishability, bulk, weight), rate of purchase and extent of the distribution of sales throughout the branch network.

Calculation of safety stock levels is based on a simple formula:

$$\text{Stock level} = \text{safety stock} \sqrt{n}$$

where n is the number of stockholding points.

It follows that by operating centrally based distribution activities the level of safety stock required may be considerably reduced. The concept is based upon the assumption that distribution (or other) failures do not occur at the rate that a business expands i.e., an increase in the number of branches will not be accompanied by a similar increase in the number of distribution failure occurrences.

Indivisibilities

Some activities, equipment or 'systems' have a minimum size and cannot be divided into smaller units. It follows that to operate a system at low capacity incurs a cost penalty in that the overhead cost is amortised over a small volume of sales. It is essential that to obtain the full benefit of such systems, management should attempt to undertake to match system capacity with throughput. Clearly this may not be possible for some projects but they should be aware of the extent of the under-utilised capacity and of its cost implications. It suggests that investment in 'indivisible systems' should consider the extent to which they may be used elsewhere in the business (currently or in the future) or even as a service to other businesses where certainly the penalties should be quantified.

Specialisation

Economies of scale due to the specialisation of labour and equipment are not restricted to manufacturing processes. It is well known in distribution that the distribution of specific categories of merchandise whose characteristics include features requiring specialist handling (e.g. frozen and chilled foods or perhaps rapid delivery under controlled conditions; pharmaceutical products) and whose rate of sale or sales distribution is low, is often undertaken by specialist 'third party' distribution service companies.

Specialist communications and research service companies have also developed within markets. The recorded music sector has specialists in promotion, distribution and market research activities. This situation has evolved because of the specific demand characteristics of segments within the market.

Managerial Economies

Clearly the range of control of individual managers can be extended and scale economies obtained. However, care should be taken in this respect. As we shall see later diseconomies can occur rapidly if managers' tasks are expanded to include new activities. Managerial economies are maximised most effectively if they are directed towards increasing the cost-effectiveness of the current task. This may be achieved by increasing the level of activity of existing functions or possibly adding tasks for which both the expertise and capacity are available. There is a 'span of control' (the number of individuals accountable to any one manager) beyond which the manager becomes ineffective. This can be increased by the application of information technology. However, this too is limited and has constraints, for example, an operations manager can obtain control data through an expanded information system, but effective control is more likely achieved by store visits, the nature of the task being an important consideration.

6.2 DISECONOMIES OF SCALE

The case for economies of scale in virtually all industrial activities is not disputed. The impact of scale on large manufacturing processes can result in substantial cost reductions. It is difficult to determine with any certainty whether or not firms also face diseconomies of scale once their level of output expands beyond a certain size.

Davies (1991) suggests that if attention is restricted to technological factors it is unlikely that diseconomies of scale exist. As throughput expands it is likely that the long-run cost curve flattens, and none of the forces which lead to scale economies are likely to begin to work in reverse at very high levels of output.

Davies argues that such diseconomies of scale that do exist are likely to be attributable to managerial factors rather than technological factors. This argument is based upon the 'span of control' (see above) which suggests that beyond an optimum number of individuals reporting to specific management activities effectiveness declines. However, as suggested above, the ineffectiveness can, to a point, be compensated by the use of technology but this too has limits and eventually *managerial diseconomies of scale* become a problem. It is possible that in process industries the point at which managerial diseconomies occur can be postponed by the substitution of appropriate technology and this point continues to be delayed as technological development of process controls advances.

However, in activities in which human resources are an important input there is a limit. The example given earlier concerning operations management is but one example. The problem likely to occur for many distribution companies is that as they restructure and replace levels of activities by technological substitution the symptoms of managerial diseconomies of scale will appear to the customer prior to becoming apparent to senior management. If this does occur, serious long-term damage to customer relationships (and possibly loyalty) may result.

Other sources of diseconomies of scale that may occur for distribution companies concern transportation costs and imperfections in the labour market. Transportation costs increase as the distance from distribution centres to branch locations is increased. It follows that an attempt to utilise warehouse capacity, or to expand the branch network, by adding branches to the service catchment area of distribution centres is almost certain to be accompanied by an increase in transportation costs. The firm can consider options, for example, suppliers' distribution activities may be more cost effective in this situation, or possibly the use of distribution service companies. The issue for the retail firm to resolve concerns overall cost and this includes control of the service aspects of inventory management. If availability or variety characteristics are likely to be affected by the change in distribution service patterns they should be examined in the overall context of customer satisfaction and the costs of achieving it.

The influence of labour market imperfections has been experienced by a number of multiple retailers who have expanded their branch network into new market territories. Some have found a shortage of labour willing to work at the planned rates for store staff (particularly in the more affluent parts of the south-east), others have found a shortage of people with the level of skills they require and have found it necessary to provide addi-

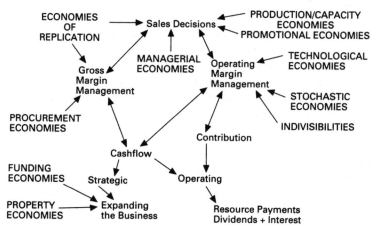

Figure 6.1 The impact of economies of scale

tional training programmes for new staff. In both examples the costs of expansion have been increased. The problem for one food multiple became sufficiently significant for the company to use a catchment profiling service to identify both market spend potential and to identify labour resource potential.

Essentially diseconomies of scale are seen to result from the problems of coordination and control encountered by management as the size of the business increases. These problems impose cost increases in a number of ways. The size of the management activity may increase greater than the increase in activity, resulting in relatively higher fixed costs.

We can see the impact of the range of economies of scale that influence the business in Figure 6.1 which returns to the model of the firm we introduced in Chapter 1. Central to the influence is the impact of managerial economies which operate in the major decision areas concerning sales generation, margins management and hence contribution and cashflow management. As intimated it is here where the success of the business is determined and for all businesses the extent (and limitations) of managerial economies should first be identified because they determine the structure of the business and establish an organisation which may then benefit from other economies of scale effects.

6.3 FACTORS AFFECTING CAPACITIES AND COSTS OF IMPLEMENTING STRATEGY

The Shape of the Long-Run Cost Curve

The foregoing discussion is influenced by the shape of the long-run cost curve. It is not suggested that companies should spend considerable time and resources in identifying individual cost curves but rather managers become aware of the implications of their decisions on the shape of the curve.

There are three generally accepted shapes that long-run cost curves might take. Figure 6.2 identifies these.

Figure 6.2a suggests that costs decrease but beyond the level at output O diseconomies of scale exist and costs begin to increase. Figure 6.2b shows a curve for which economies of scale are always available and as through-put is increased costs decrease. Figure 6.2c suggests costs decrease to a point known as the minimum efficient scale, beyond which no further scale economies have been identified. As Davies suggests there has to date been no easy way to identify cost curves and discriminate between alternative forms. He suggests attempting to use empirical evidence by using one of three alternative methods:

* Statistical estimation;
* The 'engineering' approach;
* The survivor technique.

Statistical estimation is a method by which observations are taken on the costs of producing a 'product' in firms operating at different levels of output, and uses statistical analysis to fit equations to the data. However there are problems. The first concerns the availability of data: data of this type is usually confidential, and therefore not readily available, and typically in a form which does not reflect the nature of the cost data required, i.e. activity costs and opportunity costs. Other problems involved concern the nature of the 'product' (i.e. the product mix) which clearly can have a major influence on costs, and the technology used in 'production' may differ markedly (depending upon investment capabilities, volumes, and 'product' characteristics and their requirements).

The engineering approach attempts to avoid many of the problems of the statistical approach by using the expertise of 'production' engineers (in a retailing context; distribution, operations and systems management) to design sets of 'plant' (stores and distribution centres, etc.) appropriate to the 'production' of different levels of output. Conceptually this approach has appeal but in practice it has problems reconciling conflict and confusion between accounting and economics concepts of costs. Another problem concerns the apportioning of total cost amongst different products, an

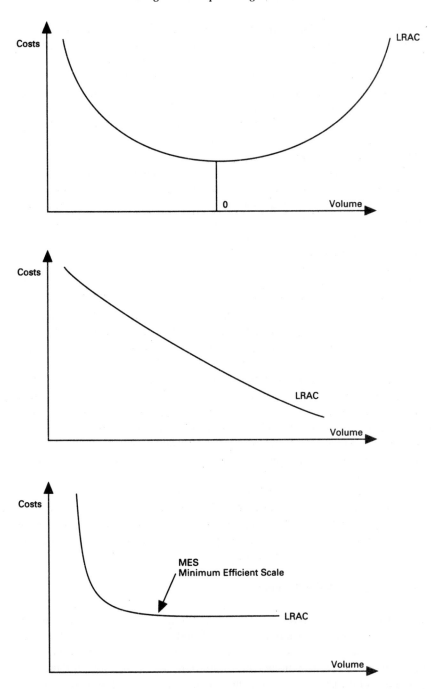

Figure 6.2 Alternative forms of the long-run cost curve

issue discussed in earlier chapters. Davies suggests that engineering and production costs are relatively easier to handle than are the costs of distribution, administration and management. Experience suggests that it is expensive to calculate costs of a wide range of options and typically efforts are directed towards identifying all known technical scale economies (thereby developing a LRAC curve shown as Figure 6.2c). Two points are estimated – the MES (minimum efficient scale) and a point corresponding to 50% MES, thereby identifying cost penalties should the 'production' volume be below the optimal scale.

Davies makes an important point concerning economies of scale and MES output levels. The important relationship is that between MES and market size. Substantial economies of scale in an industry sector suggest large companies with concentrated markets: if the MES occurs at a very large level of output then there is the possibility of a monopoly situation which would require consideration.

The Survivor technique developed by Stigler (1958) assumes that market forces work efficiently so that firms in the most efficient size category take an increasing share of the market, while firms in less efficient size categories take smaller market shares. (See Figure 6.3a.) The assumptions made by Stigler are very restrictive: all firms should be pursuing the same objectives; should be operating in a similar environment; faced with similar factor prices and 'technology' should remain constant over the period of observation, and market forces work effectively without 'arrangements' or barriers to entry.

It is interesting to note that in a period of prolonged recession it is likely that these assumptions converge i.e. similar objectives, operating environments, factor prices and technology and the survivor technique offers management a basis for considering strategy implementation with particular emphasis on short term consequences and an overall view of an 'ideal' long run average cost curve.

Stigler's research was conducted in steel manufacturing which has very different characteristics to the distribution sector, however, there is an intuitive appeal to the concept. Figure 6.3b suggests how the major firms in food distribution 'match' the criteria proposed by Stigler's work and have emerged in terms of market share.

The Concept of X-inefficiency

The concept of X-inefficiency is concerned with short run costs and is seen as a link between the behavioural model and the managerial model of the firm. Micro-economics, with its standard, neo-classical, profit maximising model suggests the firm incurs the minimum cost achievable for the level of output being produced, given the set of 'plant and equipment' which it has decided to install. (See Figure 6.4). Such a firm is said to be operationally-efficient or X-efficient.

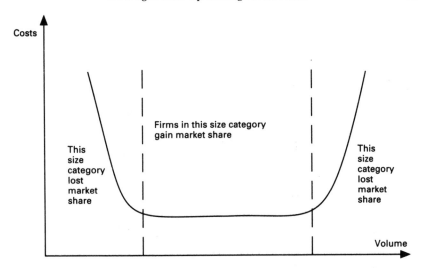

Figure 6.3(a) Stigler's Survivor Technique

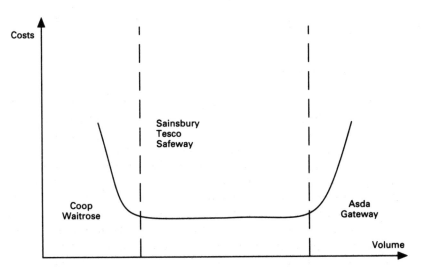

Figure 6.3(b) Stigler's Survivor Technique: an intuitive view of food retailing

However, this may not be so. Often companies maximise managerial utility and in so doing will pay higher salaries to management than is justified by the level of 'output' of the firm. If this is the case the firm becomes X-inefficient or demonstrates 'organisational slack'. There are other reasons for organisational slack to occur. For example a poorly structured incentive payment scheme which focuses more upon revenue generation than on cost control may result in a situation where the firm operates above the

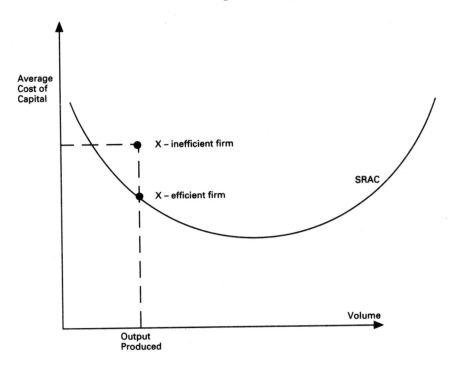

Figure 6.4 The concept of X-inefficiency

short run cost curve. Similarly if large firms are difficult to control they too, may tend to be X-inefficient, as management effectiveness is diluted as size increases. The structure of the equity holding is important. A large number of institutional shareholders could exert influence on management to aim for maximum profits and become X-efficient whereas a widely held shareholding would lack both information and the power to be able to produce a similar reaction. Competitive posture in the market place may influence X-efficiency. A market in which there are three or four similar size businesses sharing in excess of 40%–50% of the market may not be conducive to X-efficiency and if they have established significant barriers to entry there will be very few enforced penalties for organisational slack.

There have been examples of X-inefficiency in recent years within the retail sector. Salaries and benefits paid to senior management, particularly in the merchandising and buying functions, where there were shortage of expertise to meet the expanding opportunities of the 1980s. Similarly for property. Leases and entry premiums were excessively high as demand exceeded supply during the same period. The result has been large redundancy programmes and extensive closures.

Economies of Scope

Baumol *et al.* (1982) describes economies of scope, that occur when a firm can produce a number of products together more cheaply than it could produce them independently. Baumol was discussing manufacturing processes. However, the concept is equally applicable to distribution, where the production process comprises procurement, physical distribution and promotion inputs that are common to two or more merchandise groups. Economies of scope can be found outside the firm. The linkages and relationships that may be developed through vertical coordination (rather than vertical integration) have been demonstrated by the large retail multiples, notably Marks & Spencer. Vertical coordination offers all of the benefits of vertical integration *without* the commitment of the company's capital. In many instances there is not a capacity commitment: the retailer is therefore able to avoid risk to both fixed and working capital. There are examples whereby both costs and risk are reduced for supplier and distributor. Effective supply chain management, with linked information systems ensures that production and stockholding activities are managed at appropriate levels to meet customer demand. Such systems, while reducing the level of control exercised by both parties have been shown to reduce overall costs by improving availability *and* reduce excessive stockholding and the subsequent mark-downs.

Economies of scope differ from economies of scale. Economies of scope result from the identification and exploitation of intra and inter-company systems linkages. Economies of scale result from increasing the activity within a specified activity. Within the retailing sector these activities have been explored earlier in this chapter.

The Experience Effect

Experience (or learning) is also separate from economies of scale. Increased activity and familiarity with a product or a process results in cost reductions from improvements in store layout and design, quality control methods, distribution and information systems. The end result is that costs reduce with the total volume produced over time (see Figure 6.5) as well as with scale and rate of output.

However, a few aspects should be clarified. Experience develops over time while economies of scale can be calculated ahead of 'production' and are reflected in the size of the facility and the volume throughput it is designed to produce *and* actually handles. Furthermore, there has been evidence to show that companies focussing their 'production' processes on low cost output due to the experience effect do not exhibit flexibility. Their costs are low but their market offer is narrow. It follows that the experience effect benefits firms who operate in markets for which choice has low customer premium but in which price competition has a dominant role.

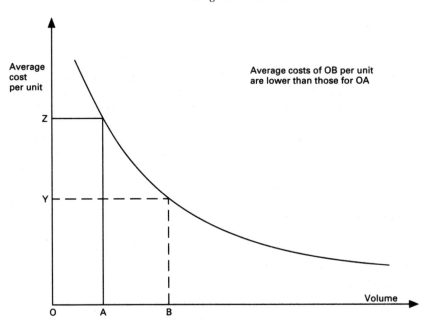

Figure 6.5 The experience effect

Experience offers other benefits across a limited merchandise range. For example, product quality and aspects of customer service can be made more specific. The essential point that emerges is that it is necessary to identify customer expectations (and their trade-off potentials) prior to implementing systems and processes that encourage management and the labour force to develop 'learning' skills.

As Figure 6.5 demonstrates average costs of production decrease as volume is increased. The concept is very useful for non-differentiated products. Its advantage is that target costs can be set for 'specific' levels of output, thus if a company can determine a 'specific' market share as an objective then many costs can be planned as can prices. Indeed exponents of the experience effect can (and do) set prices such that their target volumes are realised, resulting in the realisation of margins and cashflow objectives.

6.4   THE ECONOMICS OF MARKET SHARE AND VOLUME

The discussion so far has focused on the importance of considering the influence of volume throughput upon the overall performance of the business. Clearly sales volume is an important influence on profitability, often because an increase in sales may be achieved without a significant increase in the cost structure of the business and this results in an attractive increase in the return on capital employed.

There are quantitative and qualitative issues to be addressed: increased corporate performance characteristics such as return on capital employed, return on sales, asset utilisation and productivity. Similarly we are interested in the operational productivity of space, staff and stockholding. We shall consider these in more detail subsequently.

The qualitative issues concern relationships with customer and competitors: market share or market segment share are the issues to be considered.

Market Share

Market share is important for a number of reasons. As already suggested in Chapter 2 the volume implications of market share influence the buying margins obtained by the retail firm. These can also have a major influence on issues such as exclusivity of selected merchandise items and certainly influence the allocation of product should shortages occur. Suppliers usually have positive reactions towards large customers, for while they expect hard negotiations, they can expect lower transaction and distribution costs which (at least in part) compensate the lower margins likely to result from the negotiations.

Market share influences credibility. A large presence in a territory increases both credibility and confidence among customers. Another benefit afforded by market share is the development of specialist offers: once credibility is established with a customer group it is much easier to expand the activity by adding relevant merchandise into a specialist retail activity.

Large market shares in established markets often enable the retail firm to influence the competitive nature of the market. Once a significant market presence is established it often follows that the retailer (or retailers) then determine price levels, quality, choice and availability characteristics which 'set the rules' for competition and condition customer expectations and perceptions.

There is a particularly important quantitative aspect of market share and this concerns the volume relationship between market share and MES, minimum efficient scale. The MES concept was introduced earlier (see Figure 6.2c). It will be recalled that the MES is that point on the long run average cost curve beyond which no further scale economies are foreseen. The significance of considering both is clear. If the MES volume occurs at a level of market share (or perhaps a measure of catchment or regional share) which enables the retailer to assume an influential posture then the benefits that accrue are twofold. For not only can the firm operate with a level of throughput at which most of its costs are at a minimum, it also has the power to be able to shape the competitive profile of the sector, segment or catchment area to ensure that its own profitability is optimal. Furthermore, in such a situation the retail firm may be able to control the rate of growth of the 'market' and, because of an advantageous cost profile, may also be able to establish barriers to entry.

Sales Volume

The significance of sales volume and cost structure has been mentioned briefly. It is an important feature of strategy implementation and will be considered in some depth in this section. The issue to be considered concerns the sensitivity of both fixed and variable costs to increases in volume activity. Fixed cost issues relate to capacity utilisation and the 'costs' of capacity extension. The issues of importance concerning variable costs are their proportion of total cost and the availability of the resource represented.

An underutilised fixed asset is a disadvantage. It represents an overhead cost which must be recovered and if the utilisation rate can be increased so the recovery problem is reduced. Fixed assets usually have the problem that they are not flexible.

Implementing strategy involves management in decisions concerning resource allocation and volume adjustments. For example, a growth strategy requires an increase in volume but also requires sufficient support resources to ensure that the sales volume generated results in a satisfactory level of profit. Clearly if the support infrastructure is currently underutilised it follows that the additional throughput is incremental to the existing level of costs and as such makes an above average contribution.

However, an implementation decision involving expansion of both volume and support resources requires careful consideration. Because fixed assets such as warehouses, etc., are usually not an economic proposition if built to handle low volumes it follows that the volume forecast should be accurate and have a high probability of achievement. Often the forecasts made have a wide range of potential outcomes and the accuracy is obscured. Furthermore because of the inflexibility of such facilities they are usually larger than required initially. If the strategy implementation is slow to materialise the result may be that a cost penalty will exist which is larger than forecast, over a longer period of time.

Typically a successful format experiences slow growth in the introductory stage of its life cycle, only accelerating when outlet coverage is expanded into targeted catchment locations. As this occurs and as sales volumes expand so the amortisation of fixed costs (usually high in the initial stages of the life cycle) is spread across an increasing level of sales and the overhead recovery situation 'reaches' a satisfactory level. Often this is a planned process such that volume targets are set in order that utilisation and overhead recovery objectives are eventually achieved.

Another aspect of this issue concerns the relationship of gross margin to gross profit. Gross margin is a percentage performance measure. At high levels of sales revenue it has considerably more meaning than it does at lower levels. Small specialist retailing businesses require high margins to compensate risk. For businesses with high levels of revenue the important measure is the yield that the margins generate. Clearly measurement of gross and operating margins are essential performance measures but from the shareholders' view and indeed that of management responsible for developing the business the emphasis is upon actual cash values and profit produced.

Another factor to be considered concerns the requirement for the growth business to use economies of throughput to build cashflow and profitability. Given that the growth business will seek to reduce its overhead as a percentage of sales *and* seek to increase cashflow and profitability it should plan to do so constructively and logically. High gross margin percentages are more likely to be reflected as high levels of gross profit if the business increases its volume within existing (or closely related) product groups. This suggests that expansion should be considered such that it intensifies the utilisation of existing fixed assets (human resources as well as physical assets). It follows that initial expansion should consider the increased productivity of the buying and merchandising organisation, distribution facilities and instore space and staff resources.

An expansion of the business into unrelated product groups is likely to result only in the expansion of sales volume rather than an increase in profitability. It follows that gross margins do not necessarily convert into high profits unless the strategy is congruent with the existing business.

Strategy implementation involving rationalisation decisions that result in volume reductions require similar evaluation. It is not unknown for the outcome of such decisions to result in much lower volume throughput than that forecast which, in turn, results in serious underutilisation of the assets. Typical examples include the rationalisation of branches thought not to be performing at acceptable levels and of merchandise groups for the same reason. The result may be that the reduced level of activity leaves the remaining branches and merchandise groups unable to meet the task of recovering the overhead costs previously met by the now relinquished outlets and merchandise.

SUMMARY

This chapter has identified and discussed a number of topics that should be considered when implementing strategic management decisions. Often strategies succeed or fail because of the existing structure of the business. Perhaps the success is due to the improved utilisation of the infrastructure of the business which enables rapid implementation or possibly the opportunity to cross subsidise a new venture.

It is important that the economics of the business are understood *before* the implementation is undertaken such that planned use of the existing elements of the business occurs, thereby avoiding surprises should performance deviate from budgeted levels.

7 The Retail Business as a Component in the Supply Chain

INTRODUCTION

Retailing has experienced a great many changes in recent years and to ensure that individual companies have been able to maintain their profitability numerous ways have been sought by which customer satisfaction may be met but at the same time costs contained. The notable characteristics of customer satisfaction have been the expectations for choice, availability, quality, exclusivity (these being merchandise issues); instore services and service facilities, and store interiors in which they feel comfortable (as opposed to 'crowded') and which have a logic in their design and layout.

Clearly each of these characteristics has a cost implication and for some time during the late 1980s/early 1990s cost inflation was in excess of price inflation. This was due initially to intense competition but subsequently this was joined by decreasing sales volumes which exacerbated the pressure on margins.

However, it is inaccurate to assume that the late 1980s/1990s was an initiation period for a focus on cost management. Retailing management had for some time been very effective at cost management, this being particularly so in the distribution activity. Distribution management had been very effective in maintaining (many increasing) customer service levels at the point of sale by maximising the use of space, controlling the stocks and flows activities in distribution and seizing the opportunities offered by information management/information technology to control the supply chain. In this chapter we consider how performance may be influenced by distribution and sourcing decisions.

7.1 THE SUPPLY CHAIN

The concept of the supply chain is not new. Muller (1990) reports a series of interviews with senior distribution managers in which a view is expressed that supply chain management is ' ... much the same theory of integrated logistics that you've been reading so much about in the past few years. ... The major difference seems to be that supply chain management is the preferred name for the *actualization* of "integrated logistics" theory'. One con-

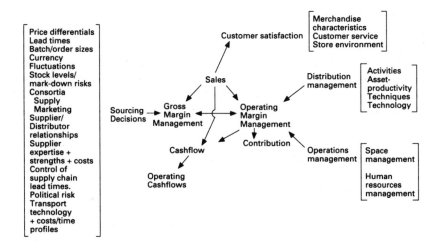

Figure 7.1   The supply chain, its components and impact on the performance of the retail business

tributor, Du Pont's director of logistics Clifford Sayre, defines supply chain management as a loop: 'It starts with the customer and it ends with the customer'. Through the loop flows all material and finished goods, all information, even all financial transactions. 'It requires looking at your business as one continuous process'. And further ' . . .This process absorbs such traditionally distinct functions as forecasting, purchasing, manufacturing, distribution, and sales and marketing into a continuous flow of business interaction. Gone are the functional "stove pipes" of corporate activity; instead departments are structured as a pipeline that stretches between a company's suppliers and its customers.'

Sayre suggests that while the theory is some twenty years or more old it has until recently, been difficult for companies to make it a reality. 'No one then believed that communication could be handled efficiently enough to link all aspects of the supply chain without gaps somewhere along the line'. That was before development in information management. 'The cost of making information available to more people has steadily gone down, while the physical costs of business, such as facilities and inventory, have steadily risen.' (Max Stenross, Xerox).

Retailing management responses can be represented by Figure 7.1. These have been noticeable in distribution management, operations management and sourcing policy. Central to the response has been the application of information technology to all three activities. Indeed it has been suggested that IT has been the driving force, so much so that it has enabled retailing management to exercise 'control by information' rather than have 'control by doing'. (Quarmby, 1985) quoted by Cooper (1992). This has enabled management to focus upon managing the core business and relinquishing the management of support functions such as distribution to specialist contractors, who have developed expertise and have used this together with the range of distribution techniques now available. (These will be discussed later in this chapter.) They have also been able to apply the benefits of economies of scale in storage, transportation and systems.

7.2   DISTRIBUTION MANAGEMENT

Distribution and Technological Developments

The role of IT in developing distribution management cannot be overstated. The introduction of EPOS systems has fundamentally changed the nature and content of many distribution management tasks and functions. The availability of EPOS data has provided the supply chain with the information on product movements (volumes and rates of flow) necessary to link the activities and close the gaps. EPOS facilitates setting performance criteria for planning and control purposes:

- Sales by department and item.
- Rate of sale.
- Hourly sales.
- Transaction size and type of payment.
- Sales by location of outlet.
- Sales by staff.
- Shrinkage over specified time periods.
- Inventory analysis.

The benefits of having this information available are quite obvious and have been discussed on numerous occasions. Briefly they relate to lower operating costs (lower staff and inventory) and improved marketing effectiveness.

However it is the increased application of EDI (electronic data interchange) that makes supply chain management function effectively. During the 1980s TRADACOMS was to establish an agreed standard structure and sequence of data for the documentation essential for trading; ordering, delivery notes, invoicing and remittance advice, along with formats for product, price and customer master files. TRADANET evolved from TRADACOMS. It provides a network for trading partners by allowing them to exchange information. TRADANET is now becoming well established as a communications link between trading partners and has clear implications for development of the management of the distribution activity as distribution services suppliers develop their links to the network. These developments will permit more delegation of distribution activities to third party service companies as the ease by which user companies (the retailers) can monitor performance increases.

This will be enhanced by the additional application of IT for scheduling and routing delivery vehicles. Computer vehicle routing and scheduling (CVRS) has demonstrated efficiencies by reducing transport costs, increasing vehicle utilisation cube and delivery time, improving service response to retail outlets, reducing transportation capital investment, and, offering a 'what if . . .?' facility. In short the direction in which IT is moving suggests that retailing management is able to devolve the operational management of distribution activities once having established the overall strategic role of distribution together with performance criteria.

Other aspects of technology tend to be overshadowed by the developments in IT. There have been (and continue to be) significant developments in warehousing and transportation technology. The developments concern order picking, handling and consolidation equipment; materials storage (capacity utilisation), control by value (bonded warehousing and other security requirements) or by temperature requirements. Similarly transportation developments reflect these moves towards cost-effectiveness. While they improve operating efficiencies and therefore increase service and/or lower operating costs they are capital intensive. As such the retailer is presented with a dilemma concerning investment in the core business or in its infrastructure. This issue will be discussed later.

Distribution Operating Methods and Techniques: JIT and Quick Response

The influence of IT throughout distribution is very strong. The availability of accurate, rapid, low cost information has facilitated the development of a range of techniques that are becoming used across the sector and which offer cost savings and increases in customer service offers. Again these techniques are seen as means by which the supply chain may be managed more effectively.

The information technology expansion was accompanied by a change in manufacturing philosophy. The Japanese Kanban (just-in-time) concept of manufacturing was originally devised to eliminate waste: any activity or process which does not directly add value to the product is seen as a cost and therefore waste, thus holding excess stocks is seen as wasteful. JIT introduced the commitment to short, consistent lead times and to minimising or eliminating inventories; but, at the same time customer service levels are maintained. The rationale behind the concept is that stocks of components (or finished items for resale) should be planned to arrive only at the time they are actually needed. In effect it saves money on downstream inventories by placing greater reliance on improved responsiveness and flexibility.

The implications for distribution management are not difficult to follow. Forbes (1991) describes the parallells between distribution and manufacturing applications of JIT. In retailing applications the objectives are twofold: to keep inventory costs down but at the same time increase customer service levels. Forbes suggests that the JIT philosophy is not entirely new, for many years retail management has been concerned with stockturn frequencies and the relationship between stockturn and stock investment. In order that customer service (merchandise availability) is maintained if not increased there is a need to replenish shelf stocks rapidly. Clearly there is an information requirement here and the development of EPOS and EDI have made the concept of minimal stocks/optimum service feasible. The total reliance on information systems is essential and if the system is to work (i.e. service objectives realised) intermediate stocks need to be removed from the system altogether and be replaced by information technology. Stock control and order processing need to be on-line and real time (rather than batch processed): such information systems can also be used for forecasting, planning, monitoring and control.

The organisational issues are important; the systems are much more effective when companies are integrated into the supply chain. Forbes proposes that there is evidence to suggest that where there is a market interface, for example between retailers and wholesale, the concept is less effective. He points to the fact that in food distribution delivered wholesaling has virtually disappeared. He also suggests there to be a role for third party distribution service companies: as the number of deliveries for each product becomes more frequent and the size of the deliveries becomes smaller, the opportunity to consolidate deliveries becomes more attractive in order to take advantages of economies of scale. Clearly the large multiples will question whether they should take advantage of these economies of scale or whether to use the investment to expand the retailing area of the business: much depends upon market opportunities, cost and availability of capital and the rates quoted by service companies. One issue that is resolved quite easily is that a JIT system with deliveries direct to retail branches would not be acceptable; the large number of back door deliveries would result in severe congestion and chaos. The exception is the large unit load, typically a volume selling commodity product, for which no cost savings would be achieved by routing through a consolidation process.

While the largest savings come from inventory reductions there are other areas in which the savings are significant. For example, the reduction in inventory holding reduces the warehousing capacity that is required. There are cost savings to be made by improved vehicle utilisation and possibly the increase in back hauling and other savings from the decreased use of outer packaging materials. Savings will increasingly occur as supplier and retailer systems are integrated.

It follows that JIT/QR offers considerable benefits by reducing the capital requirement for infrastructure investment, by reducing operating costs (and therefore improving operating margins) or improving both. There is also an impact on operating gearing to be considered (operating gearing being the proportion of fixed costs to total costs; see Chapter 9). The more capital intensive the business becomes the more vulnerable becomes the profit performance to variations in volume.

Distribution Requirements Planning (DRP)

Distribution Requirements Planning has much in common with JIT/QR in that its basic thesis is the reduction of cost by eliminating unnecessary stockholding within the supply chain. DRP is derived from another inventory and scheduling approach: materials requirements planning (MRP). MRP deals specifically with supplying materials and component parts whose demand depends upon that for a specific end product. Again, as with JIT in manufacturing the underlying concepts have existed for many years but it is only recently that IT developments have permitted the full development of MRP.

Christopher (1989) defines MRP as: ' ... a system for forecasting or projecting component part and material requirements from a company's master production schedule (MPS) and the bill of material (BOM) for each end product or module. The time phased requirements for components and materials are then calculated, taking into account stock in hand as well as scheduled receipts. The system establishes, maintains and derives priorities based upon regular reviews and updates. One of the key principles of MRP is that it works on a "time-phased" basis ... the requirements for components are established in the light of when they will be required for production against planned replenishment lead times.'

The success of MRP focused the attention of distribution planners on the opportunities that may exist for a similar approach to distribution planning. This has led to DRP which seeks to identify requirements for finished product at the point of demand and then works backwards to produce aggregated, time-phased requirements schedules for each stage of the distribution system. Hence DRP has a 'pull' rather than a 'push' philosophy, the emphasis being placed upon identifying and anticipating customer requirements at the point of demand and this requirement 'pulls' the product down through the supply channel. This is contrary to the approach which plans requirements centrally and then 'pushes' the product down the channel.

Thus the DRP concept relies upon forecasts of customer demand being generated and works backwards towards establishing a realistic and economically justified system-wide plan for ordering and processing the required finished goods demand. DRP is then a time phased plan for distributing product from plants, warehouses and other planned locations to points where it is required to maintain specified levels of customer satisfaction.

Christopher describes LRP (logistics requirements planning) as ' . . . the biggest pay-off for total systems optimisation . . .', the linking of MRP and DRP. It has, as he suggests, ' . . . an overwhelming logic . . .', but is extremely difficult to implement in practice. Much the same may be said concerning MRPII (and DRPII) systems which extend resource planning into the medium and long term. Here the intention is to re-examine existing physical facilities to match them more precisely to the streamlined materials flow planned and facilitated through requirements planning.

The components in a requirements planning system are:

The forecast: forms the basic input for requirements planning. Forecasts should be based upon demand at the lowest level in the distribution system. This may much easier for commodity, non-seasonal products for which demand is not distorted by unforeseen events. If the forecast is based upon demand rather than sales the forecast will take account of out of stock situations (i.e. demand that existed but not satisfied) and any unusual variations in demand.

Communications; are the means by which the impact of requirements at one level may be responded to at another level in the supply chain. Christopher refers to the problem being more one of organisational integration (or perhaps the attitudinal change required) in which supply chain participants make available 'confidential' information to each other. The importance of IT developments in facilitating communications through EDI has already been discussed.

System flexibility; with the surplus, just-in-case inventory removed from the supply chain the system must be capable of responding to changes rapidly. Both manufacturing and distribution systems must be able to react quickly to changing levels of demand. The retailer's distribution system exchanges large safety stocks for information flows and a transport facility capable of quick response to short-term requirements.

Suppliers and customer contact; the importance of communications and forecasting have already been noted. The greater the knowledge the supplier has of customer requirements the more accurate will be the forecast and the production scheduling. It follows that reliability will be increased and consequently the requirements for safety stock will be reduced and eventually eliminated. A number of food multiples have developed strong interdependent procurement-supply systems which have both DRP and MRP (possibly MRPII) systems working in one integrated system. See Figure 7.2.

There are a number of issues emerging from this discussion. Clearly the objectives of both DRP and MRP are to maximise customer satisfaction at an optimum supply chain cost. This requires cooperation between supplier and distributor both of whom are required to make investment decisions in fixed and current assets. Both seek to maximise ROCE (return on capital employed) and typically both are concerned with structuring their businesses such that the return to the shareholders is maximised. We shall consider the ramifications of alternative financial structures in Chapter 13 where the

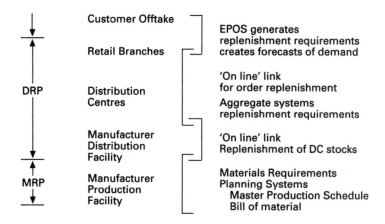

Figure 7.2 DRP/MRP, maintaining customer satisfaction through physical distribution and manufacturing systems linked by EDI

implications of financial and operating gearing will be explored in detail. At this point it is sufficient to note that both the financial and asset structure of the business should be such that the return on the shareholders' investment is maximised. In response to this fundamental objective many retailing businesses (and manufacturing businesses for that matter) take the view that they should focus their investment on the core activity of the business (i.e. retailing or manufacturing) and to delegate (or to buy in) the infrastructure/support systems activities. More companies are leasing distribution facilities (plant, vehicles etc.) or using third party distribution service companies rather than using investment resources on non-core activities. Apart from the fact that they are converting fixed assets into operating expenses the decision also has implications for the way in which assets are financed. It has been suggested that Laura Ashley will save around £1.5 million a year in distribution costs, £1 million in wage costs and some £3 million capital expenditure on systems costs by using Business Logistics, a Federal Express company. Furthermore, by September 1993 the aim was to deliver anywhere in the world within 48 hours.

7.3 OPERATIONS MANAGEMENT

Developments in retail operations management have been closely linked to those in distribution management. Indeed most have been mutually supporting in their nature. The changing nature of consumer expectations has already been noted, particularly the increased requirement for choice and service facilities. These trends have put increased pressure on sales space which has been under pressure to increase performance for some time.

There had been pressure to eliminate storage space in retail outlets for some considerable time. The rapidly rising rental costs had caused concern during the 1970s and 1980s, particularly in outlets with central locations where the productivity of selling area had to be increased if the location was to remain financially viable. Another aspect of the cost problem was that the storage areas encouraged a duplication of safety stocks and these increased costs, reduced profitability and cashflow.

The problem was addressed by multiple retailing by introducing regional stockholding locations, or Regional Distribution Centres (RDCs) which were introduced to manage the increasing volume of deliveries to stores (direct from suppliers) and which were creating unnecessarily cost penalties through shrinkage, damaged goods and returns. Such a delivery pattern also required additional staff to receive and store the shipments. Furthermore the fact that safety stock nationally existed did not always eliminate out of stock situations. The RDCs did release sales area which when allocated on a planned basis improved the sales productivity of the store. They also enabled operations management to improve labour productivity because of the control that could be imposed by phased deliveries and the planned work load.

Out of stock situations improved as more control over stock levels could be maintained. A particular problem for apparel retailers is the achievement of full margins, and the conversion of storage area into selling area together with the application of visual merchandising techniques enabled retailers to display merchandise more effectively and comprehensively. This had the effect of selling the merchandise at the planned margin, increased the value of the sale (through coordinated merchandise displays) and because labour was being used more effectively increased the operating margins. There was also a 'bulk purchasing effect' whereby the overall margin could be increased due to centralised purchasing and central deliveries. The use of third party distribution service companies has increased the margin effect and as noted earlier reduced the commitment of capital to non-core business activities and, possibly, reduced the overall capital requirements of the business and the interest changes. Clearly there have been distribution management issues overlapping these decisions but successful retailing is a process of integrated management decisions.

7.4 SOURCING DECISIONS

Returning to Figure 7.1, there are a number of factors to be considered when examining the sourcing decision. Given that management will attempt to manage costs (either to reduce them or maintain their levels) and at the same time increase customer satisfaction it suggests that three issues are underlying factors: cost-price, quality and lead times. Each of these factors has an impact upon customer satisfaction, gross margin management, or both.

Price Differentials Lead Times, Batch Sizes and Currency Fluctuations

Procurement often takes place within an environment over which the retailer has limited control. For example, in the United Kingdom because the pound sterling is a sensitive currency, and therefore vulnerable to currency fluctuation, buying decisions are made against a background of risk and uncertainty. Following the exit from the Exchange Rate Mechanism (ERM) in 1992 the fall in the value of sterling was such that the price advantages obtained by offshore sourcing were largely removed. For example, a 15–20 per cent differential is sought when sourcing from the Far East compared to European suppliers due to the factors of longer lead times, larger order sizes, and payment required at the point of dispatch (on dispatch) rather than 30 (even 90) days after dispatch. Currency fluctuations influence buyers towards quick response systems: the reduction of both stock-holding costs and mark-downs are important considerations.

It follows that financial considerations together with currency fluctuations have a major impact upon gross margin management. By considering these issues alongside those posed by distribution (and operations) management, margins may be enhanced, certainly protected from excessive erosion. Furthermore, customer satisfaction can be improved in sectors in which 'merchandise currency' is an important factor, such as the apparel markets.

Buying Consortia

There have been a number of developments among retailers in various sectors to organise cooperative groups to gain better positions for future trading. In Europe the ERA (European Retail Alliance) has been developed by Ahold (the Netherlands), Group Casino (France) and the Argyll Group (United Kingdom). The aim of ERA is not simply to pool purchasing (and thereby improve gross margin management) but to cooperate in the fields of marketing (product development), logistics and information technology, these having implications for operating margins as well as a gross margin from joint development of 'European Brands'. Ahold has also been a major force in the development of AMS (Ahold Marketing Services) which comprises the three ERA members together with Dansk Supermarket (Denmark), ICA (Sweden), La Rinascente (Italy), Migros (Switzerland), Kesko Oy (Finland) and Mercadona (Spain). The overall aim of AMS is to increase cooperation between suppliers and distributors to help reduce cost of both production and distribution. The Sears sponsored Ensemble package incorporates foreign suppliers (Brazil, Indonesia and the Far East). It offers suppliers communications links, software and manufacturing consultancy.

At issue here is the strength of the relationships that can be built between retailers and suppliers. The benefits of long term relationships that lead to a much clearer understanding of each other's business philosophies (e.g. views on quality, exclusivity, choice, coordination) and business capabilities (e.g. capacities, capabilities, consistency, creativity, credibility and competitive advantage) can only result in improved performance throughout the supply chain and customer satisfaction.

Utilising Supplier Expertise

Closer working arrangements between individual suppliers and retailers can lead to the removal of inefficient practices within the supply chain. Often these developments and resulting practices can be extended to other supplier/retailer relationships. Simon Jack (1993) reported on activities within Kingfisher companies. B & Q and Comet work with suppliers with the purpose of reinforcing their expertise and strengths. This can be particularly important with suppliers of retailer own brand products. There are some product areas (electricals) where overseas suppliers have cost benefits which if preserved by maintaining tight control over supply chain activities can utilise just-in-time production methods and enable the retailer to offer lower prices to customers.

Control and Lead Times: Cost and Flexibility

The apparel sector is more efficient if personal contact is exercised. Country Casuals has found that using supply sources that have short lead times improves the control they can exercise over manufacturing activities. The Company uses supplier/manufacturers to manufacture from its designs. In 1993 it sourced 65% of production in the UK, because of flexibility and quality considerations. Clearly there are a number of trade-off situations in these decisions. For the retailer who has a predominantly staple merchandise assortment and for whom quality specifications can be established and then left to a minimum of supervision and also for whom price is an important consideration, the need for a high level of intervention is less than for the fashion retailer. For high quality, high price (margin) products (ladieswear) the considerations are different. Short lead times and flexibility enable the retailer to make changes to production quantities if necessary, local production facilitates quality control.

Political Risk

Many retailers have established an historical reliance upon far eastern suppliers, particularly with Hong Kong, Taiwan and for some Korea. The political balance of power will shift when Hong Kong is returned to China and it is likely that the political and commercial characteristics of these countries will experience some changes. The nature of these changes is difficult to predict and consequently there has been a shift of sourcing away from areas thought to be likely to experience problems towards those with greater stability.

These changes suggest that the time is appropriate for an audit of sourcing strengths and weaknesses of available supply markets. For example, the old COMECON alliance has a large labour force with some of the skills necessary and Portugal and Greece have the added benefit of EC membership as well as a skilled labour force with relatively lower costs. The discussion can be broadened. Given that a range of skills and costs exist throughout Europe and adjacent countries it suggests that sourcing decisions may become more focused on customer satisfaction requirements. For example, sourcing locations can be selected on the basis of a range of criteria:

- High volume, low price, low skills content.
- Short run, bespoke manufactured items.
- Seasonal, speciality products.
- Specialist products with a requirement for frequent supervision.

Given these (and other criteria) the sourcing decisions become directed towards satisfying specific product attributes that match customer expectations rather than decisions aimed at maximising buying margins. Optimising margins and focusing upon increasing sales with target customer groups with a specialist merchandise range is likely to be more profitable than attempting to buy at minimum cost.

Transport, Technology, Costs and Time Profiles

The concept of trade-off management is now apparent in sourcing decisions. It was not too long ago that transportation was considered to be a necessity which should be 'purchased' at as low a price as was possible. However the requirements of the marketplace have forced the buyer to consider other issues. The high level of mark-downs that accompany large bulk orders (the size of which were often, in part at least, determined by freight rates) and other factors have made other transport modest economic.

If stock levels can be reduced significantly with attractive financial benefits, the transport cost differentials between surface and air are often insignificant. Add to these savings the additional economies, mark-downs, storage space, etc. then air freight offers worthwhile benefits.

Technology and technological developments have an important role. The evolution and rapid expansion of specialist transportation systems has enabled retailers to expand the width of their merchandise offers. The expansion of produce ranges (both fruit and vegetables) has been due in large part to the advances in chilled transportation facilities and developments by growers. The result has been to enhance product range margins by the introduction of more expensive items.

SUMMARY

Supply chain management has three important aspects. Distribution management developments have been responsible through its advances for improving the effectiveness and speed of distribution decisions. It has replaced 'control by doing' with 'control by information'. The result has been to allow management to concentrate its efforts and investment on running its core business, thereby increasing the return generated on capital employed. The application of philosophies and techniques such as just-in-time (quick response) distribution, distribution requirements planning and the realisation that the supply chain extends from raw materials to end user, managed by integrated information flows has improved efficiencies. Operations management developments have included performance improvement of space, personnel and stockholding. Many, if not most, developments have been integrated with distribution management decisions.

Sourcing decisions have also expanded within the context of their content and influences. Elements of currency futures management have combined with financial, marketing and politically influenced decisions. The retail sourcing decision can no longer be taken without recognition (and evaluation of) the complete supply chain and its organisational and financial components.

8 The Retail Business as an International Business

INTRODUCTION

Attempts by retailers to expand into overseas activities have been met with mixed success. The excursions of the 1970s and early 1980s were, by and large, not very successful. A changing economic geography has regenerated the interest. The single market and its changing economic and financial infrastructure, the North American Trade Movements with similar, if not as all embracing, movements, the Pacific Rim and of course the attempts by the COMECON block to replace their old philosophies with capitalism and entrepreneurship, all have prompted many retailers to consider overseas expansion.

Treadgold (1991) in an expansive review of the internationalisation of retailing does suggest that '. . . for many retailers, developing a foreign trading presence is often primarily a response to a relative absence of sustainable long-term growth opportunities at home rather than an overt desire to exploit any lowering of barriers to market entry embodied in the 1992 programme . . .' The point made is that many retailers see the return on limited resources becoming potentially larger in overseas markets due to a number of domestic market constraints.

Essentially there are three basic motives for looking to overseas markets: limited domestic market growth opportunities, an offer which has international appeal and, the identification of opportunities suggesting that the successful application of domestic based expertise (and possibly capacities) adjusted for local needs and requirements can offer profitable growth potential. Williams (1992) researched motives of UK retailers. His research revealed that '. . . most retailers responded to growth orientated motives and motives arising from an internationally appealing and innovative retail formula. Passive motives and those resulting from limited domestic market growth opportunities had a markedly lower degree of influence.' A rank order showed the motives as:

Retail formula has international appeal.
Senior management drive and support.
Possessed unique competitive advantage.
Long run profits.
Precise knowledge of overseas opportunity.
Capitalise on innovative retail formula.
Exploit own retail 'know how' and techniques.
Long run sales growth.
Corporate objectives included internationalisation.

Retail sector conducive to internationalisation.
Attractive future growth prospects of overseas markets.
Attractive current growth prospects of overseas markets.
Increased public standing and prestige.
Mature UK retail sector.
Overseas distribution of products.
Economies of scale.
Saturated UK retail sector.
Dominant firm in UK sector.
Offers from foreign retailers.
Unfavourable experiences from UK expansion.
Expansion goals could not be realised in UK.
Overseas visitors used UK shops.
Exploit foreign retail 'know how' and techniques.
Exploits technological advantage.
Favourable currency movements.
Increased competition in UK sector.
UK diversification possibilities exhausted.
UK competitors expanding abroad.
Surplus organisational resources.
Excessive restrictions in UK market.
Exploit foreign technological advantages.
Depressed share prices favoured overseas acquisitions.
Foreign government incentives.
UK Government incentives.

The motivation statements were generated from an in-depth review of the literature and a pilot survey. The research method was a semi-structured personal interview at which a standardised questionnaire, mainly consisting of Likert scales was used to minimise interviewer bias.

Williams concludes there to be low regard for motives based upon the perceived limitations of domestic growth market opportunities and that these are not therefore the major reasons behind the recent internationalisation developments of UK retailers. The strength of growth oriented motives and those arising from an internationally appealing and innovative retail offering implies that retail internationalisation has preference to domestic expansion.

The decision options facing retailers can be described by Figure 8.1. There are three primary elements in the alternative decisions: return on investment; resource commitment required, and; risk. Figure 8.1 suggests a decision polygon in which the decision elements which eventually describe the surface of the decision situation: Figure 8.1b is the ideal situation in which ROI is large with low risk and low resource commitment, Figure 8.1c describes the situation to be avoided, whereas Figure 8.1d shows a typical choice situation in which the hypothetical overseas investment offers a higher ROI, lower resource requirement at the same level of risk.

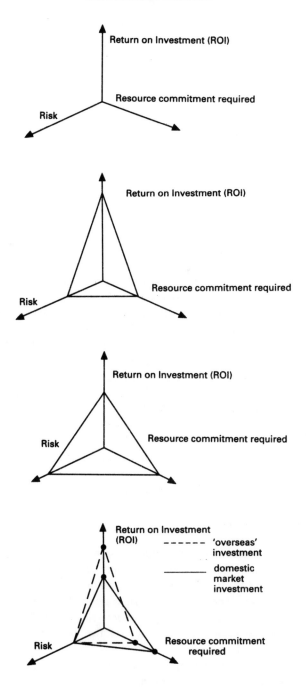

Figure 8.1(a) Decision elements; (b) the 'ideal' solution; (c) the 'most likely' situation; (d) choices

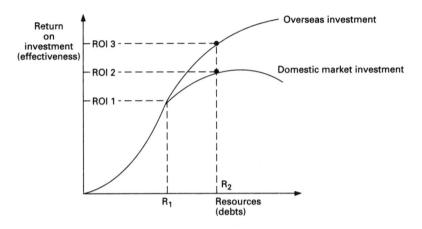

Figure 8.2   Cost/benefit approach to investment

The decision process can be seen more simply as a return to resources situation described by a cost-effectiveness curve. See Figure 8.2. In this Figure the business has developed up to R1 with a ROI of ROI1. At this point a decision is required: whether to continue to invest in the domestic market or to allocate the resources to an overseas investment. In the hypothetical situation illustrated it is suggested that expansion in the domestic market is less attractive. Competition and eventually saturation restrict the return on investment whereas by contrast the ROI on the overseas investment has a more attractive rate of growth. Clearly a more sophisticated approach is required, probably using discounted cashflow techniques, however the simple point made is that many retailers are now beginning to question the viability of their domestic markets when compared with overseas opportunities. This chapter examines the options available.

8.1   RETAILING ACTIVITIES

Treadgold gives a thorough and comprehensive review of developments in international retailing. He deals with the topic on a regional basis: Europe, North America (USA) and the Far East with a mention of the emerging activities (and interest shown) in Eastern Europe. Of particular interest to this discussion is the logic or method underlying these developments and the implications that such expansion has for the financial and market performance of the retail business.

There are a number of reasons behind overseas expansion and a number of alternative methods (strategies) for achieving the desired results. The alternative entry methods have included all of the strategy growth options typically discussed in strategy texts such as: organic growth, acquisition, joint ventures, and strategic alliances. As Treadgold (and others) have suggested the challenge for retailing is to attempt to maximise the return on investment (or the net present value of the income streams generated) '... while remaining sensitive to the important, and very durable, differences in consumer and retail environments, whether defined by reference to national political boundaries or by functional region.... For most retailers this demands making a trade-off between the desire for global homogeneity and the necessity for local sensitivity'.

This suggests a dimension to the decision criteria that may not have been given sufficient recognition during the earlier attempts at internationalisation: the store selection and purchasing decision within consumption is largely determined by cultural values and norms and one that may not be possible to change. Clearly some products are more culturally influenced than others; food shopping and consumption differs markedly throughout Europe from North to South, whereas more recently introduced products for example, durables and personal luxury items, can utilise the retail distribution systems and methods developed elsewhere.

It follows that risk has a number of dimensions. There is financial risk that surrounds the expectation of return on an investment, political risk which accompanies any overseas investment and market risk which has important cultural considerations, some of these may be far reaching. This topic will be considered in detail later in this Chapter.

8.2 THE STRATEGIC OPTIONS FOR INTERNATIONAL EXPANSION

An Overall View

There is a traditional view of international business decision options: the two opposing alternatives of being either a multinational or a global business. Theodore Levitt offered the distinction: 'The multinational corporation operates in a number of countries, and adjusts its products and practices in each – at high relative costs. The global corporation operates with resolute constancy – at low relative cost – as if the entire world (or major regions of it) were a single entity: it sells the same things in the same way everywhere.' (Levitt, 1983).

There are a range of optional market entry strategies available to firms contemplating overseas activities. Jeannet and Hennessy (1992) describe these from a general stance and suggest they range from; indirect exporting (where there is no market activity on the part of the Company); direct exporting (the company identifies and uses local intermediaries); the company overseas sales subsidiary (the company establishes a sales office and becomes its own intermediary having an inventory locally and assuming the credit risk). Licensing is the next alternative, the company agrees with a local firm for it to manufacture and/or distribute the company's products under agreed terms and conditions (thus the company establishes a market presence without equity investment). There are other advantages: time and local knowledge being the primary factors but both commercial and political risk are avoided. Franchising is a specific form of licensing in which the franchiser makes available a total marketing programme around the product-service.

Jeannet and Hennessy move onto consider manufacturing alternatives. While at first consideration these may not seem relevant some of the issues are. For example the retailer with a strong franchise that may be design (Laura Ashley) or operations led (the fast food companies) may find that these together with well supervised and managed local manufacturing agreements may have advantages other than simply to reduce the costs of transportation and stockholding (together with accompanying mark-downs and shrinkage). The equity investment is largely avoided and political risk is minimised.

Joint ventures are suggested as having advantages of shared investment and risk as well as the synergy that is created by combining the skills of two or more partners. There are problems and these stem from ownership structure and consequently control and decision making concerning future direction of the business as well as operating functions. There are a number of examples of joint ventures working with differing degrees of success. In the UK the Homebase DIY business was established as a joint venture between Sainsbury (who had the experience of locating, developing and operating superstores in the UK) and GB Inno BM who brought the DIY expertise into the arrangement. Ahold the Netherlands-based food retailer has developed a number of joint venture operations in food retailing, fast food and other sectors. Vendex with broader interests in the Netherlands (based on its department store operations) has extended both in terms of activities and geographical expansion.

A more recent phenomenon is the development of strategic alliances. Whereas in a joint venture the traditional approach in which the partners contribute fixed levels of resources and the venture (usually a corporate entity) develops from there, the strategic alliance goes beyond this and the participants explore a range of activities into which their various skills and expertise are introduced and from each expects to 'profit' from the others' experience.

Retailing Issues and Implications

Clearly these broad entry options have limited application to retailing companies. There are examples of exporting activities which have developed into established overseas businesses. The development of Marks & Spencer's business in Spain and Hong Kong began with M & S merchandise sold initially through an arrangement locally and developing into fully ranged stores.

The issue confronting retailers seeking to expand into overseas markets is the extent to which local cultural issues require to be considered. Culture is '... simply each society's solution to problems presented by life ... Products and services must solve problems and meet consumer needs in order to be viable. It is important that the marketer understand whether a need met by a product is a recognised one within a particular culture. If it is, then the cultural difference ... is not as relevant as the similarity of needs.' Reynolds (1978). Understanding cultural impact and importance is influenced by one's own culture and furthermore, cultural differences tend to stand out more than similarities; yet it is the similarities that may be more important to a marketer. More significant is the fact that in many cases all people have similar needs. These can be seen from the very early work of Murdock (1945) who identified some seventy 'cultural universals', (these including bodily adornment, cooking, courtship, division of labour, family, feasting, gift giving, housing hygiene, marriage, mealtimes, medicine, property rights, status differentiation, trade, weather control). Culture is learned behaviour, and as such is, by definition, individual. It follows that any generalisations about a culture must recognise the variation *within* a culture as much as the differences or similarities between that one and any other (Cundiff and Hilger, 1988). It suggests that opportunities to segment existing markets exist, even in well established product-markets and explains the success of niche retailing activities.

Salmon and Tordjman (1989) have used the Levitt distinction between global and multi-national businesses to define them in a retailing context. A global retailing strategy being the 'faithful replication of a concept abroad ... as if their targeted market was homogeneous, thereby ignoring all national or regional differences'. They suggest a multinational strategy to be: '... retailers consider their subsidiaries to be a portfolio of geographically dispersed retail businesses, for each of which they adapt their standard formula to fit local market conditions'.

The earlier paragraphs emphasised that the cultural differences within markets may be strong in some sectors. Within marketing theory the emphasis in segmentation theory is increasingly towards the socio-cultural issues i.e., the attitudes and perceptions of aggregate sub-groups of customers within overall markets. There is also the possibility that the basic features of the offer appeal to culture based values that can be reflected across an offer. An example of this can be seen with the strong franchise enjoyed by Marks & Spencer for whom the customer perceptions of quality, reliability and competitive price can be used to build their assortment. There are very few examples such as this, possibly the customer perception of Sainsbury quality and price is another but whether this could support a solus diversification by Sainsbury into non-related merchandise activities remains to be tested.

However, there is an argument that could be made to suggest that 'cultural convergence' is occurring. Commercial research suggests that consumer tastes, needs and purchasing patterns are becoming similar across a number of sectors. These may well be influenced by other factors which are also indicating similarities such as, demographic profiles, the decline of the nuclear family, an increase in divorce, the changing role of women in many societies and, possibly most influentially, easy access to common media (film, television, music etc.) which has the effect of accelerating the 'cultural convergence' and decreasing the effects of cultural barriers. But these changes are slow and the opportunities for global operations remain small in number.

Treadgold suggests that because the opportunities for globalisation are restricted '... the tendency amongst all but that select group of "global" retailers has been to emphasise localisation above globalisation ... this manifests itself in adopting multinational organisational structures which regard each part of a retailer's geographic presence as distinct and separate elements of the total organisation. Yet few of the benefits of trading internationally can be realised without a high level of integration between the retailer's home market interests and its foreign interests'. This suggests that the retailer should examine its operational expertise and its managerial economies of scale against its strategic, international aspirations. Figure 8.3 shows how the economies of scale discussed in Chapter 6 may influence various decision points. The importance of each type will depend very much upon the nature of the opportunity, these will be discussed in detail below.

Treadgold argues that: 'For the majority of retailers who do not possess the elusive quality of a culturally unconstrained offer, the most appropriate international strategy is one which emphasises the uniqueness of local markets. But being locally responsive need not imply adopting a multinational strategy which, by treating each country as a separate trading unit, does not allow for the possibility of realising the benefits of trading internationally to both the home market and the foreign operations. Rather, international retailers should strive to be not multinational but *trans-national* organisations ... The objective of the trans-national retailer is to reconcile the apparently conflicting aims of local responsiveness and global efficiency ... The trans-national retailer is one which presents an offer tailored to the localised demand characteristics of consumers but which is leveraging the behind-the-scenes efficiencies and benefits of being a global operator ... unlike a multinational organisation, it can be responsive to change in retail and consumer markets not only *within* nationally defined markets but also, and crucially, *between* national markets.'

Returning to Figure 8.3 it is possible to see 'how' by analysing the opportunity against the economies existing in the business. The important feature to be identified is the incremental benefit of increases in sales volume on the key aspects of the economies of scale in the business. By conducting this analysis it becomes possible to determine the range of volumes over which the economies of scale are effective and, most importantly their relative importance. For example an overseas market that allows the retailer to sell in excess of fifty per cent of its existing merchandise may have a very

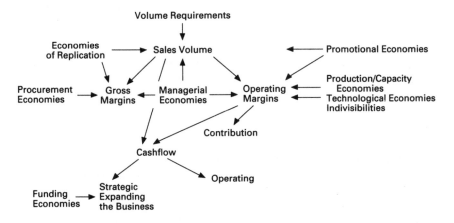

Figure 8.3 Management economies and the international expansion decision

large 'volume effect' on gross margins through large incremental *procurement economies*. The impact could be very large because fixed cost increases would be negligible, thus the increased volume would tend to be sold and to produce a 'gross to net' margin effect. Another potential benefit may appear under *technological economies* of scale, which may occur in both the operations and distribution activities. As equipment is replaced with larger capacity items the relative costs are much less, thus imposing a lower level of fixed costs to be recovered. A similar argument can be made concerning *indivisibilities*. The larger throughput volumes permit (and encourage) the use of larger, more cost-effective organisational and system structures.

The nature of multinational, trans-national and global retailing companies becomes clear. *Multinational* and typically retail conglomerates comprise a portfolio of businesses each of which is targeted towards a local national, customer group. Examples of this would be Vendex, Dairy Farm (part of the Hong Kong conglomerate, Jardine Matheson), and BAT prior to the divestment of its retailing activities. The *global companies* such as Benetton, IKEA, Body Shop and Toys 'R Us have transferable formats, across both geographic and cultural 'borders' such that '. . . it sells the same things in the same way everywhere.' (Levitt). Treadgold suggests that C & A positions itself differently in many of the markets in which it trades but its head offices exchange market and sourcing information with each other. Carrefour uses its expertise in operating its exported hypermarket format into Spain, Brazil, Argentina and the USA. It has benefited from expertise gained in these activities, e.g., fish retailing from Spain and funds handling from Brazil. For Marks & Spencer the learning process was not easy. The Paris store traded unprofitably before it was adjusted to French consumers' expectations. To this list there should be added Ahold and GIB group both having used their expertise in overseas markets either with joint venture partners or independently.

8.3 ANALYSIS FOR RETAIL INTERNATIONALISATION

There are three important considerations that should be explored prior to undertaking the decision to expand into overseas markets. These are risk, resource requirements and return, and were introduced earlier in this chapter (see Figure 8.1); however they do require some expansion.

Risk

There are a number of aspects of risk to be considered: environmental risk; business risk; market characteristics and business risk; financial structures. *Environmental risk* concerns local political, economic, legal and regulatory factors that can inhibit the overseas activity. It is important that these be evaluated early in the planning activity. For example, if it is ascertained that political instability exists the agreements reached with government and commercial parties may well be reversed should an election result in a change of political party and policies. Other issues of importance concern: government or local business participation in business development; profit repatriation; confiscation of assets; nationalisation and domestication are also topics to be explored.

Economic characteristics comprise a range of issues. These are largely macro-economic factors such as GDP trends, tariffs and quotas, currency trends, inflation employment trends, balance of payments and the structure of overseas trade, interest rates and consumer credit policies, monetary policy and fiscal policy and their management.

The legal and regulatory factors are at two levels. There is an overall view that should be taken concerning the regulation of commercial activities, commercial business structures, company taxation, and specifically the regulation of overseas companies. There is also the regulation of retailing and peripheral activities that may cause concern. Here issues such as working hours, trading hours etc. are important, but so too are regulations concerning property and location development (i.e. permitted locations, size, number of outlets) and the legal processes to be followed. Other factors such as the requirements for local content in merchandise ranges may be very important, such as control which if excessive, may prevent a company optimising its procurement economies on an overall planned basis. The consequent dilution of margins may make what appeared to be an attractive proposition one with a large amount of risk.

Market Characteristics and business risks are influenced by the size and nature of the market under evaluation. Clearly the ideal is for the targeted overseas market to be very similar to the domestic market. However, a market of similar size and sophistication may have significant cultural differences and it follows that size, population dispersion (urban and rural structures) and marketing sophistication may not quite be enough and other factors such as cultural differences have considerable influence.

Furthermore aggregate markets may not be homogeneous. Europe can be seen to comprise three trading areas:

- North-West Europe; consisting of Germany, France, the United Kingdom, Switzerland, Belgium, Austria, Scandinavia and Eire.
- Southern Europe; consisting of Spain, Portugal, Greece and Italy.
- Eastern Europe, consisting of Hungary, the Czech Republic, Poland, Slovenia, Romania, Russia and the Ukraine.

What is interesting is that while the consumer and cultural differences have been recognised for some time, more recently the importance of structural differences have been acknowledged and feature in the consideration of strategic expansion overseas by retailers. North-West Europe has more multiple retailing organisations than either Southern or Eastern Europe where independent (often family owned) retailing dominates. Purchasing behaviour differs considerably. In the North Western sector consumers follow the regular but less frequent weekly (or longer) shopping patterns of North America. In Southern and Eastern Europe purchasing is typically daily. Retail offers reflect these patterns.

Another consideration concerns human resources. Often the success that has occurred in a domestic market is due to the skills and quality of staff within the business. Any analysis of overseas opportunities should, therefore, include an appraisal of human resources to establish capabilities.

The nature of the retail offer may as a result require considerable changes if it is to be made to 'fit' and to be profitable. The structure and effectiveness of existing companies should be evaluated and in particular alternative scenarios should be constructed to simulate their possible responses to a new market entry. This requires a detailed understanding of consumer expectations and perceptions together with a thorough understanding of the competitive characteristics. The analysis should identify segments within markets and determine both customer and competitor differences across the segments, thereby identifying opportunities for differentiated offers.

Business risk; financial structures are concerned with the financial and operating gearing situations that may result by undertaking the overseas expansion. Both may be varied by considering alternative internal and external financing arrangements. From an internal aspect financial gearing may be varied by using retained earnings rather than seeking long term loans for the expansion. The external consideration may involve either funding the project locally (from government or other institutions) or perhaps seeking a partner for the venture. Operational gearing should be reviewed by considering the fixed cost content of the venture and reviewing the alternatives available: initially it may be less risky to operate with low fixed costs (by using service companies wherever feasible) until such time as there is sufficient volume to reconsider the decision. By this time the options and their impact on margins will be much clearer. Another important factor in the analysis is the analysis of incremental increases in these factors. If, as Figure 8.3 suggests, opportunities to exploit economies of scale exist then as the diagram (and earlier discussion) suggests the improved utilisation of the assets can have a dramatic effect on asset productivity and profitability. Another consideration concerns the cashflows that occur. An overseas acquisition will generate large amounts of cash quickly, whereas organic growth will require cash to be put into the venture and cashflows be negative for some time.

Resource Requirements

In Chapter 9 a model will be introduced (Figure 9.1) which essentially links the margin, asset, financial and funds flow management activities of the business. Figure 8.4 extends this model by incorporating the detail shown in Figure 8.3 and becomes a model in which the resource requirements necessary to achieve the forecast level of sales can be estimated. Using Figure 8.4 we can explore both the amount or level of resources required together with the relationships between them. (Figure 8.4 also incorporates the risk characteristics.) The discussion is continued below where capital availability and sourcing are discussed.

Return (Performance) Requirements

Determining the required return from the proposed expansion overseas is an ongoing exercise. Many of the factors considered during the evaluation of risk and the estimating of resource requirements will impact upon performance. Thus the measurement of performance requirements will develop overtime. Again, there are both marketing and financial considerations. (See Figure 8.5.)

Marketing performance is a combination of sales volume (required for critical mass to achieve gross margins performance, market credibility and visibility etc.) and customer satisfaction (perceptions of the offer, the service achievements, etc.).

Financial performance is concerned with the returns generated to both overall and incremental increases in the investment in the business. If we assume that resources are limited then the concern should be that not only specific or individual projects achieve ROI or NPV objectives, but also achieve the maximum return for the shareholders. The analysis should set objectives for the return on incremental resources and aggregate values such as gross margins, current assets and fixed assets.

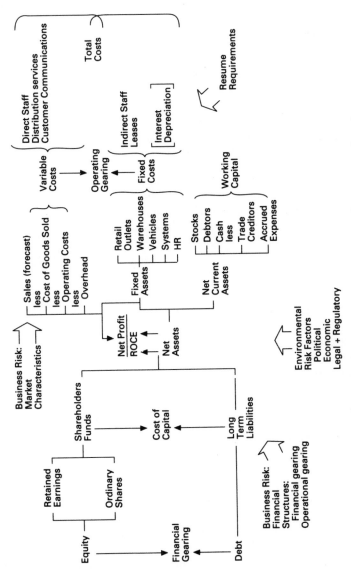

Figure 8.4 Simulation of the export business, its resources, performance and options

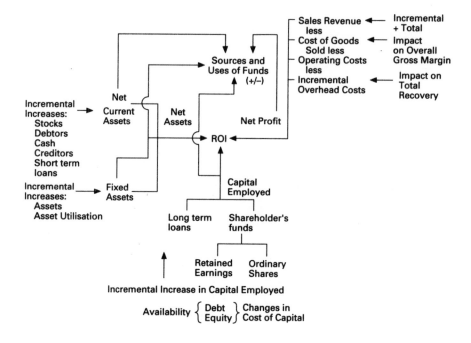

Figure 8.5   Performance issues

There are five basic alternatives. These are:

- Organic growth
- Acquisition/merger
- Joint venture
- Franchises
- Strategic alliances

The choice between these options is influenced by:

- Risk
- Time
- Capital availability
- Control
- Sourcing

Given that an opportunity has been evaluated against the criteria determined by risk, resource requirement and return, the strategic options begin to identify themselves.

Risk

The elements of *risk* that may influence a decision have been identified earlier, they clearly influence the *way* in which an opportunity may persuade a company to opt for organic growth or perhaps to acquire an existing business, whereas a high risk opportunity will probably influence the company to opt for a joint venture, franchise arrangement or an alliance with other companies. Local participation may increase the consumer acceptance of the offer, thereby reducing the risk.

Time Considerations

Competitive activity may require a retailer contemplating a market entry to consider time as a planning constraint. Competitive activity may establish a requirement for an option which facilitates rapid market entry enabling the company to acquire sites in specific locations, establish an offer and begin to create a 'branch awareness'. Alternatively a global operator e.g. IKEA or Bodyshop may have more time to establish an entry because of the uniqueness of their offer and the difficulty it presents competitors who attempt to imitate.

Clearly time imposes constraints on the choice of strategic options. Organic growth requires time, particularly if the offer being developed differs from the domestic business or if the cultural or structural differences are significant. Under such circumstances joint ventures have appeal, or if the offer is a strong brand with a well developed market positioning in adjacent territories, franchise operations are a possible option. Suitable acquisitions/ mergers may also resolve this problem.

Capital Availability

Capital is often the key resource and that which limits the expansion activities of most businesses. Joint ventures and strategic alliances offer solutions but create other problems. Joint venture arrangements typically involve the creation of a third company (jointly owned by the 'venturers'). Issues such as operating procedures, reporting methods, retained earnings and dividend policies and eventually financial structures and marketing direction, can become increasingly difficult to resolve.

Control

The issues raised in the previous paragraph are typical of those presented by any form of joint commercial activity. The need for 'control' is an issue that should be part of the initial planning activities in which financial, marketing and organisational control requirements are identified and established as part of the development plan. This approach determines the suitability of strategic alternatives e.g. quality control requirements may be difficult to establish and maintain in markets without supporting infrastructures. (McDonalds' entry into Russia required an investment in meat processing facilities as well as retail outlets). Equally quality control of service presents difficulties when there are culturally based attitudes that are not supportive to a strong customer service ethic.

Sourcing

The availability of appropriate merchandise at costs which enable the business to operate profitably and to generate funds for growth is an essential requirement in any market. The changing political/economic structures of trading areas throughout the world have resulted in shifting the balance of power between suppliers and distribution. The Single Market (Europe post–1992) has encouraged the concentration of manufacturing by major consumer goods companies such that individual retailers in domestic markets become the customers of a European supplier rather than the customer of say the UK or French subsidiary. The implications of this change are that suddenly the positions of relative power shift. From being a 20% stakeholder in the national manufacturer's business the national retailer becomes a 5% (or even smaller) business with the European supplier. The relationship changes and the influence that having 20% of a manufacturer's business infers is no longer there.

Strategic alliances have been created among large European retailers to redress this balance together with other motives. Treadgold identifies four main types of alliances: purchasing led; development led; skills based or multi-function alliances which embraces elements of all three. He suggests that the European Retail Alliance (ERA) and its sister organisation, Associated Marketing Services (AMS), is arguably the most important of the recently constituted (1990) alliances between European retailers, both for their combined purchasing potential, some £30 billion, and more importantly for the areas of co-operation envisaged by the group:

Development of existing business.
Coordination of supplies.
Coordination of promotional support.
Introduction and testing of new products.
Standardisation of product and packaging.
Coordination of distribution.
Development of merchandising and promotional materials.
Coordination of own brand development.
Material sourcing for own brand suppliers.
Assistance in production and distribution.
Operation of stockholding facilities.
Management of temporary supply shortages.
Forum for retailer/supplier issues.

ERA members comprise a core group: Argyll (UK), Ahold (Netherlands) and Casino (France). AMS extends the co-operation principle to a further group of seven retailers: Migros (Switzerland); ICA (Sweden), Mercandona (Spain), Kesko (Finland), Dansk Supermarked (Denmark) and All Kauf (Germany). ERA holds a 60% stake in AMS. The remaining 40% is split between the other members, each of which can hold up to 5%. Treadgold does emphasise that the EC has yet to make its view known concerning cross-border alliances within the Community's competition policy.

SUMMARY

This chapter has reviewed the important issues emerging in the area of international retailing. The growth of international retailing businesses has been influenced by a number of factors ranging from economic and political changes to converging consumer characteristics.

The structural or strategic postures of a retailer seeking international opportunities has been influenced by the extent to which the retailer offers a solution to culturally standard needs. There are few global retailers, companies who can export their offer without modification. More likely is the multinational approach in which companies can operate internationally but do so by adjusting their offer to meet specific local needs. The trans-national company aims to operate internationally responding to local demand but using expertise and influence obtained elsewhere and benefiting from an international exposure to experiences, ideas and emerging opportunities.

There are a number of motives for retailing to expand in overseas markets and these have been linked to the basic model of the firm in Figure 8.6. The process discussed in the latter half of the chapter proposed an approach to the overseas expansion decisions and Figure 8.7 represents the issues covered.

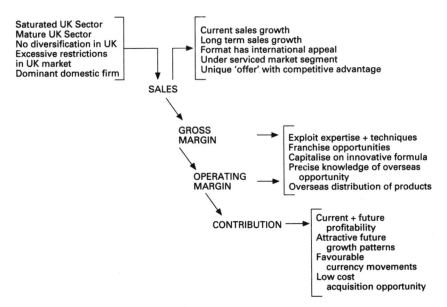

Figure 8.6 Motives for expanding overseas

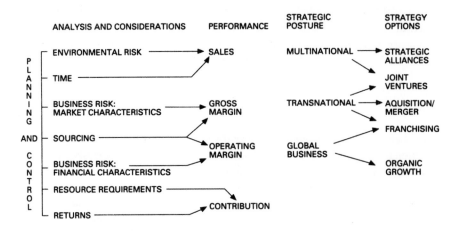

Figure 8.7 The overseas decision

9 An Integrated Approach for Management Decision Making

INTRODUCTION

In Part I we have considered the major elements of company profitability and therefore the factors contributing to the success of the business: generating sales revenue; managing gross margins; managing the operations of the business to generate a contribution to profit and overhead and the management of cashflow for operational and strategic purposes. We also considered the important topic of economies of scale, an issue which influences the management decisions concerning both the size and characteristics of the business.

In this chapter we review the implications of these decisions on the financial structure and its management. There are a number of considerations that have considerable influence on these decisions: financial and operational gearing, fund sourcing decisions and their implications. Figure 9.1 illustrates the nature of decisions management must consider. The primary task of the corporate executive is to maximise shareholders' wealth and within the parameters of the model we have used throughout the text so far we have been concerned with producing a satisfactory return to the shareholders, this being measured by net profit divided by net assets or capital employed. We shall discuss performance measurement in detail in a subsequent chapter.

The components of decision making are essentially financial. Any decision taken and subsequently implemented must be seen in a financial context: its impact on the profitable operations of the business is the eventual measure of the extent of its success. Figure 9.1 suggests that four areas of financial management are important. The management of the buying and store operations activities concerns *margin management* (gross margins and operating margins discussed in Chapters 3 and 4). *Asset management* is the response of management in the effective application of resources in fixed assets and working capital to produce profit. *Financial management* is the structure and acquisition of capital funding for the business and its subsequent management. A measure of stewardship is given by focusing upon *funds flow management* which indicates how funds are obtained and used within the decision making process of the business.

In this chapter we explore the implications of decision making on the model of the business we have developed in the preceding chapters. Particular

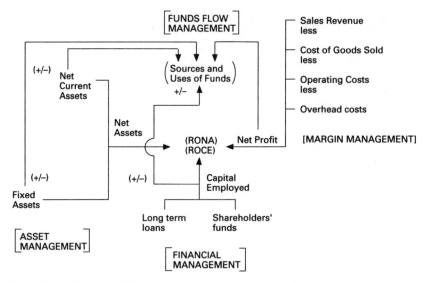

Figure 9.1   The financial management structure of the business

interest will be aimed at integrating decisions and showing the impact of such decisions.

Management should not attempt simply to maximise sales, or margins, or cashflow without considering the impact of decisions taken in one area, upon the reaction of other elements of the business and the time horizon over which they are operating. Furthermore, the financial management structure within which decisions are made is an important consideration together with the organisational requirements necessary to make it work successfully.

This chapter considers the topics of the previous chapters in Part I and discusses an integrated view of making implementation decisions, the structure issues and aspects of performance measurement.

9.1   INTEGRATING DECISION MAKING: THE FINANCIAL ISSUES AND IMPLICATIONS

The preceding chapters identified the individual elements of profitability and the success of the business. Clearly no business decision can be taken in isolation: expansion decisions have a number of interrelated components such as the implications on the utilisation of fixed assets and this in turn can be examined from the viewpoint of incremental fixed costs and the impact on margins and cashflow. An example will expand this. Consider the situation in which a multiple retailer decides to expand the number of outlets within a region or territory in which the company already has significant market penetration. We will assume that the fixed asset structure has the capacity to 'service' the expansion in sales and further that the promotional costs involved (as a percentage of sales) is not likely to increase significantly. It follows that the incremental sales revenue will produce a greater contribution (as a percentage of sales) due to the increased utilisation of existing assets and the amortisation of fixed costs over the increased sales revenue.

A closer look at Figure 9.1 identifies the linkages between the management decision areas. Decisions taken within the business which will *directly* improve the performance of that area will have an *indirect* impact on others.

Returning to the example in the previous paragraph we can see that the expansion will increase sales which in turn will increase gross margins through a volume effect and operating margins due to similar reasoning. As overheads are unlikely to expand by the same proportion as the sales growth it follows that net profit will be greater and consequently there will be an increase in both ROCE/RONA and the sources of funds. As mentioned earlier, asset utilisation will increase, thus asset turnover and asset management will improve and this improvement together with the increased utilisation of inventory holding (i.e. higher stockturn) will show an overall improvement in asset management.

It follows that there are a number of basic implications that should be considered during the evaluation of decision options. These are:

- Customer expectations.
- The critical success factors necessary to ensure that the forecast levels of customer purchasing do occur.
- The expected patterns of customer purchasing and the frequency and size of transactions.
- The implications for the cost structures of the business.
- The implications of the cost structures on the financial structure and management of the business.
- Broad parameters for financial structure and performance that will act as a guide for decision making such as;
    profitability: return on total capital; employed (net assets); return on shareholder funds;
    gearing: financial gearing; fixed assets financed by debt; operational gearing;
    cost and availability of capital: fixed capital; working capital.

These topics are expanded upon below and in Figure 9.2.

Customer Expectations

The elements of customer expectations together with a review of shopping decisions processes are discussed in depth in subsequent chapters. At this juncture it is essential to identify the issues that are important to customers. There are four basic areas from which a convincing retail offer must emerge, these are:

- Merchandise characteristics;
- Customer service characteristics;
- Store environment, and
- Customer communications.

Customer expectations will exist for each area, furthermore it is realistic to expect there to be a number of interdependencies and interrelationships between each of them; for example, merchandise decisions will inevitably have implications for customer service (e.g. delivery, installation etc.) for store environment (e.g. visual merchandising) and customer communications (e.g. message context, personal and non-personal communications). These are illustrated in Figure 9.2 which uses merchandise characteristics as an example.

Critical Success Factors

Each area will have specific aspects of concern to customers: critical success factors. Those typically found in customer research are identified in Figure 9.2. Some may be common to others in these areas, for example merchandise support and services may have common areas with both customer service and possibly store environment. Furthermore, the critical success factors may require to be detailed. This will certainly be necessary for merchandise assortment characteristics, where such topics as availability, quality, choice, etc., may be important characteristics. We shall return to this topic in more detail when we discuss the issue of implementing decisions.

Customer Purchasing Patterns

This is a topic to which considerable attention must be paid and there are a number of chapters devoted to the customer store selection and purchasing decision in Part II. At this point it is useful to consider this topic in the context of customer visiting and purchasing frequencies (clearly they may differ) and the average transaction per customer per purchasing visit. This is important for a number of reasons. First is the need to know the relationship between browsing and purchasing visits. Many purchases are decided before the customer enters the store, others result only after a period of browsing and comparison shopping followed by a period of deliberation. How the decision is made is an essential information input because it influences each of the areas (i.e. merchandise, customer service, store environment, and customer communications). The transaction size and frequency is also a major input. This information enables revenue forecasts to

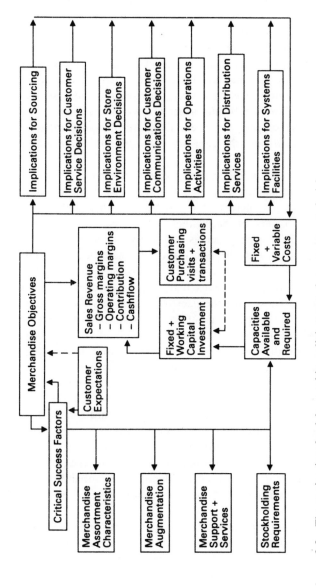

Figure 9.2 The topics involved in reaching all integrated management decisions

be made and this together with an estimate of the costs of meeting the 'shopping' needs of the customers will facilitate margin, contribution and cashflow forecasts.

Financial Structure and Performance Considerations

Cost Structure Implications

Other aspects of the business are influenced by the merchandise, customer service, store environment and customer communications decisions. Figure 9.2 identifies the interrelationships between each of these and also considers the support activities, i.e. operations, distribution and systems. Not featured in Figure 9.2, but clearly important are the human and physical resources required by the support activities. They are of course included in the *fixed and variable costs* and the capacity *available and required* topics.

Parameters for Financial Structure and Performance

The topics identified are seen as both policy and performance issues. Clearly as performance parameters they can be quantified and the financial structure and performance of the business monitored. As policy issues they have more impact in that they act as a directive to management from which a planning approach may be developed. We have then a number of criteria (see Figure 9.3) which can serve both purposes, that is act as quantitative measures and policy directives that may be used in the evaluation of decision options. These, like the decisions to be appraised, are integrated with the financial management structure of the business and as Figure 9.3 suggests they are related to the profit and loss account, balance sheet and funds flow statement all of which should be used when forecasting the expected level of activity of an alternative or option. Of particular interest are:

Gross margin (gross profit): which measures the efficiency of the buying activity by the difference between planned and realised margin resulting from business activity. If planned margins are not achieved it suggests that customer expectations were either not identified or met. The gross margin also indicates the funds available from successful sales to support the operational activities *and* contribute to overhead expenses and profit. In a planning context it is essential to identify the probability of achieving the planned margins because of the implications for the business of failure to do so.

Operating margin (operating profit): which measures the efficiency of store operations and distribution activities in achieving customer service and store environment objectives and at the same time creating a contribution to overhead and profit.

Operational gearing: indicates the relationship between fixed costs and variable costs. Operational gearing is high when fixed costs are a high proportion of total costs. It is an important measure because if operational gearing is

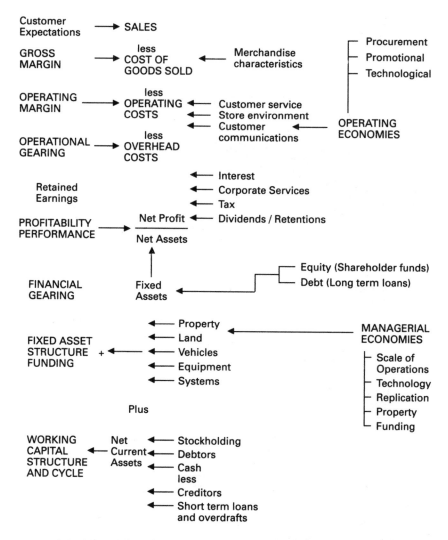

Figure 9.3 Financial performance, decisions and influences

high, profit is sensitive to changes in the level of sales (see Figure 9.4). With high operating gearing the contribution margin is larger than that for low operating gearing situations. While sales are stable and reach a forecast level no particular problems occur, however, as Figure 9.4 suggests the situation is very different should there be wide variations in sales performance. In the illustration BE_H and BE_L are the break-even volume points for high and low fixed cost situations. The shaded areas indicate the proportional differences in contribution as volume varies. Operational gearing is an important consideration in decision making. Given a choice between a high

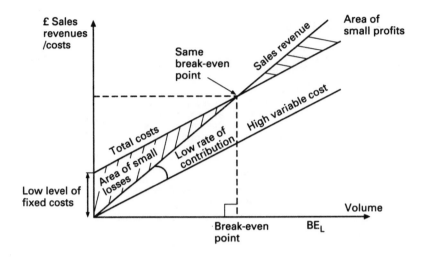

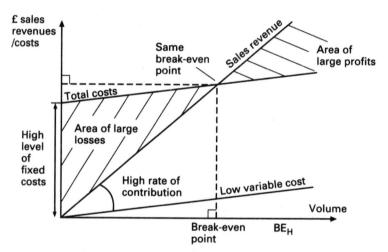

Figure 9.4   The impact of operational gearing   *Note*: Break-even points may
(a)   Low fixed costs, low operational gearing   be at the same level, i.e.
(b)   High fixed costs, high operational gearing $BE_L = BE_H$.

fixed cost structure or a low fixed cost alternative a number of issues are to
be considered. Clearly the expectations of sales achieving forecast levels
together with a minimum variation around the forecast is an important consideration. Wide fluctuations will result in large variances in contribution.
Given this may not occur other factors should be considered. Typically, high
fixed costs suggest that labour is substituted by capital equipment, or that
by applying capital equipment, for example EPOS equipment major efficiencies
will be available. Issues such as customer service and the impact of technology on the service offer are important considerations. Risk is high for niche/

differentiated retail businesses selling merchandise which is sensitive to reductions in disposable income, interest rate increases and other symptoms of recessionary periods. A high level of operational gearing can result in very serious consequences for the business. It follows that a business which requires a high level of operational gearing should have adequate gross and operating margins together with a stable revenue stream (and preferably one for which the sales forecast is reliable). Without such criteria efforts should be made to lower the operating gearing to an acceptable level provided the essential characteristics of the offer can be maintained.

Retained earnings: are the residual funds available after all costs etc. are met. They are a low cost source of funding and are important for that reason and for the influence that a regular, high level flow of retained earnings has on the confidence of shareholders and the investment market generally. Retained earnings growth is an important cashflow component and, therefore, consideration.

Profitability performance: measured by net profit divided by net assets is the primary performance measurement for the business. It follows that any project or new venture the firm may consider should be reviewed against this criterion. Performance measurement is dealt with in much more detail in later chapters, it is sufficient to say at this point that profitability criteria are an integral component in the decision making process.

Financial gearing: means borrowing to finance business operations, rather than using equity capital (the shareholders' funds). The relationship between debt and equity within the firm's financial structure influences its financial risk. It is measured by the proportion of debt to total capital employed. Management can adjust its financial risk (gearing) by changing the proportions of debt and equity in its capital structure:
Equity:

by retaining profits or paying dividends by issuing new shares or purchasing back those shares in issue.

Debt:

by borrowing more or repaying existing debt.

If the rate of return on assets financed by borrowing is greater than the cost of debt, any surplus is added to equity earnings, thus benefiting the ordinary shareholders and resulting in a higher rate of growth in earnings per share. However, if profits are declining the ordinary shareholders become vulnerable: the interest on the debt must be met, even if the rate of return on assets is lower than the rate of interest to be paid on the debt, thereby resulting in a loss from borrowing. Ideally the level of gearing (i.e. the proportion of debt within the total capital employed) should be adjusted to benefit the ordinary shareholders. This occurs when the operating profit is high, then high gearing benefits the shareholders. It follows that when evaluating a new venture the impact that funding the activity will have on the overall performance of the business is a major consideration. Any project requiring extensive funding should be considered in this way. In the earlier example (the expansion of the business by a multiple retailer) the method of funding the expansion is an important consideration. If, as suggested, the increase in gross and operating margins is to larger values than currently achieved it would be possible to fund the expansion through borrowing because if the return on the investment exceeds the debt interest it is to the benefit of the ordinary shareholders.

It is worth noting at this point that Figure 9.3 shows that a number of operating and managerial economies of scale influence the performance of the business. These were discussed in detail in the previous chapter and the reader is reminded that economies of scale may have a significant impact on profit performance. Clearly this influence is a major consideration, particularly for distribution and information systems where surplus capacity may exist and can be used.

Cost of capital: the cost of capital for the business varies with the level of debt or gearing that the firm introduces. From the earlier discussion it follows that there are three aspects to be considered: the cost of equity funds, the cost of debt and the overall, weighted average cost of capital that results from the combination of debt and equity funding. (For an explanation of how this may be calculated see Myddleton (1992).) Of particular interest to us is the effect that various combinations of equity and debt have on risk and the perceptions of investors towards risk. The essential concern of financial managers is focused on market reaction to the addition of debt to the equity base. It can be shown that for a company with no debt the addition of increments of debt to the capital structure can improve the return on equity. It follows that as the return on equity increases, so too does the company's total market value (as share price increases). However, beyond a certain combination, as debt increases significantly and the market becomes concerned at the level of interest changes to be met from earnings, the market value may be expected to decline. It follows that the market has concluded that the increased debt has increased beyond a combination they consider to be prudent. In other words, they perceive the shares in the company now to have some risk attached and consequently the share price is marked down. Evaluation of a proposal should, therefore, include an appraisal of the impact of debt financing (if this is to be considered). Unfortunately there is no theoretical approach by which the level of gearing is likely to be 'too much'. Clearly the considerations introduced earlier will obtain. An expansion of the business utilising existing expertise, together with any operating and managerial economies of scale that may prevail is less likely to cause concern than perhaps diversification into an unknown product-market using debt financing. Hence it becomes an essential part of any evaluation process to consider both the nature of the project proposal and the method of finance.

Fixed asset structure and funding: concerns the way in which assets are acquired and funded. A number of issues are of importance to decision makers. The relationship between fixed costs and variable costs (operating gearing) has been discussed earlier. Clearly this influences the fixed asset structure. A company with high fixed costs is very likely to have a proportionately larger value and number of fixed assets than one with low variable costs. The issues concerning market forecasts, sales volume amounts and stability have also been discussed. Here we are concerned with how these may be funded by the company. An increase in fixed assets may be managed by increasing either equity or debt capital (or perhaps if very large amounts are involved, a combination of both). This may be accomplished without disturbing the structure of the control of the business by using a rights issue to obtain additional capital. During 1992 some large companies made rights issues to fund expansion activities and restructuring. This effectively maintained the 'balance of power' of the existing ordinary share capital structure but provided capital for expansion without the problems of interest payment liability. The gearing implications have also been discussed earlier but an important aspect which should be added is the relationship between fixed assets and the type of funding selected. A measure of vulnerability is given by the ratio of fixed assets funded by debt. Many 'fixed assets' are specialist in their nature and consequently have a low resale value; it follows that should the project fail not only would the company have difficulty in meeting interest payments but disposal of the fixed assets would also be difficult. It is not simply high-technology equipment that has this problem: specialist retailing outlets may face similar problems, a poorly located under-performing superstore has limited appeal. (The recent [1992] dilemma of the Hatfield Galleria project is an example of this problem.) To avoid the risks of ownership (and to avoid the funding issue) 'off-balance sheet' funding has attraction. In this method of asset financing a company leases many of the fixed asset requirements. Lease payments become operating costs and while the risk is diminished it is clearly not avoided because the leasing company will be quite expert and assessing risk and lease payments will be adjusted to ensure they (the leasing company) are protected.

There are issues concerning depreciation and tax allowances that enter the decision making but so too does the issue of alternative uses (suggested above). In the example used earlier, the decision to expand the business, these topics would be considered and the issue of capacity availability and utilisation of the infrastructure and its funding methods and alternatives evaluated with a view to both performance and risk. One other alternative to both ownership and leasing is the use of service companies to provide the distribution and storage facilities required by the venture. Clearly this will increase operating costs but will obviously lower the risk. It will also lower operating gearing.

Working capital structure and cycle: the nature of retailing is such that the management of working capital is particularly important and has far reaching implications for the success of a business. Working capital is defined as current assets (inventory, debtors, cash and short term investments) less current liabilities (creditors, short term loans and payments due). Clearly because of the high value of stock the efficient management of working capital has very large implications for any management decision. An issue of importance which concerns performance (and consequently success of a project) is the basic structure of the working capital requirement. The influence on sales and current assets is shown in Figure 9.5. As a business (or a specific project) expands both fixed and current assets may be financed by long term debt, equity or by 'spontaneous' increases, accrued taxes and negative working capital (trade credit which because of rapid stockturn is paid only after the stock has been sold 'two or three times' before payment is due). Short term financing needs (often a feature of retailing caused by the seasonal trading characteristics of many businesses) should not be based upon long term facilities due to the possibility of being required to meet cash obligations, and due also to the possibility of having made a poor merchandise selection or forecast resulting in mark-downs to achieve a planned sell-through volume. The working capital cycle is also important for many businesses. For example, with retailers who source from overseas and as a consequence have working capital committed for long periods of time or jewellers, some of whom may have very slow stockturns, it is important to identify the period of time taken to convert stock purchased into cash receipts. Consider the following example showing two hypothetical companies:

	Company A	Company B
	Days	Days
Sourcing	42	7
Depot stocks	21	7
Outlet stocks	10	3
Credit customers' payment	30	10
	103	27
Less credit from suppliers	0	30
Days to finance	103	−3

Company A sources offshore because it considers the lower costs (and consequently its prices) are essential to its competitive positioning. By comparison Company B sources domestically and consequently is able to maintain

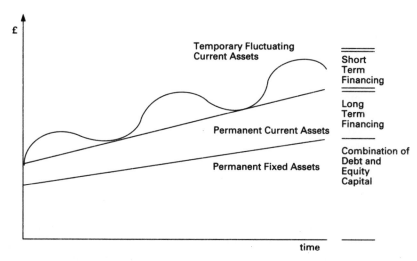

Figure 9.5   The structure of working capital requirements: fluctuating and permanent current assets

lower stocks throughout its distribution/operations system. The implications of the two approaches on the companies' working capital cycles are very clear. Company A has 103 days stock to finance whereas Company B benefits from the 'negative working capital' effect. Clearly there are other costs to be considered. Company B is likely to have a sophisticated information management/inventory management facility which clearly reduces its operating margins. However, if both companies are apparel retailers then the benefits of low stock levels and rapid response (the B option) would compensate the price advantage offered to A by offshore sourcing.

Returning to our example, the expansion of the number outlets operated by a multiple retailing business, it is likely that the working capital requirements are attractive. Given that the company would *not* require to maintain stock levels in its distribution centres to match the anticipated growth of sales (see Maister [1975]) because it can be shown that the total inventory in a system is proportional to the square root of the number of locations at which a product is stocked. Thus it follows that the safety stocks required by the expansion would only be fractionally incremental, thereby having a beneficial impact on operating margins, contribution and capital employed (net assets). Furthermore, provided the merchandise assortment profile is similar to the remainder of the business the structure of the working capital need cause no concern.

An Example: J. Sainsbury PLC

The expansion activities of one or two UK multiples offer interesting examples. Sainsbury is a particularly good example. Sainsbury has shown consistent growth of both sales and profits in recent years. It has grown organically, taking opportunities to use market penetration, market development and related product development to expand its base business. Monitoring consumer changing habits and behaviour (more working women, increased overseas travel, increasing disposable incomes (at least in the long term) rising car ownership etc.) and responding with out-of-town superstores, convenience-ready-made-meals, delicatessen and produce products has enabled the Company to increase average customer transaction values and gross margins. The development and expansion of its own retail brands has also enhanced its gross margins: the most notable development being in home laundry detergents where the Sainsbury own label has doubled its market share in a sector dominated by Lever and Procter and Gamble.

Concurrently Sainsbury have invested at the rate of £800 million (approximately) into the business each year. This has expanded the number of outlets (optimising economies of scale) but has also improved the operational efficiency of the business and in product range development.

9.2 MANAGEMENT STRUCTURE AND DECISION MAKING

Implementing management decisions is essentially a task in which management allocates limited resources to achieve specified objectives within a prescribed corporate direction. How effective this proves to be depends largely upon the management structure within which direction is given and the amount of responsibility delegated. The structure should reflect the nature of the task, i.e. planning and control of resources to achieve specific objectives, and it should reflect the different levels of responsibility throughout the organisation which are necessary if implementation is to be successful. The use of Responsibility Centres have been found to be helpful in this context.

Responsibility Centres exist in most medium and large sized companies. They comprise:

- *Investment Centres*: in which management is responsible for costs, revenues and assets employed (resource allocation policies) e.g. retail conglomerates.
- *Profit Centres*: which delegate responsibility for revenues and costs and this structure would be typical of the management of a merchandise division.
- *Revenue Centres*: are typified by activity centres in which the emphasis is on generating sales. In retailing companies the use of information technology has been such that merchandise and space planning (primary activities in generating sales) have been centralised and most multiple retailing companies opt for cost centres in field locations.
- *Cost Centres*: are used when managements' responsibility is for managing the performance of a unit at a prescribed level of cost. Typically

Table 9.1 An illustration of the typical relationship between the organization structure and responsibility accounting centres

Board/General Management	INVESTMENT CENTRES responsible for: • Identifying strategic options
Corporate Direction	• Estimating (and allocating) macro-resource requirements • Forecasting return on investment and cash flow
Functional and Support Management	PROFIT CENTRES responsible for: • Evaluating options and the opportunity costs of alternatives
Implementing Functional and Support Strategies	• Detailed resource allocation • Implementing strategy • Maximizing returns from allocated resources • Generating operating (trading) profit and cash flow
Field and Branch Management	COST AND REVENUE CENTRES responsible for: • Achieving revenue targets
Operational Implementation and Management of Management Decisions.	• Maintaining prescribed levels of service • Meeting operating requirements • Controlling costs within their budgeted levels

retail outlets operate in this way, levels of service are established and budgeted levels of expenditure determined.

It is an important feature of effective responsibility accounting systems that each manager of a responsibility centre participates in the development of the forecast of the output and the budgeted cost of achieving that output. Managers are much more motivated towards achieving profit, revenue and cost forecast and budgets if they have been involved in their determination. Examples of the de-motivation and frustration generated by situations in which managers are assigned performance requirements (without involvement) are not difficult to find. Table 9.1 describes the responsibilities of different levels of management.

Our focus is on functional and support management activities. Functional management relates to the decisions that implement positioning strategies within the context of overall strategy and corporate direction. The decisions concerning merchandise, customer service, trading format and store environment and customer communications are the responsibility of functional management. Given the corporate direction (specifically the intended positioning) a 'vision' of how each component integrates with the other component areas into a co-ordinated retail offer should emerge. Typically these are merchandise and customer service roles and often include store environment.

Support activities are those which provide facilitating services. In this context we suggest that marketing, finance, human resource management, systems and operations (together with distribution) are support activities. Their role is to provide information and resource inputs to enable functional management to operate effectively. Thus we see marketing as a service activity providing research data on customer expectations with which both the merchandise and service characteristics of the 'retail offer' can be determined with some reliable levels of accuracy.

The implementation process is also conducted at field and branch management level. Here the task role is much more one of ensuring that the task performance is achieved at prescribed levels of customer satisfaction expectations, revenue and budgeted costs. However, it is interesting to observe that with the increased sophistication of management information together with an acknowledged need to increase job satisfaction at field and branch levels, more responsibility is being devolved. Some companies are encouraging these managers to become involved in developing local merchandise offers and local promotions. It is suggested that this practice may become more widespread.

Clearly structure is important when considering strategy implementation. There are two factors to be considered. One issue concerns the position of the firm in its own life cycle. If it is the growth sector both structure and management style should be such that creativity is encouraged. Conversely in a mature stage the focus is more likely to be placed on productivity, the purpose being to increase the profitability of existing assets. The type of expansion is also important. Growth through replication requires managers who know the business well: growth through diversification will require management with a radical approach to the business. It follows that the management structure within which the process of strategy implementation takes place is very important. The wrong emphasis may result in the failure of what may have been a sound strategy.

9.3 IMPLEMENTING DECISIONS: SHORT AND LONG TERM ISSUES

The previous chapters (2, 3, 4 and 5) took a detailed view of the managerial considerations and decisions involved in the management of sales generation, gross margins and operating margins and cashflow. In each chapter, we examined topics that may influence management decisions during the process of implementing management decisions. However, the objective for

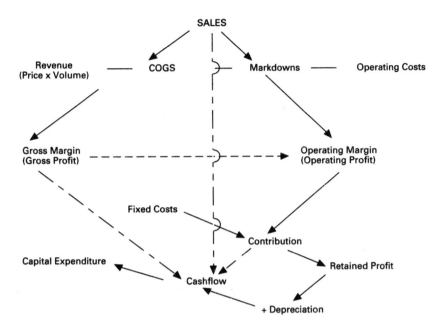

Figure 9.6   The 'accounting elements' of strategy implementation

successful implementation is to achieve an integrated performance which reflects the overall objectives of the firm.

The topics to be considered during the implementation activity are described by Table 9.1 in which the relationships between the activities discussed in Chapters 2, 3, 4 and 5 are integrated. It provides an overall model within which issues are raised and which should be reviewed both independently and with a view to identifying positive and negative impacts upon other issues and activities.

Some examples may help here (see Figure 9.6). Consider the components of gross and operating margin management. The profile of the sales revenue has an important impact upon both of these activities. A price-led offer will emphasise volume at low and competitive prices and the objectives of the merchandise and buying group will be to seek to offer a range of merchandise that is fast moving and comprises nationally known brands that can be sold at discounted prices. To achieve buying margins that facilitate this strategy the buyers may find it necessary to purchase in high quantities thereby creating a need for additional storage facilities. In some categories of merchandise they may also risk high mark-downs if their selection proves to be unpopular with the customer: this could have cost implications for operations management as space and employee time are allocated to clearance sales.

There are also issues to be considered when considering fixed costs and capital expenditure. Depending upon the market position adopted, so the costs of creating the store environment will differ. An exclusive, high level of choice offer supported with a wide range of customer service facilities will require a higher level of capital expenditure (and maintenance costs) than the one which is price-led and described in the previous paragraph. This has an impact on the level of profit generated and the cash required by the business for expanding the offer. It will also have implications for operating gearing, particularly if sales fluctuate around the break-even level of sales volume.

9.4   PERFORMANCE EXPECTATIONS AND MEASUREMENT

Earlier chapters have discussed the role of critical success factors as a means of relating quantified objectives to customer expectations. As we can see from Figure 9.7 there are two influences to be considered. Clearly the customers' needs or expectations create factors to be considered when developing and implementing strategy (see Chapter 1) but so too can the aspirations and expectations of management influence the strategic direction of the firm. While it is difficult to present examples to support the well-known Cyert and March proposals we can consider events of the 1970s and 1980s and question the rationale behind decisions taken by retailing management. An example: it was a phenomena of that period that a majority of retailing companies pursued what they perceived as a market based opportunity among aspirant C1 customer groups. That the opportunity existed cannot be disputed. Indeed it was at the end of the 1970s, early 1980s, that a rapidly expanding group emerged in terms of disposable income and propensity to

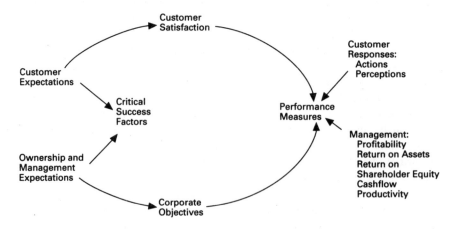

Figure 9.7   Developing performance measures

spend. However, the issue to be considered (in retrospect) is: were the companies pursuing this opportunity, and it was a major strategic convergence within the industry, capable of success? Or was the reality that while a number of retailers pursuing this group with success (which was based upon managerial capability and the company's credibility within this customer group) was a realistic response to the opportunity; others failed and did so because the response was led by 'managerial aspirations' rather than a realistic allocation of resources within a segment of the market lacking individual appeal (in the context of personal identity and preference) to senior management. Hence the C2, D and E groups were, and largely remain ignored.

It follows that a realistic view of market opportunities is the basis for the successful implementation of any strategy. Prior to allocating resources a realistic view of the credibility of the company to make an offer should be established. Provided that evidence can be found (e.g. positive consumer perceptions) then the basis for success may exist. What is required if planning is to proceed is an achievable set of objectives and critical success factors which are interrelated. For example, it is unrealistic to expect large increases in gross margins if one of the customer related critical success factors is to offer variety, and another to offer high levels of availability. Figure 9.8 suggests a framework for developing integrated performance measures. It proposes that while there are a number of expectations that may be used as the basis for developing critical success factors, two issues should be resolved: those of sustainable competitive advantage and financial viability. Clearly there is a time perspective concerning customer expectations and preferences. Some are influenced by fashion and are often short term. It can be a serious mistake to select such topics as a basis for planning. It commits resources which often could be more usefully utilised, and which once committed are unavailable for other uses. Hence the selection of critical success factors should be based upon a view of which are likely to be relatively long term factors (long term being variable from sector to sector) and more importantly those which are identified as having a major impact on the consumer store selection and product purchasing process.

Financial viability is essential. It is an indication of poor management if the financial viability of the company is compromised to pursue an opportunity which imposes unacceptable constraints on the resources of the company. Examples of this include high fashion – innovatory merchandise which is a high risk venture and may prove to have only limited success, with high levels of mark-downs and consequently poor overall gross margin performance. Another example, typical of many companies, is a high service offer (usually personnel based) which proves to be too expensive to maintain. The result is that not only do operating margins prove to be unacceptable, but that following actions to remedy the problem customers become disenchanted with the lower level of service.

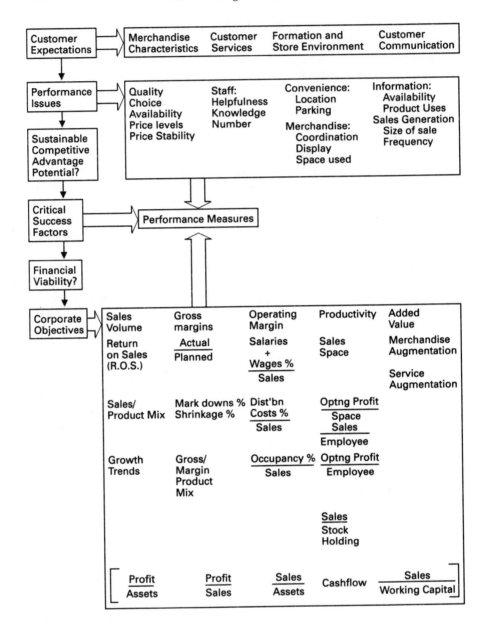

Figure 9.8   Detailed view of performance setting

It is suggested that performance measures are arrived at by a process of 'costing' the critical success factors identified as important for the business. They can be appraised from three aspects. First there is the issue: does the effective implementation of a strategy based upon these particular CSFs offer sustainable competitive advantage? What are the likely financial implications of this decision? Is there a compromise situation? In other words, is it likely that consumers are willing to consider the possibility of 'trading-off' elements of one CSF for another. For example, a customer group strongly favouring choice may well be willing to accept a lower level of availability in order to have a wider range of merchandise from which to make purchase selections. The research activity by which this may be investigated, conjoint analysis, will be discussed in a later chapter.

SUMMARY

The purpose of this chapter has been to integrate the previous chapters in Part I. Management decisions should be integrated and interrelated. No decisions to maximise sales (or margins or cashflow) should be taken without considering the impact that the action will have on the overall performance of the business. The chapter discussed the basic issues of importance to the company's financial structure showing how decisions do relate to each other within the context of accounting and financial models. The discussion also considered the decisions for merchandise, customer service, store environment and customer communications. This approach will be explored in detail in subsequent chapters.

The topic of structure discussed the role of management in the context of decision making responsibility. The need for the roles of investment, profit and cost and revenue responsibilities was illustrated in a simple model.

Finally the chapter introduced the topic of performance measurement and the influence of various groups (management and 'ownership' together with customer expectations) and how these might respond to achieving the required levels of customer satisfaction and corporate objectives. This topic is very basic to the successful implementation of management decision making and this discussion serves as an introduction to a detailed treatment later.

Part II

Understanding Customer Expectations

INTRODUCTION

In Part II we explore consumer expectations. We begin by considering recent influences on consumer behaviour; the agents of change that have had an impact on consumer developments over recent years. These are suggested to be: the expansion of the information sciences and of technology; the 'expressive revolution' (the growth of individualism and of informality) and the 'structural revolution' (changes to traditional hierarchies). These together with the external environment have contributed towards the creation of a range of social values which cover attitudes towards achievement, authority and risk taking, through to attitudes concerning leisure and work and include attitudes on equality and entrepreneurship. This is a wide ranging menu but one which influences the store selection and product purchasing decision process by providing a reference frame for identifying customer typology and qualification, customer lifestyle characteristics and customer shopping missions.

Shopping missions are the basis of a shopping visit and clearly may vary by individual and occasion. Six shopping missions are identified and described. They are: destination purchases; planned regular purchasing visits; planned comparison shopping; planned browsing visits; impulse purchasing and distress purchasing missions. An analysis of the nature and frequency of the shopping missions provides a basis for planning the retail offer, its positioning and differentiation emphasis and the attribute characteristics. The overall structure of the analysis is to provide a basis for resource allocation and strategy implementation. Clearly information is a primary input. A chapter is devoted to developing approach to the provision of information for developing the shopping missions. The alternative research methods available for developing data are reviewed together with a review of conjoint analysis, a useful technique with which the relative importance of customer expectations and from which the relevant attributes of the retail offer may be derived.

Once the retail offer has been decided upon a means of effecting delivery *and* meeting acceptable profit objectives follows. Resource allocation requires costing information and the issues of resource allocation and resource productivity analysis are explored for both strategic and operational decisions. The use of activity based costing to optimise resource allocation is reviewed and possible modifications to convert the activity based costing model into an *attribute* based costing model are proposed and evaluated.

10 Deriving Target Customer Group Characteristics

INTRODUCTION

There is a considerable literature dealing with the topic of market segmentation and with its implications for retailing decisions. Within the context of strategic decision making and implementation the management focus should be upon customer characteristics that are important to the company at this time and for future planning purposes. That is to say that the theory of segmentation is accepted and provided that segments are: identifiable; with meaningful characteristics; are reachable; have a viable size, and are stable over time, they are significant for strategic analysis and planning purposes.

This chapter will focus its attention on the issues and implications of customer responses for strategy purposes rather than to revisit the methodology of segmentation research. In order that we might introduce some new approaches to incorporating customer store selection and purchasing decision processes into strategic decision making we will consider the process (or background) to the formation of consumer and customer behaviour. This will require to be placed into a useful format in order that a workable target customer profile might be developed for our purposes.

The requirements for researching customer decision making is a major issue for retail management. It is to this issue that we direct the content of this chapter.

10.1 CONSUMER BEHAVIOUR: INFLUENCES AND RESPONSES

Consumer behaviour has an extensive literature and a discussion of the issues raised and in particular of the theory of consumer behaviour is beyond the scope of this chapter. However, we do have an interest in the 'basic issues'. Our concern is with issues such as: the cause and effect relationships between social values and consumer behaviour, between consumer behaviour and retail/business response.

In Figure 10.1 we suggest that consumer behaviour is moulded by a cyclical process. The suggestion is that it is difficult to identify cause and effect in this process. This can be expanded using the example of technology. There are a number of aspects of technology to be considered. Process technology influences the efficiency of the business, and as it does so it requires employees to become technologically literate. The use of EPOS at the point of transaction, the use of data processing to produce information to plan

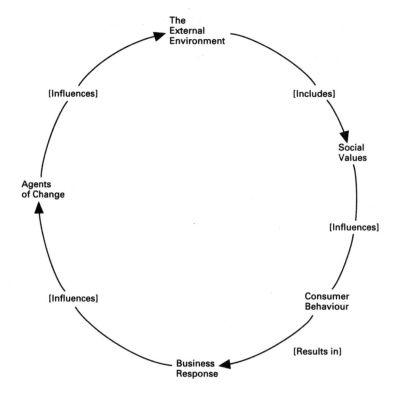

Figure 10.1   The process of social and consumer change

assortment selection, staff scheduling etc. requires a level of expertise to be developed by the staff responsible for tasks in these areas. Product technology also requires the development of a technological literacy. Development of consumer durables, leisure products and children's toys all require an increasing level of skill and understanding if the benefits of the products are to be fully realised.

Agents of change have an impact on all aspects of an individuals interaction with family, work groups and broader aspects of society. They are fundamental to the overall process of change within the external environment. Figure 10.2 identifies four agents of change or 'revolution': information, technological, structural and expressive. Together they influence these issues and trends which are fundamental components of society and which create the environment within which social values develop.

Over time these new and novel characteristics become part of *consumer behaviour* i.e. expectations and preferences, perceptions and attitudes, and decisions and actions. 'Culture is the most fundamental determinant of a person's wants and behaviour' (Kotler, 1984). The process of socialisation involves exposure to efficiency and practicality, material comfort, freedom

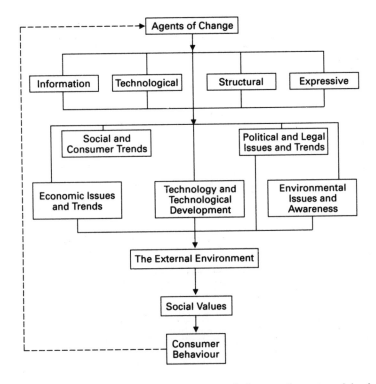

Figure 10.2 The relationship between agents of change, the external business environment, social values and consumer culture

(of time), etc. as well as exposure to achievement and success, individualism, humanitarianism and youthfulness, the elements of individualism within consumer culture.

Consumer culture is monitored by successful businesses. The *business response* reflects the individual company interpretation of consumer expectations and preferences and is demonstrated by the positioning statement which describes the 'offer' made to the customer group targeted by each company.

Over time is arguable that many of the responses become incorporated as components of the agents of change and evolve as significant issues in the external business environment. Figure 10.3 illustrates the broad relationships between agents of change, the external business environment, and the formation of social values and consumer culture.

Agents of Change

As societies develop there are basic elements that influence the direction and rate of change within the society. The effect of these influences has been significant and over time the period over which the influence has

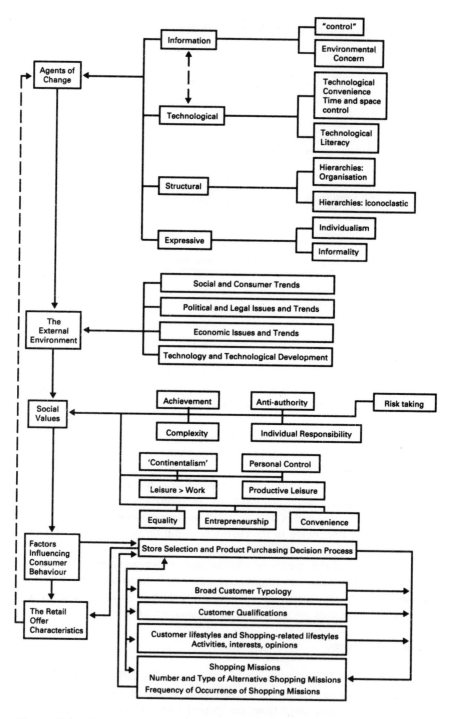

Figure 10.3   The elements of social change and consumer behaviour

operated has varied. For example, the fundamental changes to society which were ushered in by the Industrial Revolution were major in terms of the nature of their impact and the period of time over which they had influence. It was this period that created a social and economic environment upon which modern society was built: urban living and commerce were established as a basic lifestyle, both of which remain as the primary elements of western societies.

Technology was the basic *agent of change*. In the Industrial Revolution period, technology in the form of production method was responsible for the changes that occurred. Over time it has remained significant. However, the 'freedom' that it has created over time has in turn fostered other agents of change. During the nineteenth century transportation played a major part as an agent of change and, together with other 'agents', expansion of plumbing, sanitation and electrification of towns was responsible for major changes in society, e.g. hygiene, health and increased life expectancy.

The growth of *information* sciences and their application to business and domestic activities is a major issue. Closely linked to technology (which has facilitated the application of information sciences) this agent of change has been responsible for increasing the amount of control that individuals and organisations can exert over their activities. The basis of the increased control is in the time and accuracy with which information can be made available. A very obvious example is the use of EPOS systems' output to 'control' merchandise ranging and stocklevels and the 'control' of labour within retail stores. For consumers the CEEFAX and PRESTEL systems provides a range of information sources with a constant update service. In France the MINITEL system offers a wider range of information services together with a facility to transact goods and services. The growth of information awareness has been responsible for an increase in an expansion of information requirements. The consumer has become aware of issues of environmental concern (environment being used in a very broad context). So we see a demand for information on product ingredients which has created an awareness of 'healthy' products and 'environmentally friendly' products.

Technology. In the context of change it has been largely responsible for the application of information sciences to business and domestic situations. However, there are other issues. Technology has provided the facility to control time and space. Simple technology (simple in a relative context) has enabled food processing and preparation to be suspended (freezer technology) and accelerated (microwave technology). The VCR has enabled us to move and to hold time and events such that they may be recorded and experienced at a more convenient time and as frequently as desired. Technology has been accompanied with the need for new skills to be developed and technological literacy has become a major requirement in industry, commerce, education and the home.

Structural changes have occurred in both institutions and attitudes. Within organisations the structural changes that have occurred have primarily been the replacement of formalised relationships (supported by authority and 'rank') by informal relationships. The informal structures are no less effective, they merely reflect a progression in the working relationships between management and staff. The artefacts of these structures have changed. Dress is less formal in many organisations, such that levels of authority and responsibility are not visually apparent and the view of many commercial organisations towards 'corporate clothing' is influenced by the need to identify staff who can help customers, rather than it is to construct a hierarchy. The 'hierarchies of attitudes' have also changed. Institutions and publications were once viewed as authoritative. For centuries the church was seen as a major source of authority and influence but post-World War Two that influence and position rapidly declined. Legislators and the law enforcement function were considered almost as infallible, however, more recently their decisions and actions have been challenged. Other aspects of this structural change can be seen in the challenging attitudes directed towards the media. Both news and promotional media were, in the past, also considered to be 'authoritative' (as were institutions) but both are subject to critical challenges as a matter of routine.

A growth of *expressiveness* as an agent of a change has had significant effect. The 'individual as an individual' with rights and views is a significant issue in society, as is the expression of those views. The expression of views can take a number of forms. Clearly one is the facility to access organisations empowered to implement central and local government mandates and to make views and opinions known to the organisations' officers. Another form is the use of the media: both national and local media (printed and electronic) are more accessible to the consumer with much more two way communications activity, thereby encouraging feedback of views. Informality is another aspect of the expressive agent of change. Informality can be demonstrated in a number of ways and it has a number of facets. A basic view of informality concerns the structural aspect discussed in the previous paragraph. In this context individuals 'express' the informality in the way in which they conduct themselves with their superiors and their subordinates and the way in which they present themselves (i.e. dress). This topic has a little in common with the technological and information agents of change as well as with the structural agent. There are a number of activities in industry and commerce (particularly information management skills) which are either scarce and (or) have emerged from more recently developed parts of the educational system. For some time computer and systems personnel were considered as quite a different breed and in many ways their response – to create a mythological cult around themselves and their activities was accepted, as was their self-expression and informality in dress and attitudes at work.

From this discussion it follows that *agents of change* have an influence on the external business environment. They can facilitate change as in the case of the information and technological agents or they may be responsible for changes within the external business environment as have both the structural and expressive agents. They all provide opportunities and threats for the development of the business environment and as Figure 10.3 suggests respond to the changes that eventually occur in consumer culture.

The External Environment

As we discussed the components of the external business environment in considerable detail in a previous Chapter, clearly there is no need to repeat that discussion. What is of interest to us here are the time perspectives over which various components effect their influence, which we will call the external environment.

For each of the components of the external environment there will be both short and long term effects. For example, within social and consumer trends we can see the long term effect of home ownership. It is considered to be a measure of a number of things: achievement, status, personal wealth, freedom and individualism. Home ownership has assumed such a high level of priority within UK society that the financial institutions (possibly encouraged by government) were over-zealous in their actions in facilitating new home owners to manifest their aspirations and for existing home owners to extend their ownership. Other issues and activities develop, for example the expansion of DIY, of consumer durables and other home-based retail markets have been developed from expanded home ownership.

As well as the temporal consideration there is also the relationship that exists between the external environment and the agents of change. From the discussion of this topic in the preceding paragraphs it is clear that agents of change have a significant influence on the environment. Some of this influence is overt. The changes brought about by information and technological developments can be seen to result in shaping the business environment. However, the covert effects may have more significant implications and here the examples are numerous. The growth of environmental concern (Information) has resulted in the explicit activities of manufacturers and distributors to recognise both the need and concern for production processes and products which are environmental and consumption friendly and can be seen to conserve the environment. The activities of Body Shop, whose merchandise offer is based upon these issues, is an example of the extent to which both environmental and social concern is part of the corporate philosophy. Contributions of effort and profits are directed towards conservation (the Brazilian rain forests) and towards work in the community (within the area of their stores).

It is also possible to identify changes in the establishment institutions, namely the church and the law, where both are responding to pressures towards less formality and to incorporate emergent attitudes and views.

Political and economic developments have equally reacted. The free enterprise and competitive marketplace of the Thatcher 1980s was modified for the 1990s with changes in both policies and personnel.

Together the agents of change and the external environment create the business environment structure within which industries operate (discussed in Chapter 2) and provide the moves by which it conducts itself. (At a higher level of significance they work to create the legal system which not only industry must adhere to, but also creates and develops the society.) Social values are developed through societies' response to the agents of change and the external business environment. It is essential that the environment be considered within its commercial context. Society, or the individuals comprising it both buy its 'products' and sell their labour and skills and clearly their living standards are largely influenced by their abilities to do so. They are influenced in their decisions by their understanding of and responses to the agents of change and the external business environment. It is their understanding and responses which when considered in aggregate create social values and a consumer culture.

Social Values

Attitudes to work, leisure, authority, achievement etc. are constantly shaped and modified by society at large. They become the values by which a society lives. Values are, therefore, shared beliefs or group norms that have been accepted by groups of individuals. That values change over time has the support of a number of researchers and commentators. (See Engel, Blackwell and Miniard [1986].) Engel *et al.* suggest there are core values held by societies and these change over time. For example, pre-World War Two consumers experienced the depressed 1930s and possibly some World War One. As a result consumers whose lives were influenced by these events tend to hold values that emphasise security, patriotism, and the acquisition and protection of material goods.

The consumers whose formative years were the 1950s and 1960s express awareness and concern for other people. This manifests itself in social concern on issues of civil rights and equal opportunity. However, fashion is also important, influenced by so much social contact at the time.

The 1970s and 1980s produced the 'self values' generation in the USA. The core values held by this group place emphasis on the 'self' – self-expression, self-realisation, self-help, do-it-yourself. The influences responsible for this development include the energy crisis, high and persistent levels of inflation, feminism, Watergate, and an expanding tax and social welfare system. The authors suggest the core value to the egoism or the moral philosophy that when individuals take care of themselves and leave others to do the same, society is more likely to thrive (subsequent evidence suggests that it may not survive!). They also suggest that Reagan's offer in the 1984 election had strong appeal to the 18–24 age group who considered that job prospects and maintenance of their life-style were higher under individualistic policies than those favouring welfare programmes.

The influences can be seen in the UK. The reason for the similarities is not surprising. The depression, World War Two, the post-war austerity, the expansion of the 1960s followed by the energy problems of the 1970s were experienced on an international basis: furthermore, Reagan and Thatcher shared similar views concerning the responsibility of the individual to assume a self-help role.

The Taylor Nelson Futures group suggests a number of trends for the 1990s. They suggest:

- An increase in informality;
- An increase in aspirations;
- A move towards individualism;
- More exclusivity;
- A shift in the concept of value with criteria based upon quality rather than quantity;
- A focus upon mental and physical well being;
- A decline in the importance of status;
- A wider range of interests;
- More entrepreneurship;
- Increased concern with conservation and the environment.

A number of issues arise. The first concerns the relationship between culture and social values. Culture has been defined widely, in the context of consumer behaviour Engel *et al.* suggest '... Culture ... refers to the complex of values, ideas, attitudes and other meaningful symbols that serve humans to communicate, interpret and evaluate as members of society. They are transmitted from one generation to the next ... The essential elements of culture are those that are learned and shared among social groups.' Within the range of definitions one suggests that culture includes both abstract and material elements. Abstract elements include values, attitudes, ideas, personality types and constructs such as religion and political beliefs. Material components include books, computers, tools, buildings, in other words 'products'. The material elements have been described as 'cultural artefacts' or the material manifestation of culture. Clearly this aspect of culture has major implications for understanding consumer behaviour where the interest is to focus upon the elements of culture that shape consumer preferences: the store selection and product decision.

A second issue follows. If we can identify clusters of social values that are meaningful in a retailing sense (i.e., those social values that influence the formation of *consumer behaviour*) then we can define consumer segments in terms of characteristics that may be responded to with a 'retail offer'.

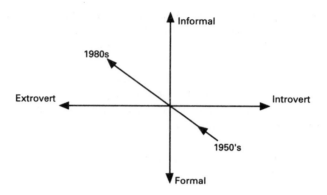

Figure 10.4   A hypothetical social values map

A third issue relates to the second. The characteristics identified should relate to the decisions to be made when developing a retail offer. The characteristics should also be close to each other in order that the customer groups shared core values influence an aggregate response. Consider the example suggested by Figure 10.4. Here we have a hypothetical plot of the way in which this society has changed on two important dimensions: it has moved away from formal attitudes when much of the population saw itself as introvert (1950s) towards less formality and has become more extrovert (1980s).

From this broad picture we can identify retailing implications. The move away from formal attitudes is likely to change attitudes towards views held about formal vs. informal occasions and situations: specifically views concerning appropriate forms of dress. The shift towards more extrovert views and behaviour suggests that dress may become more flamboyant as the individualism becomes demonstrated by the more extrovert.

A fourth issue is important. The clusters of characteristics or dimensions should share congruence. In this way the targeted customer group will seek basic merchandise, service and store environment characteristics that will be shared by both the customer group and the offer characteristics. If this can be achieved there will be a coordinated and coherent positioning statement made by the related offer components to a target customer group whose preferences and expectations are based upon shared value characteristics. Figure 10.5a illustrates a situation in which customers in each of the four departments are closely clustered. This means that there can be a coordinated and coherent positioning statement made with specific and related offer characteristics. However, in Figure 10.5b the mapping suggests four quite different customer groups whose preferences and expectations are not reflected by their perceptions of the offer.

Returning to Figure 10.3 we have included the issues suggested as being important characteristics in the formation of social values for the 1990s. It is clear that each characteristic will have more or less significance to indi-

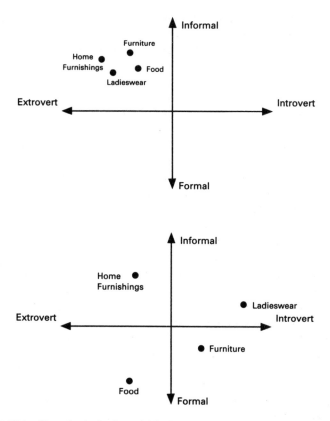

Figure 10.5(a) Hypothetical plot of ideal customer type profile by merchandise
                  group
         (b) Hypothetical plot of situation whereby merchandise groups have
              appeal to a range of customer types

vidual companies. For example, *achievement* will be an important characteristic to a number of companies. Manufacturers and distributors of 'status
artefacts' (e.g. motor vehicles, 'designer' clothes and durables) would be
interested in how achievers *demonstrate* the fact that they have arrived. On
the other hand *how* achievers achieve is of interest to companies or institutions providing distance learning services. The trend towards individual responsibility and collectivism has interesting commercial implications for
service products retailers. Individualism and self-responsibility suggests an
increase in interest in health insurance and financial/pension plan products.

'Continentalism' – the acceptance of Europeanisation – raises important
issues. It suggests that the one-market concept and the potential for Ger-
man, French, etc., products and retail outlets is unlikely to be met with
much resistance. However, some caution is necessary and that is based upon
the concept discussed earlier whereby core values exist. Furthermore, as we

suggested at the beginning of this Chapter (Figure 10.1) many social values
are influenced by the business response of manufacturing and retailing. For
example, convenience has been developed by superstore retailers and is seen
as an important selection characteristic by consumers in other shopping
situations. It follows that any 'imported' retail offer should recognise the
importance of core values and include them.

The issue of work and leisure is important. A 'synthesis' of research in
this area would suggest a number of issues. First, while there is a tendency
towards favouring an increase in leisure time it is not unanimous. Those
with 'interesting and responsible jobs' tend to work increasingly longer
hours. This offers opportunities to service-oriented retail offers to identify
the members of this group and to make an offer to them which demonstrates time saving. The increase in desire for leisure has a caveat. Leisure
(for many) should be productive in that it offers an opportunity to improve
'body and/or mind'.

There are many aspects and facets to the components which comprise
social values. Some are specific in their implications and have a fundamental impact on some businesses. Clearly these characteristics should be
identified and sensitivity analysis be applied to investigate the optimistic,
pessimistic and realistic performance probabilities and expected values.

Our interest here has been to establish the importance of social values in
the development and modification of consumer behaviour. We do emphasise
the point made on a number of occasions during the discussion, that the
topics differ in the intensity of their importance and influence and should
be evaluated with this in mind. The approach used by a number of companies
is to use Environmental Scanning – a systematic observation of the external environment to identify emerging trends that may affect the future of
that organisation. An environmental scan would include the agents of change,
the external environment, social values and their impact on developing consumer behaviour. It would also consider the inter-relationships and influences
that each has on another. Clearly the objective is to derive a series of specific
issues that have major influence for current and future activities. This is
often best achieved by considering macro-contributions for companies such
as Taylor Nelson Futures and the Henley Centre's Planning for Social Change.
However, at the end of the day it is the management's responsibility to interpret these issues and establish pertinent scenarios and planning assumptions.

10.2   STORE SELECTION AND PRODUCT PURCHASING PROCESS

As we have seen there is a wide range of influences upon individuals and
it is not surprising to find that a wide range of customer types exist. Furthermore, each customer demonstrates an equally wide range of customer behaviour patterns. Consider Figure 10.6, which illustrates how attitudes towards

Shopping attitudes

Store selection and purchasing decision process	Task -oriented (convenience dominated) ← → Pleasure-oriented (environment dominated)	
Pre-purchase Search Comparison	Convenient location Ample parking Close to other task-oriented stores Relevant merchandise selection	Exclusive store merchandise Wide choice Prestigious image
During purchase Product augmentation Transactions Facilities	High availability Competitive prices Rapid cash handling	Ambience and excitement Visual merchandising In-store facilities Product-services centres Credit facilities
Post-purchase Delivery Installation Use extension Evaluation Repeat visits	Product displays and customer advice areas	Theme displays and customer advice areas

Figure 10.6   Attitudes towards shopping influence trading format and store environment strategy decisions

shopping influence customers' preferences depending upon how the customer views the shopping activity. Food shopping is often seen as task oriented and consequently the consumers' dominant preference is for convenience. Conversely, apparel shopping is environment dominated, because the consumer is influenced by the type of shopping activity and it follows that the offer made to the customer should reflect the expectation of customers. It is also clear that customer expectations and preferences vary for the individual customer and customer visit. The notion of categorisation of goods and services is not new. Figure 10.6 reproduces the product-patronage mix proposed by Bucklin (1963). In this matrix consumer preferences and store types are matched. Bucklin's suggestions are a little restrictive in that he proposes that each of the store types can satisfy the range of customer shopping activities. This could be seen as stores attempting to be 'all things to all men' in that each of the stores has an offer to meet each of the consumer shopping purposes. With the benefits of 30 years experience, improvements in information technology and customer research sophistication, we have the facility to become more focussed in customer profiling and targeting. The changing lifestyle habits of consumers

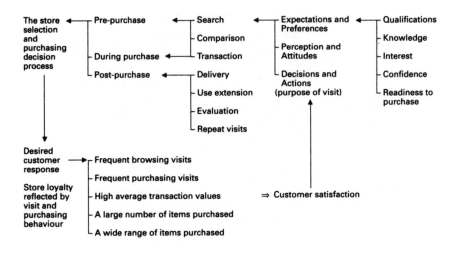

Figure 10.7   Customer expectations and response

and their need to budget time and expenditure suggests that there is scope for a fresh look at these issues.

This suggests that there are a range of shopping trips that may be taken by anyone individual and that they will vary depending upon the circumstances in which the individual happens to be. It follows that a young mother who is accompanied by pre-school age children while shopping for food and other similar items will favour the store that offers convenience. Convenient parking, shopping and customer services that have small children in mind. On another occasion the same person may be shopping for clothes (without the children, possibly with a friend). On this occasion the exercise is much more pleasure oriented and her preferences are more for entertainment and the purpose of the exercise may not necessarily be to make a planned purchase. Thus the fact that individuals' shopping visits can vary considerably suggests that conventional segmentation methods e.g. demographics, socio-economics reinforced with psychographics is not sufficient and that additional information which describes the purpose of the visit and customer's 'qualifications'. This is described by Figure 10.7 where the elements of the store selection and purchasing decision process are illustrated. The outcome, the level of customer satisfaction achieved, will influence the perceptions and attitudes of customers and will be used when the customer is considering future purchases.

The store selection and purchasing decision process suggests that additional information would be helpful for planning purposes. Given the earlier discussion concerning the elements of consumer behaviour and their influence on buying decisions we suggest that to develop a target customer profile

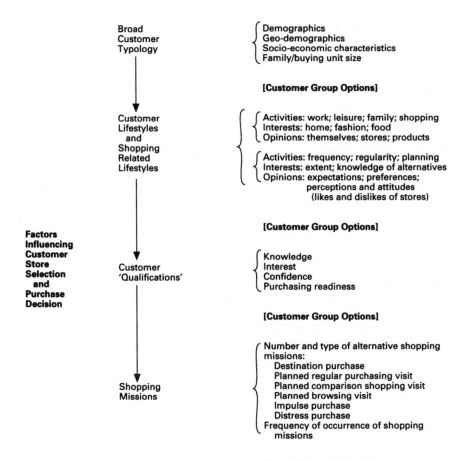

Figure 10.8 Profiling target customer groups

(or target customer profiles) much more information is necessary rather than simply helpful. The information inputs suggested are shown in Figure 10.8. There are four components which are sequential in that at each step the target market focus is narrowed progressively.

10.3 FACTORS INFLUENCING CUSTOMER STORE SELECTION AND PURCHASE DECISION BEHAVIOUR

Broad Customer Typology

An initial review of the market will identify customer groups that are attractive. For example, food retailers will be interested in the *demographic* group aged 25–44: it represents a large proportion of the population, has family responsibilities and therefore has a high average spend on a frequent, regular basis. *Geo-demographics* identify the occupancy of types of residences. This can be very useful because purchasing activities have been shown to be similar in similar geo-demographic areas. It follows that motor vehicle distributors and home improvement retailers may find geo-demographics helpful as may 'specialist' and 'exclusive' retailers seeking to locate in areas with characteristics found to be particularly suitable and previously identified using geo-demographics. *Socio-economic* characteristics assist in the evaluation of both the type of store and merchandise likely to be favoured, and also indicate the ability to *make* the purchase commitment. The *family or buying unit size* is important for a number of reasons and should be considered alongside the other information components. Clearly larger buying units suggest high volume purchasing. However, this does not necessarily imply high average rates of transaction as the buying unit (or family) may be from a low socio-economic group. It follows that they may be both selective and price sensitive and that average contribution per transaction is low. An analysis of the customer segment will identify those elements which offer potential and which are likely to respond to the type of 'offer' currently made by the company, or to that 'offer' which the company has the capability to make. An important and additional element of information that should be identified at this stage concerns not simply the likely purchasing volumes but the qualitative characteristics that customers seek. Here the geo-demographics and socio-economics components will be helpful as indicators of the range of merchandise characteristics and nature of customer services required by the groups identified.

Customer Lifestyles and Shopping Related Lifestyles

Clearly these are linked because the 'macro' considerations of lifestyles do influence shopping lifestyles. In addition to this the activities, interests and opinions are interrelated. A person with a very senior level post in a business is unlikely to demonstrate a high level of interest in shopping nor to have much knowledge of shopping alternatives. It follows that preferences would be for a high level of convenience for pre-purchase, purchase and post-purchase activities. The alternative providing this 'integrated convenience offer' would create very positive responses for perceptions and attitudes. Conversely, the family oriented person, one with more leisure time to allocate to shopping is likely to demonstrate high levels of interest and knowledge together with quite different preferences and expectations.

The shopping related lifestyle characteristics are clearly much more retailing focussed. Activities should identify the detail involved in planning shopping activities, identifying the extent to which the shopping function is a planned rather than an impulse activity and the reasons for this. For example, the housewife with a family is more likely to have some structure in shopping planning with a routine to maximise the use of time. Conversely, a 'single' person is likely to be more haphazard in shopping behaviour tend-ing to fit needs around work and leisure schedules. Similarly the levels of interest (extent of interest in shopping as an activity and knowledge of alternatives) will differ. Opinions, the expectations, preferences, perceptions and attitudes will reflect the overall lifestyle pattern and likes and dislikes will develop being based upon shopping needs.

Customer 'Qualifications'

There are four factors comprising customer qualifications. The extent of the level of customer qualifications provides a number of useful data. For example, very high levels of interest and knowledge would suggest a customer whose above-average interest would suggest that they make frequent browsing visits and respond to knowledgeable sales staff within a specialist activity. Clearly depending upon merchandise type they may devote considerable amounts of leisure time to using and reading about the product and its 'activity' use: it is an important feature of their lifestyles.

The high level of knowledge and interest may extend into confidence but not necessary so. For example, the situation described by Figure 10.6 may well obtain. The task oriented situation, where shopping becomes a necessity and not a leisure pursuit, is probably one where because of frequency and regularity the level of customer confidence is high. This would occur for customers for whom, say food shopping is a large proportion of their budget and consequently they become both knowledgeable and confident about the activity.

Levels of confidence, knowledge, interest and readiness can be measured by using scaling techniques. Figure 10.9 proposes a consumer purchasing behaviour map which is helpful from two aspects. It can identify customer groups who have an ongoing, specialist interest in the merchandise group

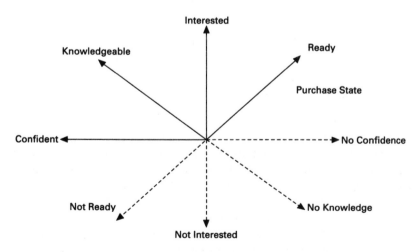

Figure 10.9   Consumer purchasing behaviour mapping

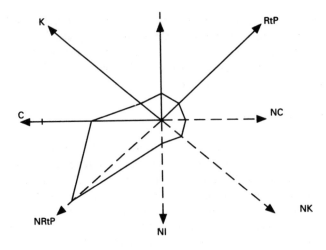

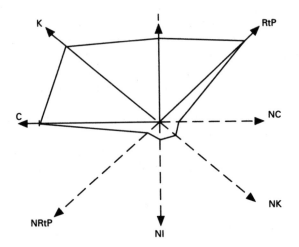

Figure 10.10   Consumer behaviour maps, durables
         (a)   No purchase planned
         (b)   Purchase imminent

and who would respond to, and support, a specialist offer. Some examples are given in Figures 10.10 and 10.11. Figure 10.10 suggests the profiles of customers in the consumer durables market: Figure 10.10a describes the situation for customers not planning a purchase in the immediate future. Figure 10.10b is the map profile that would be expected among customers planning purchases and to do so have gathered together information on alternatives, having during the process increased both knowledge and confidence levels as they become 'ready to purchase'.

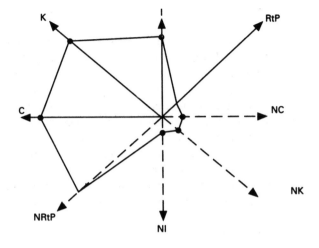

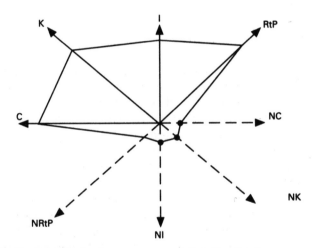

Figure 10.11   Consumer behaviour maps, specialist (Angling)
    (a)   No purchase planned
    (b)   Purchase imminent

The specialist activity customer map profiles are illustrated in Figure 10.11. In Figure 10.11a the levels of confidence, knowledge and interest are very high while no purchase appears imminent. In Figure 10.11b the customer moves towards making a purchase.

It follows that by plotting customer qualifications management will be able to determine both short term and long term prospects for their business. The mapping approach can also be extended to (or combined with) tracking studies which provide quantitative measures of expectations and relative preferences.

Shopping Missions

The notion that store visits vary by purpose for individuals was introduced earlier. It will be remembered from that discussion that we suggested that store visits vary with customer requirements. A planned purchase to a specific store to make a specific purchase, following a process of the evaluation of alternatives, differs markedly from an impulse purchase of a magazine while shopping for food or from a planned browsing visit to look perhaps at clothes or furniture but with no purchasing in mind. Each alternative can be viewed as a *shopping mission*. It follows that retailers would find it useful if they were able to aggregate customer shopping missions because it would facilitate both merchandise assortment selection and store planning (visual merchandising, merchandise density and service offer). We suggest six shopping missions:

- Destination purchasing visit
- Planned regular purchasing visit
- Planned comparison shopping visit
- Planned browsing visit
- Impulse purchase visit
- Distress purchase visit

Destination purchases are those where both the store and the product have been selected and the purpose of the visit is to make a transaction.

Planned regular purchases are those made for food and other everyday requirements. As we commented earlier these are often task oriented and convenience is a primary requirement.

Planned comparison shopping occurs when a purchase is imminent and the mission purpose is to obtain knowledge and build customer confidence prior to making the purchase.

Planned browsing visits are leisure oriented 'escapes'. They typically are visits to department stores and others of interest. The mission purpose is entertainment rather than information gathering or purchasing.

Impulse purchasing occurs without prior needs having been identified. The value of the purchase may be minimal or indeed very high.

Distress purchases are, again, unplanned. They are prompted by an immediate requirement, e.g. a meal ingredient has either been forgotten or has 'run out'. Alternatively the item may be required because of a DIY emergency, plumbing, electrical, etc. Convenience is again the primary requirement.

The frequency of occurrence of shopping missions is an important input when planning the retail offer. A predominance of one particular shopping mission would prescribe the merchandise and service facilities. For example a small hardware store located in a suburban shopping area could well find it profitable to offer 'distress items' and a 'distress service'. It would follow that, assuming the competitors were located some distance away, the benefit to customers of a close, convenient DIY store which invariably has the distress product when needed and offers high levels of service (opening hours and advice) would be repaid in the form of store loyalty manifested in regular purchases of other items.

Conversely, a centrally located department store, with considerable adjacent competition, would probably discover that two shopping missions dominated. These would be planned comparison shopping visits and planned browsing visits. The merchandise assortment and store planning decisions should reflect the regularity and frequency of the occurrence of these two missions.

Having evaluated the customer group options by considering, broad customer typology, customer lifestyles and shopping related lifestyles, customer 'qualifications', and dominant shopping mission types a target customer group (or groups) can now be decided upon.

10.4   FACTORS INFLUENCING RETAIL OFFER CHARACTERISTICS

The customer analysis discussed in the previous paragraphs provides us with details on customer shopping missions (and expectations). From these data we can begin to consider the positioning characteristics of the retail offer. There are four factors to be considered in Figure 10.12.

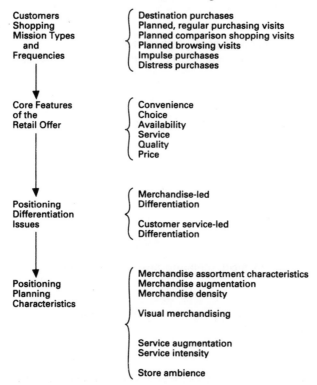

Figure 10.12   Factors influencing retail offer characteristics

Customers' Shopping Mission Types and Frequencies

The first factor, customer shopping mission types and frequencies is simply a decision based upon the frequency of each shopping mission. This information can be derived by conducting focus group discussions with a structured sample of customers or alternatively with instore research using questionnaires. The purpose of this analysis is, as we have already established, to identify the merchandise; customer service; store format and environment, and customer communications mix most appropriate to meeting the customers' expectations.

Core Features of the Retail Offer

Given the shopping mission (or missions) that the offer should address the core features of the offer can be defined:

Convenience
  location and parking (travel time);
  store layout and display;
  store opening.

Choice
  core product ranges and product characteristics;
  to reflect mission requirements (i.e., width and depth issues); branding.

Availability
  core product service levels;
  to reflect mission requirements (distress purchases).

Service
  advice;
  transactions;
  product-services;
  service-products;
  delivery;
  credit;
  specific services to meet shopping mission requirements.

Price
  compatible with the shopping mission expectations;
  competitive prices;
  stable prices.

Clearly the precise nature of these features will be determined by the types of shopping mission(s) the business is attempting to satisfy. Other issues will influence the features. For example, store size, location, availability of parking, etc. are important issues to be considered.

Positioning Differentiation Issues

We have already discussed the role of differentiation in creating competitive advantage. The conclusion reached was that essentially differentiation would be either merchandise or service led. This is not to suggest that the differentiation be specifically one or the other but rather that one would assume a dominant role in the positioning decision. The shopping missions would determine the core feature requirements.

Positioning Planning Characteristics

Having decided upon the positioning strategy the role of the positioning planning characteristics is then considered. These are:

- *Merchandise assortment characteristics*; merchandise features that meet customer expectations for choice, quality, exclusivity, style, availability, etc., at price levels that are seen as competitive.

- *Merchandise augmentation*; features that add value to the merchandise by the selective addition of services and the inclusion of appropriate service products that are relevant to the range. It creates benefits for customers that are not available from competitors and thereby creates competitive advantage through merchandise led differentiation.

- *Visual merchandising*; reinforces the company's positioning statement within its competitive environment. It uses merchandise displays to inform customers, to arouse interest, encourage comparative shopping and to move the customer towards a purchase commitment. Visual merchandising should coordinate the merchandise offer into an integrated message which reflects customers' expectations. It should also classify merchandise into related groups (or departments) which reflects customer shopping missions.

- *Service augmentation: information*; is a combination of both customer service and customer communication. The communications task is twofold: it both persuades and informs the customer. It should be directed towards that aspect of communication which is identified as most effective and is preferred by customers. Customer research will identify their preferences but often it is the information content which is most influential.

- *Service augmentation: facilities*; the interest here is the range of supporting facilities that are offered to customers. These are not directly supporting the merchandise offer but are indirect service features that can influence customer store selection because of the added value they offer during customer visits.

- *Service intensity*; relates to the number of staff (sales and service dedicated) within a department or store. The issues concern the impact on sales and profitability of additional levels of service staff.

- *Store ambience*; should reflect the planned market positioning in the store's 'mood', character, quality and atmosphere. It should be tailored to the target customer group. It has no specific components but the store ambiance reinforces the merchandise and service offers. Customer communications should be coordinated to transfer the ambiance to the customer by creative and subtle use of media and design.

In Chapter 2 we discussed the hierarchy of strategies. It will be remembered that functional strategies for merchandise, customer service, trading format and store environment, together with customer communications were focused to create a positioning strategy. The positioning strategy being the company's response to the expectations and preferences of the target customer group. Figure 10.13 illustrates the role of merchandise and service led differentiation in developing a positioning strategy. It also illustrates the component positioning planning characteristics.

SUMMARY

We can summarise this chapter by referring to Figure 10.14. The elements and influences acting on individuals, their backgrounds, education etc., result in their belonging to a number of broad customer groups which develop a range of lifestyle attributes. They also are responsible for influencing the level of interests and knowledge. Consumer behaviour and lifestyle also has an influence on time budgets (the amount of time consumers are able, or willing to allocate to shopping activities). These are seen as shopping missions for which customers develop expectations and preferences. The retail offer is an explicit response to shopping missions and is developed from a considered positioning strategy and the strategy is implemented by allocating resources to the positioning planning characteristics.

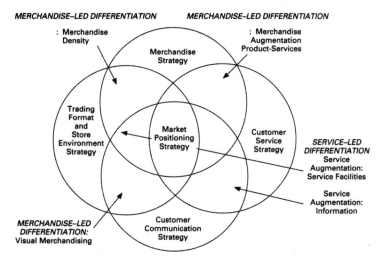

Figure 10.13 Positioning strategy and the role of merchandise and service differentiation

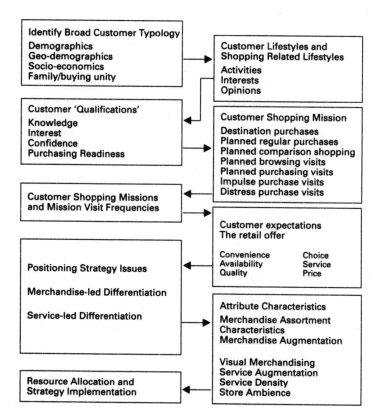

Figure 10.14 Consumer behaviour, shopping missions and planning the retail offer

11 Interpreting Customer Expectations

INTRODUCTION

In the previous chapter we discussed the issues concerned with deriving target customer group specifications and introduced the notion of shopping missions as a means of identifying the most frequent aspects of the target customers' store selection and purchasing decisions.

We identified six mission types:

- Destination purchases
- Planned regular purchasing visits
- Planned comparison shopping visits
- Planned browsing visits
- Impulse purchases
- Distress purchases

Knowledge of the frequency of the occurrence of these missions and the expectations of customers provides vital information inputs for deciding upon the differentiation approach; the balance between merchandise and service led differentiation. Once this is decided the positioning characteristics can be considered in sufficient detail to be able to derive a positioning strategy, together with detailed functional strategies for merchandise, customer service, trading format and store environment and, customer communications. Figure 11.1 describes this process.

It is important that we consider the role of information in helping to define both the shopping missions and the dimensions of customer expectations. This raises the role of information system and issues concerning data generation.

11.1 RESEARCHING SHOPPING MISSIONS: INFORMATION NEEDS

Clearly the expectations and the behaviour of both existing and potential customers provides valuable insight into the way in which their shopping missions are formulated. Detailed knowledge would provide the information required to plan merchandise ranges (and their assortment characteristics) and the trading format and store environment that would maximise customers, expectations and their satisfaction. An additional benefit would also be available: that of being able to determine the contribution made by each of the shopping missions.

174

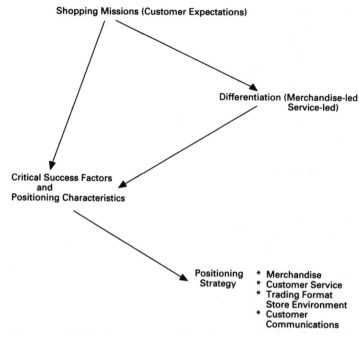

Shopping Missions (Customer Expectations)

Differentiation (Merchandise-led
Service-led)

Critical Success Factors
and
Positioning Characteristics

Positioning   * Merchandise
Strategy   * Customer Service
                  * Trading Format
                    Store Environment
                  * Customer
                    Communications

Figure 11.1   Developing a positioning strategy from shopping missions

There is a requirement for timely information in sufficient detail and with considerable accuracy if this is to be possible. In aggregate terms we need information that identifies:

number of customer visits – browsing and purchasing; departments visited;
transaction numbers and average spent per transaction; the composition of each purchase;
    number of items) in departments
    range of items) shopped
a measure of customer loyalty.

Much of this information is available (in aggregate form) from transaction records and the benefits of EPOS information outputs can add considerably to the total information available. However, we do have problems measuring customer loyalty and if we were to try to identify the store selection and purchase decision process of any specific customer or customer group we would have considerable difficulty.

If we add a few more 'ideal' information topics we begin to see the need for a more formalised approach to data gathering, the need for a structured customer data base. Consider the additional information topics:

Customer characteristics;
  demographics;
  geo-demographics;
  socio-economics;
  general lifestyle topics;
  shopping lifestyle topics.

Shopping characteristics;
  day and time of visit;
  visit duration;
  departments visited;
  frequency of visit.

Purchasing characteristics;
  browsing/purchasing activities;
  size of transactions;
  range of purchases over time;
  purchasing occasions;
  customer services purchased and/or used.

This is of course the customer profile described in Chapter 10 and provides the basis for deriving the shopping missions discussed in Chapter 10.

Identifying Information Requirements

It follows that if we seek to maximise customer satisfaction at levels of contribution that are acceptable to the company we must identify the information that is required. In Figure 11.2 we have structured the information set necessary to derive shopping missions. Some of the data is already available from which the required information can be obtained. However much of it is not available from sales records, furthermore some data will be difficult to obtain and will require a specific effort. With this in mind we suggest that a 'data matrix' be built. Many companies conduct an audit of their decision making activities and match the output with the information currently available. Clearly there are always gaps and before a decision is made concerning *how* the desired information can be obtained an analysis of its worth is made: this will identify *if* it is worth obtaining. Thus an information sensitivity analysis is conducted to evaluate the value of the required information. The following questions are asked:

Does the availability of the information improve:

the merchandise offer (e.g. choice, availability)?
gross margin and profitability?

CUSTOMER CHARACTERISTICS

(Target and Secondary Customer Group Profiles)

Broad Typology	Shopping Missions Determinants	Customers' Shopping Missions Determinants
Demographics Geo-demographics Socio-economics	*Shopping Visit Activities*	Browsing / purchasing visits and occasions
	Day and time of visit Visit duration	Size of transaction
Customer Shopping *Characteristics*	Departments visited Size of purchase Frequency of visits	Range of purchases
General lifestyles Shopping lifestyles:	⇓	Aggregate purchases over time
Expectations & preferences Perceptions & attitudes Customer 'qualifications'	*Shopping Missions:*	Customer purchases of service products and services
	Destination purchase Planned regular purchase Planned comparison shopping Planned browsing Impulse purchase Distress purchase	

Figure 11.2   An ideal customer profile information set

customer service (i.e. identify qualifying and determining aspects of service)?
the store environment and visual merchandising?
customer responses (e.g. increase spend and increase the favourable perceptions)?
customer satisfaction?

If so at what cost?

The costs of obtaining information are a function of time and accuracy requirements. The pattern of the costs differ. The relationship between time and cost is inverse: as the time requirement is reduced so the cost of obtaining the information increases. For increased accuracy there is also an increase in cost. Clearly availability, accuracy and time, together with cost, should be considered and compared with the decisions made at various levels of the business and should be considered in the context of their potential impact upon the business. The total impact is a combination of sensitivity and profit contribution.

Returning to the content of the information required, the audit should

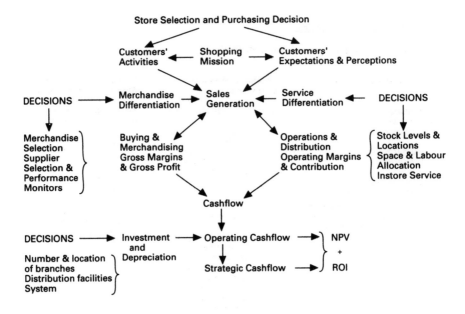

Figure 11.3   Decisions and the business

consider the decisions to be made throughout the business. Figure 11.3 uses the model introduced earlier as the basis for developing the audit by using the decisions made at various levels within the business. Figure 11.3 addresses the problem at an aggregate level, from this there follows a process in which decisions are disaggregated to match responsibilities within the organisation structure. This activity is clearly specific to the individual company and its sector of the marketplace and will vary by segment activity. For this reason we cannot take the topic very much further other than to suggest that there are a number of issues to be considered:

- The *sensitivity* of the business to the accuracy and timing of decisions;
- The *feasibility* of obtaining the required information;
- The *cost* of obtaining the information;
- An estimate of the *competitive advantage* that having the information offers the business;
      in the short term;
      in the long term.

Upon completion of a review of decisions taken throughout the business a customer information matrix (see Figure 11.4) can then be constructed. The matrix should identify *customer characteristics* together with *customer store visiting and purchasing activities*. The purpose of the matrix (and the various information inputs) is to identify the data necessary to make effective

Customer Characteristics	Visit Characteristics					
	Number of Visits			Departments		
	Total	Browse	Purchase	Browse	Purchase	Not Visited
Demographics						
Geo-demographics						
Socio-economics						
Buying unit/family size						
Lifestyle Characteristics 　Activities 　Interests 　Opinions						
Shopping Lifestyle Characteristics: 　Activities 　Interests 　Opinions						
Customer Qualifications in Product Areas: 　Knowledge 　Interest 　Confidence 　Purchasing 　　readiness						
Other Stores Used: 　A						
B						
C						
D						
Media use: 　Newspapers 　Journals Magazines 　Television 　Radio						

Figure 11.4   A customer information matrix

buying and merchandising decisions, and effective long term resource allocation through investment in property, systems and human resource development. The information suggested by Figure 11.4 is a more general example. Specific applications will differ depending upon the nature of the business (for example, time, location and competitiveness will be influential), its sensitivity to particular elements of information and the cost/benefit relationships of information, decisions and business performance.

11.2   OBTAINING INFORMATION: THE CUSTOMER DATABASE

Customer database management is a topic which has received considerable attention. The important feature of any customer database is that it should be cost-effective. It should offer decision makers an information service based upon prescribed service levels for availability, accuracy and time. The service levels should be determined after the audit activity has identified the decision making process within the business and the sensitivity of the

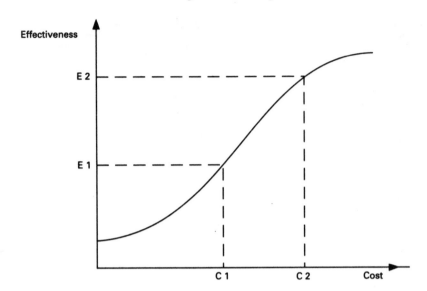

Figure 11.5   Cost-effectiveness relationships for information system decisions

decisions made to availability, accuracy and timeliness of data.

The basic cost-effectiveness relationship in information management does not differ from that in any other form of business. In Figure 11.5 we depict the familiar 's' curve which describes the situation in which decreasing returns occur eventually, following a situation in which the effectiveness of the information characteristic (e.g. accuracy or time) is enhanced by increasing the budget allocated to obtaining it.

Once again we have a situation where it is clear that while the relationship is common to all businesses the specific relationships and information requirements will differ. For example a multiple food retailer will accept that because of the broad customer base using the store, there is no great competitive advantage to be obtained from detailed customer characteristics information. However, if that retailer operated a chain of delicatessen stores targeted at a specific customer group then the advantages that would accrue from detailed customer knowledge involving expectations, perceptions, detailed store selection and purchase decisions activities would be significant. Similarly a department store could find similar benefits and these would differ across the range of the departments within the store.

There are examples of very detailed information systems in specialist ladieswear retailing. For these businesses data is developed around *individual customers* with a view to offering a complete service. Thus by identifying preferences on a merchandise basis (e.g. styles, colours, etc.) the retailer is able to contact customers individually as and when merchandise of specific interest becomes available. This is an example of specialist database marketing whereby comprehensive files are maintained on customers. It follows that to be worthwhile (i.e. cost-effective) the customer spend and customer loyalty factors have to be considerably higher than they would be for a multiple ladieswear business.

Obtaining Information: Information Sources

To be useful data must be structured before it has utility as information and intelligence. It is also essential that the cost-effectiveness of the data be considered (discussed earlier) and with this in mind the alternative sources of data should be explored. Kotler provides an excellent survey of the subject.

Essentially there are two basic sources of data. *Secondary* data is information that already exists somewhere, having been collected for other uses or even users. *Primary* data is original data comprising original information for the specific task on hand. Clearly there is a cost-effectiveness issue to be considered. Secondary data, being available will cost less to access than primary data, however, its effectiveness may be considerably lower than would be so for data specifically collected for the decision maker. The criteria of availability, accuracy and timeliness are important factors when evaluating secondary data cost-effectiveness.

The selection of data sources should comprise part of the audit. The audit should identify and evaluate sources of secondary data to discover the extent to which the information needs are partially or wholly satisfied by the data available. There are numerous sources of secondary data:

Internal Sources
Financial account reports;
Management accounting reports;
EPOS data, detailing sales (time, outlet, merchandise group and type);
Purchasing/procurement records;
Inventory levels;
Payroll data, detailing:
    salaries and wages;
    hours worked;
    full and part-time employees;
  Customer records, detailing:
    store visits;
    purchasing patterns and volumes;
    service used;
    credit records;
  Research reports:
    ongoing (diary studies, tracing studies, etc.);
    commissioned (specific project reports).

External Sources
Government publications: a range of information is available from the government. Its usefulness varies with the type of business seeking information, it is also aggregate in its nature and consequently may not provide specific answers to problems; this can be resolved by approaching the publisher who often will provide disaggregate data at a cost. Notable government publications that are of use to retail management include:

   Social Trends
   Family Expenditure Survey
   Household Consumption Statistics
   The 'Retail' *Business Monitor.*

Commercial data sources: there are a number of companies providing data to retail companies. The data may be sector oriented and published for general availability, examples being:

   Verdict
   Mintel
   EIU
   Jordans

Each of these companies publish detailed sector market studies, some on an annual basis, which review market activities in varying levels of detail. They are available on a one-off or a subscription basis. Other sources in this category are data service companies, who offer data structured to meet specific problems. Some of these companies are helpful in offering a consultancy service which will work with client companies on the identification of problems prior to recommending data requirements. Examples of this type of company include:

   CACI
   A C Neilsen
   AGB
   BMRB (with Target Group Index)

In addition there are companies who offer specialist research services. Their specialisation may be by sector or by type of research method.

Periodicals and books: there is within the distribution activity a range of trade and consumer journals whose staff have considerable experience within their specialist sectors. Their journals can be very useful because they identify issues and trends and comment on competitive and consumer topics. In addition to the periodicals themselves there are press cutting service companies, for example, McCarthy, who offer subscribers a service based upon major informed newspapers and journals across a wide range of companies, activities and products/services.

Secondary data provides a starting point for developing an information base. Typically it is low cost and offers rapid access: it also offers a 'trend' facility and as such makes a sound foundation for a corporate data base. However, the precise data required may not be available, it may be out of date, incomplete or not sufficiently detailed. In such an instance the research to collect primary data. The cost will be greater, so too will be the time/availability; however, this will be compensated with accuracy and, or course, relevance.

Primary data can be collected using a number of methods:

Observation: whereby researchers 'observe' behaviour, listen for unsolicited comments and reach their conclusions based upon unprompted 'responses'. This method is used to identify customer store shopping behaviour: individual customers are followed around the store and their actions and behaviour (browsing and purchasing, etc.) logged. Aggregated data provides useful 'maps' of store usage and indicates customer preferences.

Survey research: offers the facility to learn about people's preferences, expectations and attitudes. Continuing the example from the comment on observation; survey research would be used to ascertain why the observed behaviour occurs.

Experimental research: comprises controlled research whereby matched groups are exposed to different situations and their behaviour and responses compared. This approach enables cause-and-effect relationships to be identified. It would follow the survey research. To continue the example; a revised store layout would be designed and installed in a location which would be selected because of its similarities to another which would become a 'control' store. Customer attitudes and behaviour responses would be monitored in both stores and comparisons made.

An important issue that should be resolved prior to collecting data during survey and experimental research concerns the nature of the data. This in turn is influenced by the use of the information that the decision maker will make of the information eventually generated. Managers typically prefer quantitative data, they claim that it is more meaningful than qualitative research data. In other words, they prefer to work with the knowledge that 60% prefer store environment A to store environment B. However, the reasons for those preferences and the customers' expectations of retailing environments often offer a more comprehensive understanding of the issue. Furthermore, it is quite possible to obtain a quantitative measure of the data. These issues and applications will now be considered in detail.

11.3 RESEARCHING SHOPPING MISSIONS AND CUSTOMER EXPECTATIONS

Both expectations and perceptions can be obtained using qualitative techniques. There are a number of methods typically used. The information can be gathered most effectively by a combination of personal interviewing to identify issues that underlie customer expectations and perceptions and then a combination of self administered questionnaires by store users and individual interviewing for non-store users, or for a sample away from the store (not necessarily all non-users), personal–individual interviewing.

Essentially we are attempting to quantify topics that are qualitative in their nature. The topics can be generated by using focus groups. By using this technique the groups can be 'focused' either on their shopping activities (i.e., the group can be 'oriented' towards discussing attitudes and behaviour directly concerned with shopping missions) or alternatively the focus or orientation may be upon types of stores or specific retailers (i.e. to obtain data concerning the use of the stores and the reasons for the type of use made). The output from the focus groups provides input for the next stage of the research exercise.

The structure of the groups and the number of focus group sessions should reflect the complexity of the research task and the geography involved. Clearly the larger the number of groups interviewed the more reliable is the data that is generated, however, there will be budgetary constraints to be considered and the cost-effective use of the budget is essential.

Groups should be structured by user type, that is by:

  demographics
  geo-demographics
  socio-economics
  store user/non-user

If regional differences are expected then geographical differentiation should be considered.

The output from the focus groups should enable us to design a structured questionnaire that will provide quantitative data concerning:

  For shopping missions:

Purpose of shopping mission (type of purchase);
Accompanied (number and age, relationships);
Time availability;
Number of shopping missions of this type typically made (estimates);
Stores usually visited;
Features expected/preferred.

For store types we would seek information concerning:

Typical use (shopping mission);
Reason (store features and/or life style issue);
Number of visits (range of missions);
Time spent on each type of mission;
Number of persons accompanying (age, relationships).

To obtain the information there are four scaling-based techniques that may be considered:

Likert scale: a statement is presented to the respondent who indicates their amount of agreement or disagreement, e.g.: When shopping for those items you have forgotten rapid check outs are essential.

Strongly Agree	Disagree	Neither Agree nor Disagree	Agree	Strongly Agree

Semantic differential: a bi-polar scale is presented to respondents who are asked to select the point that represents the direction and intensity of their feelings:

Convenience shopping requires:

slow service _____ fast service
wide choice _____ relevant choice
parking _____ no parking

Importance scale: a scale that rates the relative importance of some attribute:

When shopping for clothes for myself choice is:

Extremely Important	Very Important	Reasonably Important	Not Very Important	Not at all Important

Rating scale: a scale that rates attributes from 'poor' to 'excellent':

Customer service at 'Shopfast':

Excellent	Very Good	Good	Fair	Poor

The use of a scaling technique provides the basis of quantification. The scale options are numbered for analysis and these can be used to quantify the respondents, attitudes and perceptions. The issue of significance or of relative importance can be dealt with by using the rating scale to ask respondents for a rank ordering of features that are important to them. This should be obtained for aggregate features of the offer, those identified as being particularly important to respondents in the focus group activity.

It is important to obtain trend data which, over a period of time, indicates changes that may occur in the consumers' perceptions of offer features (and their relative perceptions of the company's offer to that of major competitors). Tracking studies are particularly useful for this purpose (see Figure 11.6). Tracking studies can be used to monitor perceptions and attitudes to the company's offer, on a relative basis, relative to competitors, or as shown in Figure 11.6, relative to an ideal. Whichever measure is used the method of interpretation is similar: the greater the distance that occurs between the company's score and the comparison data, the larger the problem for the company.

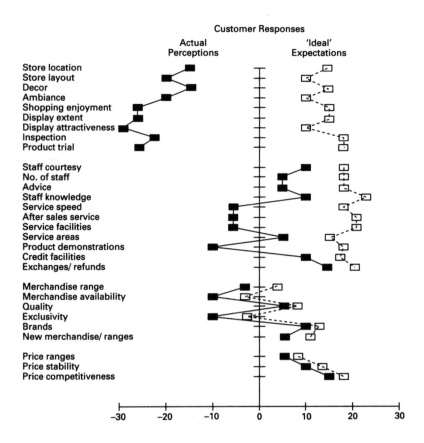

Figure 11.6   Hypothetical tracking study

In Figure 11.6 the topics are allocated to four areas; store environment, customer service, qualitative merchandise features and quantitative merchandise features. The example suggests that the hypothetical company has hardly any problems concerning quantitative (price) features, but does not meet the customer 'ideal expectations' for environment. If a rank ordering (rating) of macro features identifies store environment as an important feature in the store selection and purchase decision process, then clearly this company has major problems to address.

A review of ideal expectations together with relative perceptions of existing market competitors is a particularly useful exercise for a company to undertake as part of a pre-entry evaluation of a new market. The study can be structured to indicate the expectations (and perceptions of current offers) for the components of both merchandise and customer service differentiation. This is particularly useful for resource allocation decisions because it indicates both the key areas of consumer preferences *and* (therefore) the areas in which resources should be focussed.

We now have sufficient information to be able to identify the dominant shopping missions, their frequencies, the value of purchases and contribution rates and customer characteristics (both in aggregate and by shopping mission): see Figure 11.2 for the structure of this information. It follows that with this information the merchandise and service characteristics to which customers will respond can now be identified. This provides the basis upon which differentiation may be decided upon.

Obtaining Information: Methods and Equipment

While the basic sales information data can be used to indicate not just sales of products, by data, time and quantities, it can also be useful for labour scheduling and for store layout decisions. The electronic point of sale data capture systems are very effective provided a sales transaction occurs. However, retailers require customer performance information as well as merchandise information. Clearly if a customer visits the store and leaves without making a purchase no record of the visit occurs and more importantly the reason for the visit and the reason for no purchases being made are unknown. We can record customers' visiting activities by using affinity-type cards (similar to those used by the airlines at check-in desks). Affinity cards can be issued to customers to encourage store loyalty and to record their visits and purchases. The card does not necessarily need to offer credit facilities.

The card operates through incentives. Recorded visits are rewarded by allocating points for both visit frequency and time spent in the store. Clearly purchases are also rewarded in a similar way. The initial 'application' will obtain broad customer characteristics and subsequent analysis of the use made will provide data to help with defining shopping missions pursued by customers.

An alternative to the affinity card is a diary panel. A structured sample of customers is motivated to complete a diary of shopping visit and purchasing activities. It has the extra advantage of providing data on competitors' stores that are visited. Accuracy can be a problem, so too is the problem of collecting the data from a representative sample because such groups are notorious for their panel decay problems.

Other alternatives are based upon specifically commissioned research that is conducted either on a regular or irregular basis. Such studies may be conducted by the retailer's own staff or by a research company. The benefits of using staff are familiarity with the store, its merchandise, etc. and with the need to generate the data. It does of course add to staff costs (or their opportunity costs). The use of an external research organisation avoids these problems but usually is more expensive. However, research companies can and do process data more rapidly.

The decision concerning method and system depends very much upon the decision makers needs *and* the costs of the competing alternatives.

11.4   DERIVING SHOPPING MISSIONS AND POSITIONING CHARACTERISTICS

Earlier we used Figure 11.2 to demonstrate an ideal customer profile information set. From the information available there are data which can be used to define shopping missions. Customer shopping determinants are derived from an analysis of customer shopping characteristics and their shopping visit activities. These, in turn, provide a basis for determining the type of shopping missions that identify customers' store selection and purchase decisions and their expectations. This process is described by Figure 11.7. Once identified, customer expectations provide the information necessary to decide upon positioning differentiation and from this the components of the positioning characteristics.

An example may be helpful. Consider a hypothetical retail company operating two outlet types. Its *large central stores* are located in the centres of towns with populations of 50 000 or more and typically have between 15 000 and 20 000 square feet of sales and service area. Its *local stores* are located in small towns with populations of between 10 000 and 20 000 people or are in off-centre locations (suburban areas) of larger towns and cities; they average around 5000 square feet of sales and service area. Their merchandise and service offers reflect the needs of the shopping missions observed. While the example that follows is not based upon any one retail company the issues raised are based upon observations of similar store types.

There are eleven merchandise groups and the company's policy is to use the merchandise and customer service offers to match the customer expectations of the shopping missions. The merchandise groups are:

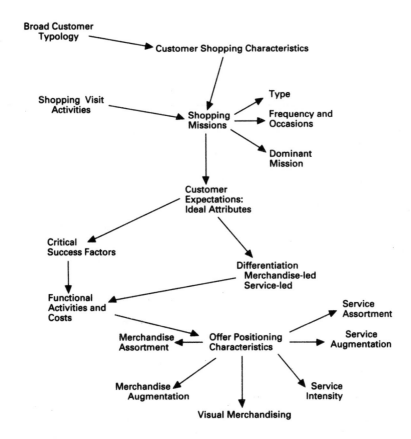

Figure 11.7   Deriving shopping missions and the offer positioning characteristics

Audio/visual, CD, tapes, etc.	Toiletries
Confectionery	Stationery and books
DIY/hardware	Haberdashery
Household/housewares	Toys
Gardening	Seasonal merchandise
Children's clothes/footwear	

The large central stores carry a complete merchandise assortment aiming to offer choice, quality and availability. The local stores carry a representative assortment adjusted to meet local needs (i.e. dominant shopping missions) and competitive opportunities and threats. The customer service offer aims to be minimal at a 'qualifying' level in both outlet types.

Ideally the customer database will provide the necessary data, however, if this is not available, or if we are considering a new activity, observation of customer activities, together with customer research can identify

Table 11.1 An example of how positioning characteristics can be related to customer shopping mission expectations

Merchandise Group: Audio/Visual
Store Type: Large Central Stores

Broad customer typology	Customer shopping characteristics	Shopping Missions			Customer expectations	Positioning differentiation
		Type	Freq & occasion	Occurrence % of total		
Male and female (50–50) Aged between 15–24 C1/C2 group.	Highly interested in a specific type of music. Well informed and very confident and ready to purchase.	Destination Purchase	Weekly Lunch breaks Saturdays	75%	Expects latest 'hit' to be available. Item is pre-sold; alternatives do not exist. No service requirements. May browse and purchase other recordings.	Primarily merchandise-led. Service facilities may influence store selection and store loyalty.
Male and female (40–60) Aged between 35–54 C1/C2 group.	Low interest in music. Requires 'easy listening' recording for self or as a gift.	Planned Browsing Visit.	Very infrequent.	15%	Not likely to have specific selection in mind. Will look for artist or title or recording that they may recognise.	Primarily merchandise-led.

customer shopping missions. By focussing on the customer store selection and product purchasing activities, the allocation of resources can be made to be more effective. The effectiveness will be increased because the positioning planning characteristics will reflect the specific shopping mission expectations, rather than be an overall response across the retail offer. Thus it allows the response to be adjusted to meet more specific expectations, being either merchandise-led- or service-led depending

Functional Activities

Merchandise Assortment Characteristics
High level of availability is essential for CD & cassettes. Wide assortment may increase consumer confidence. T-shirts etc.

Merchandise Augmentation
T-shirts, magazines etc.

Visual Merchandising
Chart displays for 'albums' and singles. Merchandise displayed by themes and by artists. Co-ordinated recording products with accessories.

Service Augmentation: Information
Chart information. Perhaps an ordering facility will help.

Service Augmentation: Facilities
Facilities to listen to music (books) may add to the offer. Coffee bar could help encourage customers to meet in the store and spend more.

Service Intensity
This customer is unlikely to require anything other than minimum transaction attention. They are knowledgeable and supremely confident.

Store Ambience
The store should be exciting and entertaining. The customer is young and responds to an exciting atmosphere.

Merchandise Assortment Characteristics
Wide choice in the 'easy listening' ranges. Availability less essential. Probably not concerned too much over artist or specific tracks.

Merchandise Augmentation
None required

Visual Merchandising
Would expect to be able to find the 'easy listening' and 'compilations' sections.

Service Augmentation: Information
Would require advice and an ordering facility.

Service Augmentation: Facilities
May require a facility to listen prior to purchase.

Service Intensity
May need some help in finding appropriate product – especially if it is a gift.

Store Ambience
Unlikely to be of major importance – unless it is very noisy. It is an infrequent purchase and it is unlikely that the customer will develop store loyalty.

upon the needs of the dominant shopping missions.

The hypothetical example described by Tables 11.1, 11.2 and 11.3 use three of the merchandise groups; they are:

- Audio/visual
- Children's clothing and footwear
- Confectionery

Table 11.2   A further example of how positioning characteristics can be related to customer shopping mission expectations

Merchandise group: Children Clothes and Footwear
Store Type: Large Central Stores

Broad customer typology	Customer shopping characteristics	Shopping Missions			Customer expectations	Positioning differentiation
		Type	Freq & occasion	Occurrence % of total		
Female Aged 30–40 married. Accompanied with young children. C1/C2. Buys to a budget.	She is well informed of comparative product quality and prices. This is a task she has performed on numerous occasions and is confident and ready to make a purchase decision.	Planned Comparison shopping visit for leisure clothes for the children.	Every 3/4 months.	80%	Expects to be able to make a choice from a range of styles and colours. Her price/quality range was established prior to the shopping mission. Once her choice is made she expects it to be available.	Merchandise differentiation should consider limited but adequate choice. This customer type is reasonably well off but has a price/quality set in mind. Thus is willing to trade-off choice for better price/quality value.
					She requires some service: advice on new materials (quality and washing instructions).	Service requirements suggest that while confident, help is appreciated.
					May need to keep children amused.	A facility to amuse children would be appreciated.

To make the example manageable the shopping missions for the large central stores are featured. The purpose of the example is to explain the concept. Clearly for retailers (such as the one featured in this example) who have a range of store location types, the shopping mission analysis should be undertaken by broad outlet location type.

For each merchandise group customer characteristics together with shopping mission type, frequency and rate of occurrence are identified and followed by customer research to identify the customers' expectations and

Functional Activities

Merchandise Assortment Characteristics
A core range is essential. This should offer basic leisure wear items on a seasonal basis. This would comprise core styles and colours in all sizes. Availability is an essential feature.

Merchandise Augmentation
Theme accessories, hats, socks etc. may be attractive if personalised themes are very popular. (Toys and sports equipment.)

Visual Merchandising
Co-ordinated displays featuring either activities or by theme personality. This will increase transaction size by proposing a complete outfit. (Toys and sports equipment.) Should be adequate to convince customer of 'authority' but not so high that locating size or style etc. becomes frustrating and detracts from presentation, there should be sufficient space to move and 'feel' the products.

Service Augmentation: Information
No major requirements. Ordering facility for out-of-stock items. Garment care sizes.

Service Augmentation: Facilities
Children's play area would be appreciated by mothers with two or more children. Changing rooms.

Service Intensity
Dedicated sales personnel who have (or understand) children. They should have adequate product knowledge.

Store Ambience
This area of the store should appeal to both the mother and the children. Therefore it must be seen as efficient for selection and transaction purposes as well as being exciting for the children.

preferences for merchandise, customer service and store environment features. The research may be conducted either by observing behaviour and deriving shopping mission features or by using focus groups for the initial research and reinforcing and validating the findings by instore research by observation and questionnaires.

From the data generated the planning executive must consider a number of issues:

Table 11.3   A third example of how positioning characteristics can be related
to customer shopping mission expectations

Merchandise group: Confectionery
Store Type: Large Central Stores

Broad customer typology	Customer shopping characteristics	Shopping Missions			Customer expectations	Positioning differentiation
		Type	Freq & occasion	Occurrence % of total		
Female Aged 30–40 married. Accompanied with three young children. C1/C2.	Beyond basic quality concern, she has very little interest. She does not consider this to be a purchase requiring much information or confidence beyond the satisfaction that the product is not harmful. She has very little time to spare, often by this time in the shopping trip she is very harassed.	Planned regular shopping visit: children's treat on regular shopping trip.	Weekly	50%	Expects safe products and acceptable quality. She also expects the product to be exciting for the children. Displays and self-service systems should be part of the excitement. No services other than fast customer handling is required.	The 'offer' should be primarily merchandise-led. Wide choice, quality and 'excitement' at pocket money prices are the essential features. Service content is limited to staff to ensure that rapid selling lines are replenished to avoid disappointment.

- The range of shopping missions within each merchandise group.

- The degree of congruence between shopping missions across the merchandise groups.

- The implications of these for developing a coherent positioning strategy: consideration of merchandise and service adjustments to maintain coherence throughout the offer.

- The cost-effectiveness of resource allocation and the measurement of resource productivity.

These issues will be discussed in the following chapter. However before

---

Functional Activities

Merchandise Assortment Characteristics
Variety is essential, but sales should be monitored to identify core items that become 'favourites' for a significant period of time. Quality assurance is essential and information to this effect is essential. Price is important as this mission is

Visual Merchandising
Attractive displays are an essential feature. Displays using characters known to the children will add even more to the excitement. Safe displays are essential.

Department should be located such that it is very visible and accessible to children.

Store Ambience
This area of the store should be designed with 'kid' appeal in mind. Bright and attractive offering new and exciting treats at competitive prices for parent appeal.

Merchandise Augmentation
None required.

Service Augmentation
None required other than clear product information.

Service Intensity
Sales assistants available to maintain the availability of the merchandise.

Rapid transaction services.

---

doing so we should discuss the possibility of identifying combinations of retail offer attributes that are acceptable to customers.

11.5 IDENTIFYING ACCEPTABLE ALTERNATIVES TO THE CUSTOMER

Having identified the attributes favoured by existing and potential customers is not the whole solution to retail offer planning. The issue remaining concerns whether or not the business can actually afford the cost structure implied by the researched expectations. Clearly it can be argued that the business often cannot afford not to 'afford' to meet the expectations of targeted customers but this claim can only be pursued once the cost structures and

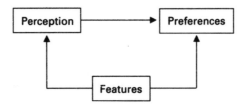

Figure 11.8   Features, perceptions and preferences

revenue potential have been evaluated. Furthermore such a proposition suggests there to be no possibility of compromise. Often the customer is indifferent between two features of a product or service beyond certain minimum levels of performance. Some examples are very obvious, particularly those concerning price and other features such as quality, exclusivity and choice. The research issues that emerge are: what are the minimum levels of 'performance' that are acceptable and what are the levels of performance beyond which the customer will consider a 'trade-off' between performance features. One possible approach is to try all possible combinations and see which one is preferred: the expense involved and the confusion caused for customers are but two of the objections to such an approach.

Conjoint analysis is a method which studies the linkages of features to preference and of features to perception (see Figure 11.8). Conjoint analysis uses expectancy value models (a rating by consumers of their preferences for specific product preferences) and preference regression (a statistical model that 'best' produces observed consumer preferences). Such models can produce the relative importances of perceptual attributes necessary for 'product' development, to study the linkage of features to perceptions and preference.

Having used factor analysis (a method of identifying a number of dimensions that represents the information given by a much larger set of attribute ratings) to identify the perceptual dimensions that consumers use to evaluate product/offers it is often necessary to explore the sensitivity of consumer perceptions and preferences to changes in product/offer features (i.e. their 'utility functions'). By examining the utility functions of product/offer features the manager can obtain insight into which features are important to the customer when selecting either an existing or a new product/offer. Typically we look for those features which give the greatest gains in preference at the lowest cost.

In Figure 11.9 the principle is illustrated. 'A' describes a response which suggests that provided a minimum level of the attribute is available an additional increase in the value of the attribute does not greatly increase the utility perception of the respondent. However, the reverse would appear to be the case for 'B'. An increase in the value of B has a significant impact upon the utility perception of the subject.

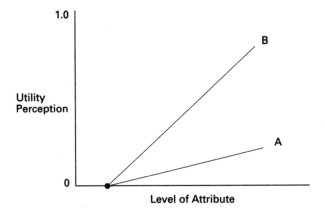

Figure 11.9   The relative importance of attributes

It follows that customers demonstrate different levels of utility for different attributes of the retail offer. This is important from two aspects. The first concerns the cost of providing an increase in utility levels and the response it receives. The second consideration concerns the usefulness it offers for market segmentation on the basis of benefits. Clearly a large response (in numbers of customers *and* customer expenditure) may suggest a viable segment exists and is one to address provided that other issues (e.g. competitive advantage) are equally attractive.

Trade-Off Analysis

There are one or two research applications which probe the 'trade-off' potential. Urban and Hauser (1980) offer a review of these (and do review the concept of conjoint analysis very thoroughly). Essentially we attempt to obtain aggregate information from the target customer group concerning their rank ordered preferences. The techniques vary depending upon whether or not there is a high level of interaction. Again the reader is directed towards Urban and Hauser for detailed discussion of the techniques available and the conditions of their application.

The usefulness of conjoint analysis (specifically trade-off analysis) to planning the retail offer is that if we can identify those elements of the offer that provide greater utility for each incremental increase, then given the cost for providing incremental increases in utility we can estimate (from customer research) the likely impact on revenues and profits. Moreover, we can use trade-off analysis to probe the acceptability limits of customers to the substitution of one attribute by another. Consider the situation described by Figure 11.10. We have two preferences for two merchandise characteristics. Customers appear either to prefer quality or to prefer choice. Figures 11.10a

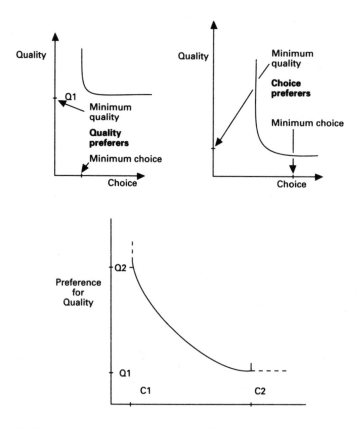

Figure 11.10   Trade-off potential between offer attributes
    (a)   Quality preferer
    (b)   Choice preferer
    (c)   Preference for choice

and 11.10b illustrate the strength of their preferences and the range over which the respondents are prepared to 'trade-off' one for the other is shown in Figure 11.10c. In Figure 11.10c it is clear that Q1 and C1 are minimum levels of quality and choice that are acceptable. The shape of the individual preference curves (Figures 11.10a and 11.10b) suggest that while some customers and 'quality preferers' and others 'choice preferers' there is a range over which they are prepared to 'trade-off' quality for choice and choice for quality. This occurs between Q2 and Q1 for the 'quality preferer'. At high levels of quality (Q2) a minimum of choice is expected (C1). However, the 'quality preferer' will accept incremental increases in choice (C1 towards C2) for which a decrease in quality if acceptable (Q2 towards Q1). At Q1 there is a level of quality below which no amounts of increase in choice is acceptable. A similar argument explains the situation for 'choice preferers'. The issues for the retail manager are the costs of meeting customer expectations across the range of each attribute and the minimum levels of each that are required.

We can envisage a situation in which considerable cost differentials may be found. For example quality control costs are very high for retailers who source from overseas. Even the very minimum level (Q1 in Figure 11.10a) may be costly to offer: any increases in quality should be met by a large response from the customer which will justify this expenditure. However, if it is relatively less expensive to offer choice, and if (again) there is evidence to suggest that 'quality preferers' will trade-off a little quality for choice without an accompanying reduction in total expenditure with the firm then customer satisfaction may be maintained but at a lower overall cost. The techniques of conjoint analysis facilitate such evaluation and developments in management accounting (such as activity based costing) are approaching the level of sophistication to be able to cope with the evaluation of costs.

We must remember that if we are approaching the customer research activity by using shopping missions care must be taken to ensure that the eventual combination of retail offer attributes reflects the characteristics of the customers within the prominent shopping missions. Thus it is possible, indeed likely, that distress shopping expectations will have different trade-off functions to those of planned comparison shopping missions. The difference in customer expectations concerning the shopping missions has been discussed earlier. Conjoint analysis probes areas of trade-offs which may identify areas between attributes where compromise exists and where costs may be reduced overall.

SUMMARY

In this chapter we have considered the role of information in effective decision making. We developed the shopping mission concept by considering the type of information that is necessary for effective offer planning. The discussion began with the structure of the information (its content and frequency) and considered the issues which have an impact on cost-effectiveness; these were sensitivity, feasibility, cost and competitive advantage benefits.

A matrix structure for data assembly was developed which identifies customer characteristics together with customer store visiting and purchasing activities from which the implications for shopping missions may be derived.

The sourcing of information was discussed in some detail, again the cost-effectiveness of information was emphasised. Sources of information were also discussed together with the techniques available for developing specific information requirements, in this context the information necessary for the definition of shopping missions was considered in depth. An example of how the information may be gathered and utilised was given.

Finally the issue of customer preference ratings was raised and conjoint analysis was described as a helpful technique by which consumer preferences might be rank-ordered.

12 Allocating Resources to Meet Customer Expectations and Create Added Value for the Customer

INTRODUCTION

In this chapter we consider the problems of matching resources to customer expectations. Having identified the target customer group by the type of shopping mission the task becomes one of combining resources to ensure that customer expectations are met appropriately and that their subsequent perceptions exceed their initial expectations: this, it will be recalled, is the basis of competitive advantage.

To achieve this objective we must link customers' expectations and corporate resources by (and with) the activities and elements that are recognizable by the customer (and which will therefore obtain a response from the customer) and which are manageable by the company. In other words we are seeking to identify and satisfy the benefits or attributes that comprise the expectations of the customer group.

Given the attributes a detailed specification of the 'offer' most likely to meet the expectations of the customer group may then be derived. Clearly management's task is to respond to customer expectations by using resources such that corporate expectations may also be met successfully. These issues are the subject of discussion in this chapter.

12.1 CORPORATE CONSIDERATIONS

Before we discuss the detail of customer expectations and the link between these and the company we should be clear about corporate expectations. Essentially the company is seeking to create a situation in which the resources allocated create competitive advantage as well as creating added value for customers. Porter (1985) suggests:

A business can be viewed as a collection of activities that are performed to design, produce, market, deliver and support its products or services.

The business's activities convert inputs from suppliers into outputs for customers through the activities at lower cost than competitors or by providing a differentiated product or service which a customer is prepared to pay a higher price for.

This can be viewed simply as Figure 12.1, where there are two dimensions for differentiation suggested. Clearly the company is concerned that both are considered. It is essential that productivity differentiation be demonstrated to the owners of the business and to potential investors. Typical indicators of productivity-led differentiation are given by the performance of sales margins, contribution compared with resources, such as space, employees, stockholding etc. Similarly customer- or market-led differentiation requires an indication of effective performance and here the indicators are sales and profit performance comparisons, market share increases, customer spending activities and customer perception measures. Figure 12.2 shows these in the context of the productivity and customer-market-led differentiation dimensions. Performance expectations can be viewed as strategic and operational and this topic will be expanded in the next chapter. At this point we need to establish the need for the company to recognise its responsibilities to the owners of the business and the requirement to produce an impressive performance for the 'City' and potential investors.

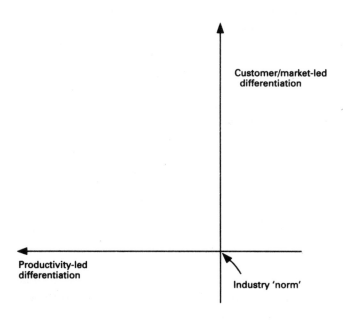

Figure 12.1   Relative differentiation to create competitive advantage

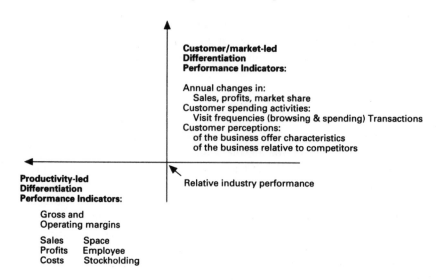

Customer/market-led
Differentiation
Performance Indicators:

Annual changes in:
   Sales, profits, market share
Customer spending activities:
   Visit frequencies (browsing & spending) Transactions
Customer perceptions:
   of the business offer characteristics
   of the business relative to competitors

Relative industry performance

Productivity-led
Differentiation
Performance Indicators:

Gross and
Operating margins

Sales	Space
Profits	Employee
Costs	Stockholding

Figure 12.2   Performance indicators of relative differentiation and competitive advantage

12.2   CUSTOMER EXPECTATIONS

It will be recalled that in Chapter 1 Kotler's interesting approach to prod-uct characteristics was briefly introduced. This is particularly useful in con-sidering the ways in which added value can be developed around the retail offer. Kotler suggests that products have three dimensions. The *core prod-uct or service* is the benefit (or cluster of benefits) purchased. For example '... purchasing agents do not buy quarter-inch drills; they buy quarter-inch holes' (Levitt). The point being made is that any alternative which is more cost-effective would be purchased, the need is for a quarter-inch hole and the drill is one alternative for achieving or acquiring the need. Hence com-munications and decision support needs are reasons for purchasing com-puter equipment. It follows that the drills and computers are the *tangible products* which manifest the benefits purchased by the customer; the core products. *Product augmentation* seeks to identify additional services and benefits that make the 'product' attractive to a specific customer. Typically these features include delivery and credit, installation (and removal of re-placed product), after sales service packages, etc.

The increased application of market segmentation and customer profiling makes product augmentation an increasingly important characteristic in de-veloping added value. It can be made to be specific to a target customer group need and it is a particularly attractive dimension to be added because unlike the tangible aspects of a product the augmentation features are in-tangible. This has the advantages of being customer specific and less viable.

It may also be attractive because of the improvement to margins that may be realised. Often product augmentation features can add more to the selling price of a product than their inclusion adds to cost. This may be due to economies of scale within the supply chain as well as within the retail company. The increasing practice of retailers selling furniture from a supplier's depot stocks is an example. Rather than maintain expensive stock levels of furniture that may be damaged during handling and delivery activities, many retailers are attracted to trade terms/service packages in which the supplier maintains sufficient inventory to service retailer sales and *they* deliver sales to customers thereby eliminating costs of stockholding and delivery.

Figure 12.1 can be modified once more. This time we can use it to illustrate the three dimensions discussed, (see Figure 12.3). The vertical axis becomes a measure of relative added value which may be measured objectively by appraising the added value features of the 'offers' of competitor companies. The horizontal axis remains a productivity or cost-led measure. The measurement of competitor added value may be quantitative, for example; price levels, range width and depth, quality and exclusivity are all visually identifiable and quantifiable as are market sales and share performances. Customer perceptions may require qualitative techniques but these two may be quantified using the scaling techniques described earlier.

Differentiation is a managerial judgment based upon interpretation of customer preferences. It follows that market segmentation is important and may be used as a basis for identifying the preferred added value characteristics of the market-place and subsequently using them as a guide for the allocation of resources which then interprets the company's positioning responses. In this regard segmentation may be considered as an influence in the planning and development of the retail offer. For some, e.g. essentially commodity based offers, it is likely that very little influence will be achieved by expanding the offer of utility by the addition of excessive product augmentation. It is likely that beyond the basic proposition of the core and tangible characteristics of the offer no major competitive advantage will be available.

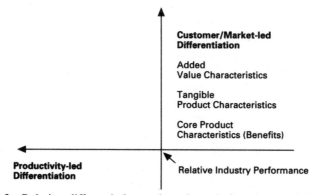

Figure 12.3   Relative differentiation and product-service characteristics

12.3   CONSUMER PREFERENCES AND CONSUMER BEHAVIOUR

It follows that consumer preferences will be a strong influence on the purchasing process. There are a number of reasons why we should attempt to understand the theory underlying consumer choice. Two of the most obvious concern the issues of market segmentation and added value. By identifying a group of customers with similar preference characteristics we can focus on their preferences and create a viable business (assuming the group to be large enough). Clearly if we understand their preferences we can define the characteristics of their preferences of the product/service that are important. However, a thorough knowledge of how preferences are derived and manifested are two reasons of similar importance. By identifying their primary attributes, those for which there can be no compromise or trade-offs together with their secondary attributes, those for which their is a willingness to be flexible, a much more cost-effective approach to product/service development can be achieved. Economic theory can offer some interesting insights into consumer decision-making and two approaches in particular are of interest. They are:

Indifference analysis;
The 'product characteristics' approach.

Indifference Analysis

Indifference analysis assumes that while unable to assign precise utility values to different amounts of a commodity, they are able to decide upon which combinations of commodities they prefer to others. They know which combinations of goods (or attributes of a particular product/service) maximises their satisfaction. It is possible to generate a set of indifference curves showing the combinations of different amounts of the two 'goods' which consumers are indifferent between. In Figure 12.4 we show the 'hypothetical' combination of product/service attributes; quality and service. At point A the combination leaves the consumer satisfied. The concept of indifference is based upon that of diminishing marginal utility: as consumers experience successively less additional satisfaction from each additional unit of a good the indifference curves will be concave upwards. If the consumer has 'excess' quality (point B) or 'excess' service (point C) it suggests that the consumer would be prepared to trade quite a large amount of quality for a relatively small increase in service, or conversely, a large amount of service for a relatively small increase in quality. The argument is that at points B and C diminishing marginal rates of substitution are demonstrated.

Indifference analysis can be expanded considerably to consider the impact of budget constraints and price differentials (and price changes) upon consumer preferences. Clearly there is an interest for us here. If we are

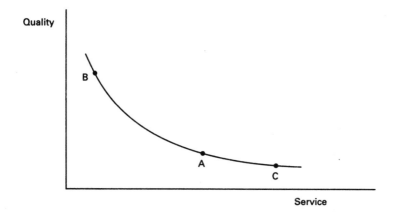

Figure 12.4   An indifference curve

able to determine indifference curves for groups of customers, we can segment markets *and* identify and cost product-service attributes. We shall return to this aspect of indifference analysis later.

The 'Product Characteristics' Approach

An alternative approach has been suggested by Lancaster (1979) who suggests that consumers demand bundles of characteristics rather than products.
In Figure 12.5 three products offer differing levels of the two characteristics quality and service. By considering the available budget and the consumer's preference between the two characteristics a balanced purchase will
result such that the consumer's level of satisfaction will be maximised. In
Figure 12.5 three products are shown, each with differing levels of the two
characteristics or attributes; quality and service. Points on a–b show combinations of quality and service that may be achieved when the consumer
allocates all of the available budget on different mixes of brand A and
brand B. Similarly b–c shows the combinations available for expenditure
allocated between B and C. The line a–c shows combinations available
from purchases of a combination of A and C; however, as this lies inside
the line a–b–c it is offering a lower level of satisfaction by giving smaller
amounts of both characteristics than can be had by spending the same income on the other combinations and would not be chosen by a consumer
seeking more, rather than less of each characteristic.

The line a–b–c becomes a budget line, similar to that in indifference
analysis. Shifts in relative prices or changes in disposable income will be
reflected in the change of the position of a–b–c. Watkins (1986) suggests
that by applying indifference analysis to this approach a useful market research

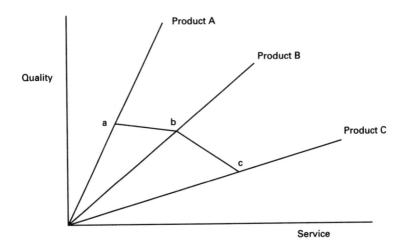

Figure 12.5   The 'product characteristics' approach

tool may be developed. A detailed exploration of this possibility is beyond our objectives. However, it is clear that such a combination would reduce the risks involved in product/service development by specifying and quantifying the product/service positioning attributes required.

The approach is useful when competing in markets segmented on the basis of product-service characteristics. By identifying the space in which competitors' offers are clustered it is possible to identify an adjacent location where, given an appropriate offer, there is potential to capture customers from competitors. A knowledge of customer preferences will permit the introduction of an offer which adds emphasis to the important features of the existing offers sufficient for the customer to switch loyalty. Clearly the larger the number of offers in close proximity to each other the more precise the research (and the subsequent differentiation) must be.

This discussion returns us to the topic of differentiation through added value characteristics. If we assume, as Kotler suggests, that products, services and retail offers are purchased because they represent an attractive set of benefits or attributes we may consider the merchandise, customer service, store environment and customer communications characteristics as attributes that may be aggregated in such a way that they represent an attractive offer to a particular customer group.

Returning to the proposition made in Figure 12.1, we can now consider these characteristics within the framework discussed earlier. In Figure 12.6 we identify the attributes developed earlier within the Kotler framework. *Core product benefits* are seen to be benefits realised by the shopping mission. For example, a distress purchase shopping mission is satisfied by the customer being able to purchase a forgotten meal ingredient at a time when

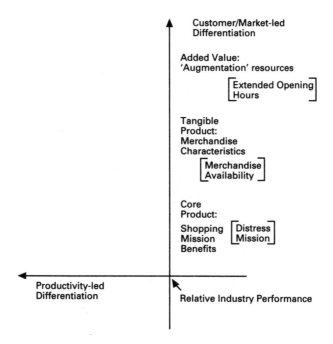

Figure 12.6   Using Kotler's framework with shopping missions

it is needed locally. Alternatively, a destination purchasing mission is accomplished when a specific need is satisfied without compromises being made to brand, size, colour, price etc. *Tangible product characteristics* are the resources made available materially to satisfy the demand: the merchandise, the service etc. *Added value* is created by enhancing the purchasing experience by using resources to add value through informative visual merchandising and the inclusion of related accessory products and services. Figure 12.7 places these activities in context and provides examples of tangible product and added value characteristics. Clearly there may be other components within the attributes suggested. However, it is unlikely that any retailing offer will not offer an element of each of the attributes.

12.4 CUSTOMER EXPECTATIONS AND CORPORATE EXPECTATIONS

Customer expectations and corporate considerations must be considered together. Clearly it is realistic to assume that unless both are satisfied it is unlikely that in the long run the business will continue.

In Figure 12.8 customer and corporate expectations are considered together. The customer expectations are based upon the nature of the shopping

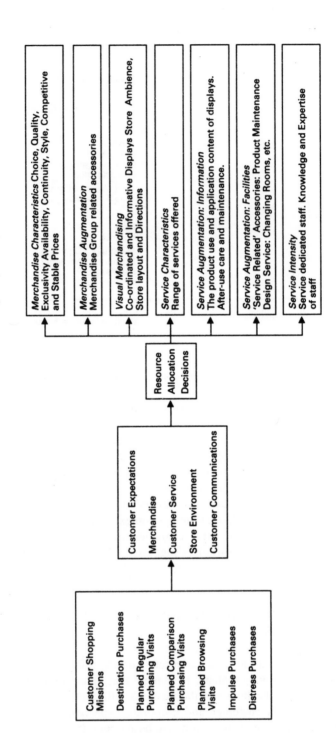

Figure 12.7 Matching customers' shopping mission expectations with attributes of a retail offer

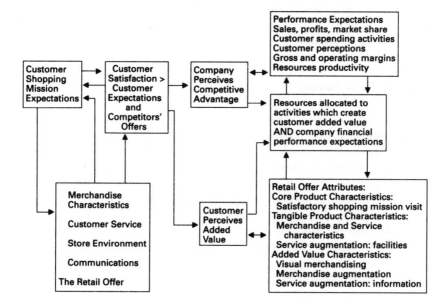

Figure 12.8   Creating customer added value and corporate competitive advantage

mission that the customer identifies the store with and hence their expectations of the offer should be reflected in the offer made. Provided the retail offer meets customer expectations customer satisfaction will either match or exceed their expectations. If expectations are simply just met, then it is likely that the store will remain one of a number within the customers' reference group for purchasing visits. However, if a situation can be constructed whereby customer satisfaction exceeds expectations and exceeds competitors offers *both the company and the customer* perceived benefits. The customer will consider there to be added value to be obtained from the visits and transactions. The company will have established competitive advantage.

Customer Satisfaction

Customer added value results from a combination of tangible product characteristics and added value characteristics such that the shopping mission is satisfactory and both tangible product characteristics and added value characteristics together make an offer to the customer which is clearly preferred to that of any competitor. If this situation is reached it is then very likely that the customer will consider the retailer as a first choice store and this will remain so long as the combination of attributes continues to meet customers' requirements. Clearly changeover time and monitoring research should be undertaken continuously to ensure that offer and expectations remain congruent.

Corporate Expectations

Corporate expectations are based upon the criteria established in previous chapters. Provided the company continues to meet the objectives it has set for itself for both financial performance criteria together with its market performance and productivity requirements it will be in a position whereby the competitive advantage it has created will be sustainable. Again the caveat concerning research of customer requirements on an ongoing basis obtains. Failure to identify changes in customer expectations will result in competitors challenging the business' market position.

It follows that the 'link' between customer satisfaction and corporate expectations is the resource allocation process. Resources are allocated to activities which meet customers requirements by creating a combination of attributes that once aggregated represent a coherent response to the customers' expectations. It was argued earlier that the shopping mission is the basis for planning and this argument is repeated here. Given that the customer 'sees' a specific purpose in undertaking a shopping mission visit it follows that the successful retailing business is that which understands the nature of the customer decision making process, the store selection and product purchasing activity, and allocates resources to provide maximum customer satisfaction.

12.5   CUSTOMER RESPONSES TO RESOURCE ALLOCATION

If we consider that to be cost-effective, resource allocation decisions should demonstrate a return, the customer response is one way of measuring the effectiveness of resource allocation. Customer responses may be measured by a change in their perceptions of a product or retail offer and in the change in their purchasing activities as well as by an increase in sales revenue customer responses and by increases in visit and purchasing visit frequencies, average transactions, and purchasing characteristics (both range and items).

It was argued earlier in this chapter that the purpose of effective resource allocation was to enhance added value for the customer such that customer satisfaction exceeds customer expectations. Figure 12.9 suggests a situation in which resources have been allocated to an activity (for example; merchandise choice). The level of customer satisfaction may be illustrated by either curve (A) or curve (B). Clearly the situation represented by (A) sug-

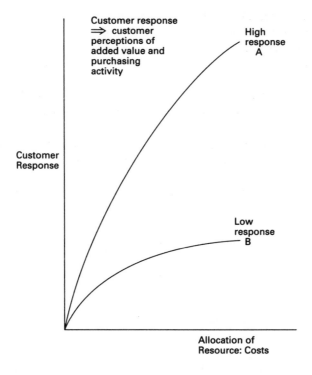

Figure 12.9   Customer response and resource allocation

gests that the decision has been successful whereas a response such as that represented by (B) would suggest that choice is not a merchandise characteristic held very high in the customers' selection criteria and does not create added value for the target customer group.

It follows that management should set itself simple operating criteria; it should first:

Identify and evaluate the key factors of customer satisfaction expectations: the factors which create added value.

Identify the 'attributes' within the business which create customer satisfaction and added value.

Link expectations – attributes – activities – resources.

To do this effectively requires knowledge of the customer (and customer store selection and purchasing criteria) together with a detailed knowledge of the cost structures of the business activities which will deliver customer satisfaction through added value for the customer. This suggests that the conventional approach to resource allocation and accounting may differ from that required. However, the point should be made that typically the cost data exists and all that is required is its restructuring for more effective use. An approach to implementing this proposal would be:

Identify and understand customer expectations of and for added value by understanding customer responses to added value features;

Identify the attributes, e.g., merchandise and service characteristics, merchandise density, service density and intensity, etc.;

Identify the activities which create the added value attributes within the 'offer';

Focus resources on these activities;

Reduce or eliminate those activities which do not add value – or which do not contribute to customer satisfaction;

Monitor activity performance.

Before developing this approach in more detail we will consider some of the issues concerning customer response and resource allocation.

Attribute Cost Profiles

In Figure 12.10 the proposition made by Figure 12.9 is expanded. Figure 12.10 emphasises this effect and suggests how an approach to resource allocation might be approached. At RA_0 the level of customer satisfaction, or perceived added value is PAV_0. At this point added value is optimised. It is a level of resource input that we classify as a *qualifying level* i.e. the minimum level of added value acceptable to the customer. The addition of resources may be met by a range of responses. Assume that RA_0-RA_1 and RA_1-RA_2 are equal amounts of resource increase then we can see that the customer group with response CR_3 clearly finds the offer (or this aspect of the offer) very much more acceptable than CR_1 and, to a degree, CR_2.

The reasons for these quite different responses are in many ways the basis of segmentation: that customers respond in quite different ways to marketing offers based upon their expectations and these will be influenced by the shopping mission. Clearly in Figure 12.10 the customer group represented by the response CR_3 has quite different selection criteria from the group responding at CR_1. Knowledge of the nature of the responses gives valuable planning input to management. Assuming we are targeting one or other of the customer groups (i.e. the group responding at CR_3 or that with

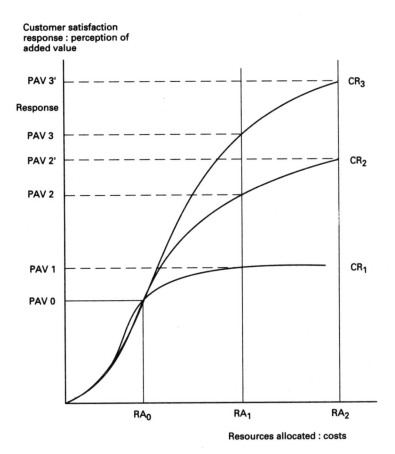

Figure 12.10   Alternative response patterns to incremental allocation

the response shown as CR_1) then our resource allocation planning would be quite clear cut. For customers with the CR_3 response we should commit resources to the level of RA_2 because this clearly adds value for this particular customer group. However, if we are targeting the customer group with the CR_1 response the resource allocation should be contained at RA_0 and should not be extended beyond RA_1. The approach suggested earlier based upon identifying and understanding customer expectations of and for added value and subsequently focusing resources upon the activities which create the added value is clearly illustrated in principle by Figure 12.10. The decision concerning *which* group is targeted depends upon the strategy of the company which will clearly be influenced by the revenue and profit potential of each of the segments, the competitive situation in each segment and of course the capability of the company to establish credibility with the target market. In the discussion which follows it is suggested that

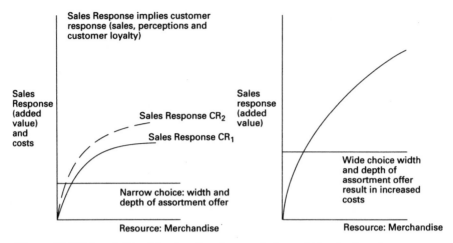

Figure 12.11(a) and (b)   Merchandise characteristics: width, depth and providing service

customer perceptions of added value are measured in part by their purchasing activities i.e. purchasing visit frequencies, average transactions and items and range of merchandise purchased. Clearly customer perceptions should also be measured and positive changes towards the added value initiatives be seen as favourable responses. For this measurement tracking studies (discussed earlier) would prove valuable.

Merchandise characteristics (choice, quality, availability, exclusivity, etc.) is a resource allocation activity that can create added value. In Figure 12.11a the response to narrow choice is suggested by the sales response CR_1. Customer research could establish (and justify) that an expansion of the merchandise assortment would increase the response to CR_2. This is illustrated by Figure 12.11b. Clearly an increase in customer choice would require additional resource allocation.

Another merchandise characteristic, merchandise availability is considered by Figure 12.12. It is well known that the relationship between stockholding costs and the level of stockholding required at high levels of availability is exponential: costs at high levels of availability increase markedly, in the author's experience they have been in the order of a 15% increase in stockholding costs to achieve an increase of two per cent availability from 95% to 97%. Concurrently the cost of lost sales declines rapidly and the two cost curves combine to give the U-shaped curve in Figure 12.12. Customer responses are shown as CR_1 and CR_2. If the response is that shown by CR_1 then the 'contribution' (the shaded area (double hatch)) is quite small and the level of availability should be maintained at OA_1. However, with a response similar to CR_2 the availability requirement can be justified at the higher level of OA_2. It is very clear that excessive availability can be very expensive, this refers not simply to stockholding costs but to both

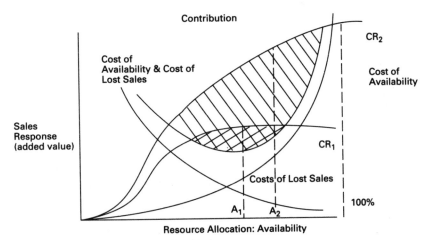

Figure 12.12   Merchandise characteristics: availability

Note: The notional contribution is maximised by offering a level of availability such that the vertical distance between the customer response curve and the combined costs of availability and lost sales is maximised.

selling area and distribution storage space. It is also likely that mark-downs will increase in order that excess merchandise is sold, thereby reducing gross margin achievement. Opportunity costs are involved which increase as resources are allocated to providing increased availability.

Merchandise augmentation, the differentiation of the merchandise offer by the addition of related products or accessories is described by Figure 12.13. The diagram suggests that merchandise augmentation is an additional fixed cost (as is service augmentation). The responses shown are those that would be expected: for an 'investment' of O-MA$_1$ the response is CR$_1$ an increase to O-MA$_2$ will have appeal to a different customer group with more success.

Service augmentation with information and facilities have similar issues. Both have fixed and variable cost components (see Figures 12.14 and 12.15). For facilities service augmentation the fixed costs relate to the installation of service facilities and the variable costs their maintenance. Service augmentation fixed costs include service literature and other media and may include initial training of service personnel and the variable costs will reflect continuation training.

Finally we consider the customer response and cost issues raised by visual merchandising activity decisions. The primary inputs concern merchandise and space and Figure 12.16 illustrates the hypothetical situation posed by the choice for management between merchandise group based visual merchandising and a theme approach. We can safely assume (from research) that the theme-based approach will have higher fixed and variable costs due to the fact that more space is usually required, together with additional

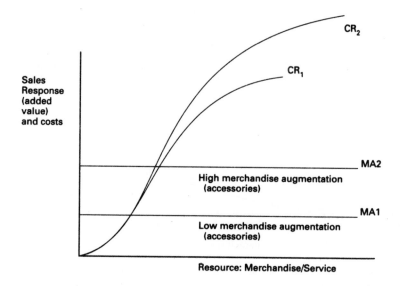

Figure 12.13   Merchandise augmentation and service augmentation

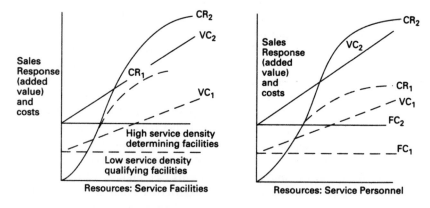

Figure 12.14   Service augmentation
facilities

Figure 12.15   Service augmentation
information

fixtures and often uses more merchandise due to duplication etc. within the
themes in the store. Management's decision is concerned with first identifying the dominant shopping mission and then deciding upon which approach
will create more added value for the customer. The added value should be
based upon advice and information on how clothes might be coordinated,
interior design and furniture combined and product applications. An example of the success of creative visual merchandising can be seen in Japanese
and North American department stores where the use of space and mer-

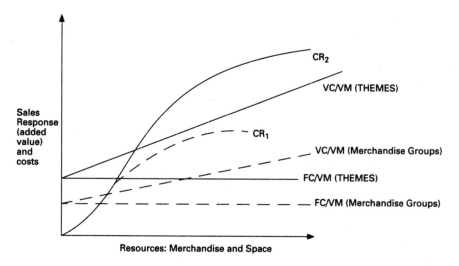

Figure 12.16 Visual merchandising

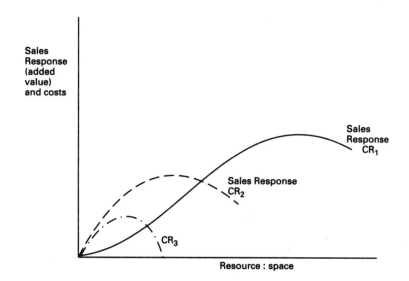

Figure 12.17 Merchandise density issues

chandise is combined into an effective response to customer expectations for advice on product uses and combination.

Merchandise density is a consideration here and the issues are represented by Figure 12.17. The response illustrated by CR_1 suggests that by increasing the amount of merchandise available in display areas sales increase steadily then gradually decline. There is probably a diminishing resources effect involved in that the combination of merchandise space reaches an optimum at which customers have sufficient space *and* merchandise. Below this optimum level it suggests that perhaps choice or availability are insufficient and that by increasing the amount of merchandise the customer response is improved. Beyond the optimum combination sales response decreases reflecting the possibility of consumers' dissatisfaction with an overcrowded store or perhaps the confusion created in customers' minds results in their purchasing elsewhere. Similar but more dramatic responses are illustrated by CR_2 and CR_3.

By contrast, a department store might find planned browsing to be a dominant shopping mission. Here the merchandise assortment requirements are very different: extensive ranges with considerable choice in each will be necessary if browsing is to be converted into purchasing. Furthermore in this situation the retailer may consider it necessary to identify elements of customer service that are 'determining' items rather than 'qualifying' items and which create competitive advantage as well as converting browsers into purchasers. Essentially we are attempting to identify those aspects of the company's offer which add value for the customer and which enhance the level of customer satisfaction achieved.

To do this with any certainty requires an accurate knowledge of cost details. Specifically we need to know the costs of providing the attributes that are important elements of the retail offer.

12.6 DEVELOPING AN APPROACH FOR COSTING CUSTOMER EXPECTATIONS

Management accounting has been tackling the needs to provide management with appropriate and timely information for planning and controlling the business from both operational and, more recently, strategic perspectives. A number of contributions are of interest but it should be said that much of the work conducted in the field of interest has been directed towards improving the accuracy of overhead allocation by developing a costing system known as Activity Based Costing (ABC). Activity Based Costing analyses current product cost structures and attempts to allocate significantly more of the overhead costs to products directly.

Underlying ABC is the technique of activity based management. The philosophy of ABM is a reshaping of companies' costs. By understanding its activities the company exposes opportunities for performance improvement that conventional cost accounting systems are seldom able to detect. Cost management is improved by identifying the components of the firm's resource conversion process and tracing the cost of activities with more accuracy. Brimson (1992) suggests that '... The traditional view is that costs are best controlled by department managers who are responsible for minimising the variance between budgeted and actual cost by cost element (salary and wages, travel, supplies, and similar costs). The emphasis is on *efficient* use of resources. The ABM view is that costs are best controlled by managing the workload, eliminating non-value added activities, managing the factors that drive cost, continuously improving value added activities, and streamlining management. The emphasis on *effective* use of resources.'

Understanding the nature of customer expectations i.e., the attributes that comprise the customers' view of a product-offer takes ABM closer to the customer. Instead of improving the cost profile of an existing product-offer the pro-active firm seeks out where it may gain competitive advantage – and what it will cost the company. Reactive companies can only achieve, at best, competitive necessity.

A more useful approach is to attempt to identify the attributes which comprise the customers' expectations of the retail offer and to use these as the basis for 'product' costing.

A full discussion of ABC is beyond the scope of this text. Much of the context of the concept, its philosophy and techniques may be gained, albeit superficially from the explanation of the model which follows. For those interested the contributions of Brimson (1992), Bromwich (1992) and Cooper and Kaplan (1991), Hiromoto (1988) and Ward (1992) should be studied.

An important element of activity analysis and activity accounting is an estimate of *cost behaviour patterns* which attempt to relate input costs with the changes of output volumes over a relevant range of activity levels. These were considered earlier in this chapter. *Attribute-Based Costing* uses these concepts in an approach to product/service costing that first identifies the customer expectations of a product/service (the retail offer) by its components (its attributes). The cost of providing the combination of attributes is derived by using the techniques of activity based management.

However it will be helpful as an introduction to the topic to consider some of the conceptual issues. Cooper, Kaplan and others have been suggesting for some time that the changing nature of both manufacturing and distribution has been increasing the proportion of fixed costs out of the total costs of production. This they suggest has been responsible for an increasing level in the inaccuracy of product costs. It has been suggested that fixed costs have increased as a proportion of total costs from 30% to in excess of 60% for some products. Cooper and Kaplan have argued that '... traditionally fixed costs were relatively small and the distortions arising from inappropriate overhead allocations were not significant. Information processing costs were high and it was, therefore, difficult to justify more sophisticated overhead allocation methods'. The thrust of the proposal is to identify activities involved in the production of a productor service, the thesis being that managers can better manage activities than they can costs!

An *activity* is, therefore, a combination of resources (manpower, technology, raw materials and environment) that produces a given product/service. Activities describe what the enterprise does: the way resources are allocated and the outputs of the process. *Activity analysis* comprises the breakdown of what the enterprise does into manageable segments for detailed analysis regarding cost and performance. *Activity accounting* is then, the collection of financial and operational performance information concerning the significant activities of the enterprise.

Activity Based Management is an approach to management that uses activity analysis to identify information on:

How activities consume resources during the production of outputs;
The extent of the activities' support of strategic objectives;
The performance improvement potential that may be achieved by:
eliminating waste;
minimising cost drivers*; and
emulating best practices.
How they support operational and strategic decision making.

12.7 APPLYING THE CONCEPT

The model which is to be developed is based upon many of the concepts discussed by the proponents of activity based management and activity based costing. Its major benefits are, an opportunity more closely to identify the activities and costs of providing a specific retail offer and to be able to consider alternative activities and costs by which the offer may be delivered. During the process they are, of course, identifying the resources required as well as the costs and this offers management a choice. The choice is based upon cost-effectiveness and opportunity cost considerations and explores the extent to which the company can actually afford to meet customers' expectations. Trade off analysis (conjoint analysis) will identify customers' rank ordered preferences and their 'price tolerances'.

The model is described by Figure 12.18, which is an outline of the components of an activity based management model. Its objective is to identify optional resource allocation combinations that meet criteria established by customer expectation requirements. The essential features are the *customer expectations* which prescribe the attribute components of their aggregate expectations and they also identify specific elements of the 'delivery service or mechanism' which are essential if the offer is to be effectively managed. These are *critical success factors*. They are indications of aspects of competitive advantage that should not be overlooked when planning or reviewing resource allocation decisions. Typically critical success factors point towards facilitating elements such as effective distribution facilities which

---

*A cost driver is a factor whose occurrence creates cost.

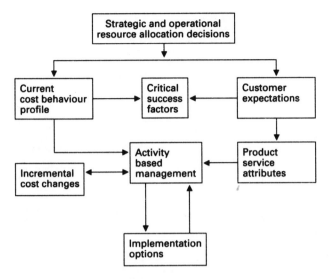

Figure 12.18 Activity based management: major components

provide cost-effective availability, or perhaps merchandise selection expert-ise which can provide 'exclusivity' in the merchandise assortment. Critical success factors can identify areas of investment in both fixed and current assets that are necessary if competitive advantage rather than competitive necessity is to be established.

An examination of the behaviour of the current costs of activities and current cost behaviour profile, enables the management to consider cost/volume and investment/capacity issues and, based upon the attributes iden-tified, what the nature and size of the incremental cost changes required will be if the activities are restructured to meet the level of performance required by the attributes. The process will identify the range of activity relationships and cost structures (together with forecasts of cost implica-tions) that are available to meet customer requirements.

Figure 12.19 expands the basic model and proposes specific areas of interest and investigation. These are then expanded in subsequent diagrams. Customer expectations and shopping missions are featured in Figure 12.20. The shopping missions should be used to determine the relevant aspects of customer expectations that will be used in turn to identify the attributes that are important and will provide the basis for arriving at an offer which is acceptable to the customer in that it meets their requirements for mer-chandise, customer service and store environment characteristics and, at the same time, meets the marketing and financial requirements of the business. Clearly shopping missions and customer expectations are linked: the cus-tomer expectations of comparison shopping missions will differ markedly from those of a distress purchase. They are also linked by customer purchasing

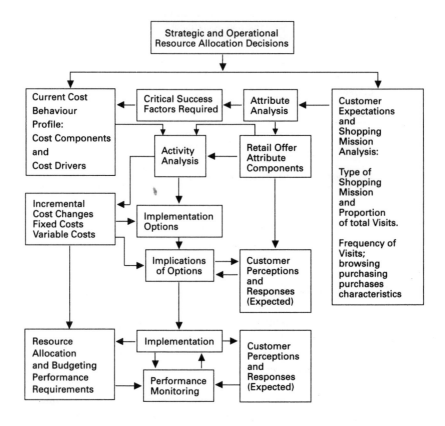

Figure 12.19   Activity based management and attribute costing

behaviour which will provide an indication of the 'economics' of customer shopping mission visits.

Given both shopping missions and customer expectations the retail offer may be disaggregated into attributes. Table 12.1 suggests the range of attributes that may be derived together with specific elements that may comprise each attribute. The purpose of the attribute analysis is to identify those critical success factors which require to be in place if the company is to develop sustainable competitive advantage within the sector or segment. These may well be an indication of the extent to which fixed investment is required or should be renewed. As suggested earlier the critical success factors may comprise fixed assets of either human or physical characteristics in nature such as a quick response distribution system, a sophisticated management information system (with highly trained management capable of its use) or perhaps a highly experienced buying/merchandising group capable of interpreting market needs.

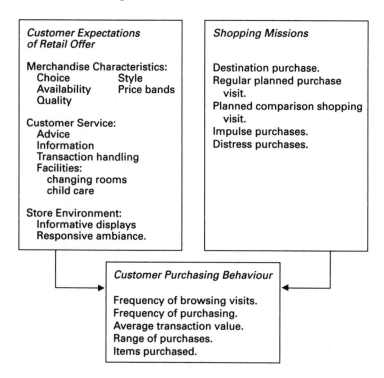

Figure 12.20 Customer expectations and shopping missions

Activity analysis follows and is described by Table 12.2. It will be re-called that activities are the components of the enterprise's processes which create added value and customer satisfaction. As such they have costs which must be explored in sufficient detail to be able to investigate the impact of changes of levels of performance on the cost behaviour of the activities. This analysis is undertaken by identifying cost drivers (factors that are a prime cause of the level of activity) and the cost elements which comprise the aggregate activity cost. Table 12.3 provides an hypothetical range of activities and their component cost elements. Care should be taken to iden-tify the fixed and variable elements and to ensure that overlap between cost elements and between activities does not occur. The relationship between cost elements and critical success factors is part of this analysis. The criti-cal success factors are facilitators rather than cost entities: they are essen-tial to the operational success of the business but their accounting is likely to be across a number of activities. However, they may be significant in the examination of incremental cost changes, particularly where capacity increases may involve an increase in fixed asset investment.

The process will result in a range of options (activity options) that will be available. These may be evaluated for customer response by using focus

224

Table 12.1 Attribute analysis: components of retail offer

Merchandise Characteristics		Merchandise Augmentation	Visual Merchandising	Service Augmentation: Information	Service Augmentation: Service Intensity	Service Augmentation: Facilities
Choice Quality Exclusivity	Availability Style Price points	Accessories Related products	Merchandise application Coordination, etc.	Merchandise performance details Comparative performance details Customer support programmes	Availability of skilled and knowledgeable staff: customer 'purchasing' customer transactions	Service facilities: Changing rooms Child care.

Table 12.2 Activity analysis

Merchandise and Merchandise Augmentation	Customer Services	Store Development, Design and Display	Systems Support	Distribution Support
Effective merchandise selection based upon market, supplier and customer requirements research.	Provision of information and advise on product use and application through a range of media. Rapid and efficient transaction service at the point of sale. Rapid, efficient and 'fair' after sales service.	Informative displays of merchandise together with relevant 'services'. Convenient location and parking. Comfortable ambiance.	Current and relevant flows of information for merchandise and operations decisions sales, stock levels, stock locations, store activity levels.	Provision of pre-determined levels of merchandise availability and delivery reliability in both store and distribution locations.

Table 12.3 Current cost behaviour profile: activity based cost analysis

Merchandise (and Customer Services) Merchandise Augmentation Merchandise Selection	Customer Services: Information, Help and Advice	Customer Services: Transactions	Customer Services: After Sales	Store Development and Design and Display	Systems Support Service	Distribution Service: Warehousing	Distribution Service: Deliveries
Cost Driver: Number of items stocked. Cost Elements: (Fixed and Variable). Merchandise characteristics (e.g. range dimensions, quality levels, price points). Merchandise stocks Buying/Merchandise staff costs. Space costs for visual merchandising. Space costs for dedicated services. Dedicated staff costs and recruitment etc. Dedicated market research projects. Equipment (EPOS etc.) (Depreciation).	Cost Driver: Number of customer enquiries handled. Cost Elements: (Fixed and Variable). Dedicated staff and recruitment costs etc. Dedicated equipment (Depreciation). Service support training. Information materials. Space costs for service function.	Cost Driver: Number of customer transactions handled. Cost Elements: (Fixed and Variable): Dedicated staff and recruitment costs etc. Training costs. Equipment costs (Depreciation). Space costs for transactions handling.	Cost Driver: Number of product returns/ service visits. Cost Elements (Fixed and Variable): Dedicated staff and recruitment costs, etc. Training costs. Dedicated equipment (Depreciation). Materials. Replacement products. Loan product stock.	Cost Driver: Unit space utilised (Square feet, linear feet). Cost Elements (Fixed and Variable): Store development, building, and fitting costs. Store design, layout and visual merchandising costs. Dedicated staff and recruitment etc. Display merchandise. Rents, taxes (less items charged to merchandise). Dedicated equipment (Depreciation). Dedicated research.	Cost Driver: Number of items of information provided. Cost Elements (Fixed and Variable): Dedicated staff and recruitment etc. Staff training. Equipment (hardware, software and consumables) Dedicated staff and (Depreciation).	Cost Driver: Cubic feet of merchandise throughput. Cost Elements (Fixed and Variable): Warehouse development, building and equipment costs (Depreciation). Dedicated staff and recruitment etc. Staff training. Rents, taxes.	Cost Driver: Number of store deliveries. Cost Elements (Fixed and Variables): Vehicles and equipment (Depreciation). Dedicated staff and recruitment costs etc. Vehicle and equipment maintenance.

groups during which the customers will be asked for a view of their likely response to a range of offers and attribute combinations. Clearly the range included in the research should include those options for which the cost profiles are acceptable and those which meet, or are very close to, the original expectations expressed by customers. The responses will provide the basis on which to plan and budget the appropriate retail offer.

Performance measurement criteria will be discussed in detail in the next chapter. It is essential that while the criteria set reflect the activity cost drivers selected because of their response to activity level changes, they should also be capable of being related to the performance measures commonly used within the business. Thus a measure of visual merchandising may be derived from a sales density objective (i.e. sales per square feet) and a merchandise density objective (i.e. stockholding per square feet). An alternative measure may involve two separate ratios involving merchandise density: one reflecting merchandise stockholding in sales areas and the other for the total (sales and services) area. The characteristics of the business will determine the most effective measures to be used, for example for a department store the interest will be on the effectiveness of visual merchandising in increasing the range of items and the value of an individual sale. By contrast the food discount operator will be interested in sales and merchandise density values. However, the important factor is that the criteria are useful in planning and controlling the offer and are related to data presentation in use in the business.

SUMMARY

This chapter has covered a considerable number of issues. It has discussed differentiation as a means by which the company may create competitive advantage and the ways in which customer/market led differentiation and productivity led differentiation may be measured were considered. Customer expectations were considered within the context of product characteristics. This discussion reviewed Kotler's approach and applied it to the differentiation model. Consumer preferences and their implications for their purchasing processes were considered within the context of micro-economic theory which reviewed indifference analysis and the 'product characteristics' approach both concepts led the discussion towards a consideration of conjoint analysis in the development of a rank ordering of customer expectations.

The discussion also considered the relationship between differentiation and customer expectations. Kotler's view of product characteristics was applied to the attributes discussed in earlier chapters and the topic expanded to consider customer expectations and resource allocation decisions. At this point the topics of customer and corporate expectations were linked to the topic of resource allocation.

13 Customer and Corporate Productivity: Measuring Customer Satisfaction and Corporate Performance

INTRODUCTION

The issues arising when considering implementing decisions and their implications for the business were discussed earlier. In this chapter we address performance expectations and measurement. It is suggested that corporate success is a combination of meeting customer satisfaction criteria and the achievement corporate performance requirements. Figure 13.1 illustrates how these are interrelated. We shall expand the notion suggested by Figure 13.1 by linking customer satisfaction and corporate performance requirements by considering how they share mutual performance measures.

Clearly the process of realising corporate success should aim to achieve customer satisfaction (this has already been established as being the basis of competitive advantage) and meet the expectations of a 'corporate coalition' (the sales and profitability performance expectations of the shareholders, managers, the City, its suppliers and employees). We know that customer satisfaction comprises positive perceptions of a retail offer and purchasing activities. Sustainable competitive advantage is developed when customer perceptions exceed their expectations and those of competitive offers.

Differentiation and competitive advantage have been discussed in the previous chapters. It will be recalled that there are two components of competitive advantage. Customer-led differentiation is where customers' actions suggest that the added value benefits from the company exceed those offered by competitors. Productivity-led differentiation occurs when the utilisation of the company's resources (i.e. the property, labour, inventory, and managerial expertise) is superior to that of competitors. See Figure 13.2 for this perspective. It follows that productivity-led differentiation performance will be demonstrated by a superior return on sales, gross margins, operating margins and cash generation and it is this performance that enables the company to create and maintain a position of relative competitive advantage. To do so requires the company to establish as a priority activity an optimal level of resource allocation, which ensures that both strategic and operational productivity objectives are achieved. The principle of this decision process is described in Figure 13.2. Sustainable competitive advantage can

227

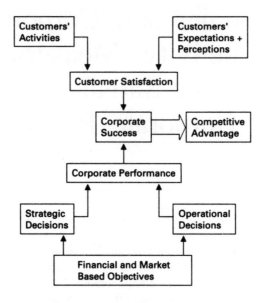

Figure 13.1   Corporate success is achieved when both customer satisfaction and corporate performance are at mutually satisfactory levels

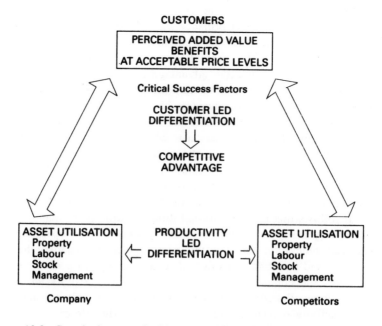

Figure 13.2   Developing sustainable competitive advantage

only be maintained i.e. customer-led differentiation maximised, provided that resource allocation is such that productivity in both the short and long run can support the strategy decisions taken to maintain the position. There are two essential requirements of concern for the company. The offer should contain added value features that provide 'real' benefits and which are a specific response to customer expectations. The second requirement is for cost-effective asset utilisation which follows from selective resource acquisition and allocation to meet the researched customer expectations. Identifying the critical success factors essential to providing customer added value will be influential in achieving cost-effective resource allocation because the process will result in identifying the most effective asset base structure to achieve this.

13.1 PRODUCTIVITY AND RESOURCE ALLOCATION

In essence productivity reflects results as a function of effort, such as the allocation of resources to implement strategy. An increase in productivity implies that more results are obtained for a given amount of effort. '. . . In a classical sense, productivity is defined as a ratio such that the output of an effort under investigation is divided by the inputs (labour, energy and so forth) required to produce the output' (Brinkerhoff and Dressler, 1990). Brinkerhoff and Dressler suggest '. . . There are many particular needs and situations that precipitate productivity measurement efforts. But almost always, the long range purpose is to enhance productivity.' Some of the more frequent applications they report are:

- Identifying productivity declines for 'early warning';
- Comparing productivity across individuals, units, organisations and industry to make management decisions;
- Linking management and labour in productivity improvement efforts to build common awareness and responsibility;
- Demonstrating productivity gains to interested stakeholders;
- Supporting incentive and bonus plans with objective productivity data.

Productivity measurement can be carried out at any level within an organisation. Regardless of the level of analysis the same principles apply: outputs and output quality are measured and are compared (through a numerical ratio) to measured input consumption. However, there is an important fact to consider. As Brinkerhoff and Dressler identify '. . . It is crucial that productivity measurement facilitators recognise the differences amongst the many levels within the organisation . . . and that they recognise the level where they are in fact operating.'

The concept of the 'customer' is integral to productivity measurement.

Customers are the ultimate consumers of a product or service, without customers there is no purpose for the operation to function, let alone measure its productivity! Customers should be identified for two reasons. First, identifying them helps to clarify *which* outputs of a unit are most important and which attributes are important to them, and as such, which should be focussed upon for measurement and productivity improvement. Secondly, quality characteristics (aspects of customer satisfaction) may be identified and from which measurement criteria can be developed. Customer expectations, needs and preferences also form the basis of long term store loyalty thus making it even more crucial that they are identified and measured.

Productivity is of interest to other stakeholders. For example, shareholders and investors generally have an interest in the overall productivity of the company's assets. Employees' interests are focused on their own and the company's performance: often they are paid by their performance output (or at least receive performance related bonuses) and their long term employment prospects are dependent upon the overall productivity of the business.

13.2   CORPORATE PERFORMANCE

We shall first introduce the elements of corporate performance and their indicators. Corporate performance can be viewed as having two components: strategic productivity; the use of resources to achieve long term objectives and to measure overall resource application and operational productivity; the measurement of specific resource allocation of a much shorter time span. Clearly there are areas of overlap such as market performance and operations effectiveness. Figure 13.3 indicates the areas of interest and the topics that are of interest at strategic and operational levels. Specific ratios and indicators are detailed in Figure 13.4.

Strategic Productivity

The long term performance requirements of a business are typically expressed in financial terms. Hence we should concern ourselves with measuring the productivity of key financial parameters. These we suggest as being return on assets (asset productivity), return on sales, and cashflow generated from sales. The 'owners' of the business are interested in its performance as an investment and how its performance compares with competitors and companies in other industry sectors.

The internal concern (that of the board) is with the performance of the business against its objectives, and the ability to undertake one or more of the strategic options available to it and the financial structure that will be 'cost effective' in achieving its objectives. It also suggests that the task of the operating managers is to provide the company with an operating profit

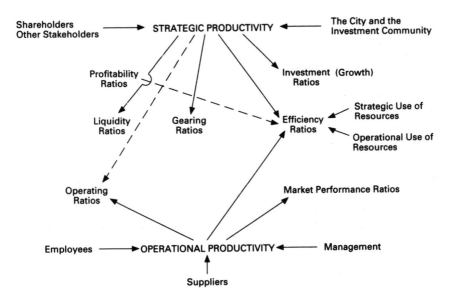

Figure 13.3   Measuring corporate performance

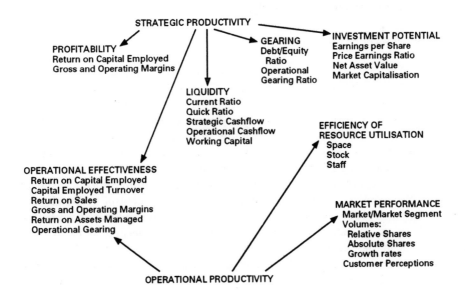

Figure 13.4   Specific measures of strategic and operational productivity

(contribution) which, when compared with the total capital employed (its allocated resources), provides another financial productivity measure.

The four key performance areas which measure the financial productivity of strategic decisions taken by the business are:

- Profitability
- Liquidity
- Gearing
- Investment (Growth)

Of particular importance when monitoring long term performance is the financial structure of the business and the effectiveness of this in generating profits, the return made on investors funds (and the ability to maintain an appropriate level of investment for growth) and the ability to meet the costs of running the business.

Profitability Ratios

Profitability ratios include return on capital employed (a measure of the return earned from investors' funds); gross margin (the indication of how effective the profit earned covers the costs of corporate overheads, branch operations, distribution activities, loan repayment and to create sufficient cash for reinvestment in the business) and net profit (the effectiveness of financial management to finance the business; i.e., its costs of capital) and to minimise the company's tax liability.

Gross Margin Return on Investment

The gross margin measures the efficiency of the buying activity and indicates the amount of initial contribution there is from which to meet operating costs, dividends, taxation and provide a reserve of funds for development purposes. It is also important to consider the effectiveness of inventory as an investment. For all retailers inventory or stock investment is a significant element of their investment in working capital and as such should be monitored on the basis of the 'return' generated.

The concept of measuring a gross margin return on inventory investment was discussed as an effective means of planning and control by Doody and McCammon (1969) and by Sweeny (1973). They suggested that as a retailing business is evaluated in terms of the efficiency in generating profit from investment the return on investment criterion should be extended to the financial performance of individual departments and merchandise assortments.

Just as the notion of a return on investment may be separated into:

$$\text{asset turnover} \times \text{'profit' margin}$$

so too can gross margin return on inventory investment:

$$\frac{\text{gross margin } (\pounds)}{\text{net sales}} \times \frac{\text{net sales}}{\substack{\text{average} \\ \text{inventory} \\ \text{investment}}} = \substack{\text{gross margin (GMROI)} \\ \text{return on inventory} \\ \text{investment}}$$

There are a number of advantages claimed for using GMROI as a perform-ance measure. First, it enables management to relate directly the perform-ance of buying and merchandising activities to the overall performance requirements of the business by establishing merchandise objectives which reflect the company's positioning response to customer expectations (for example, width, depth and availability vary directly with customer expecta-tions for choice and inventory service). Secondly, it follows that this gives an opportunity to link buyers' performance with the investment for which they are responsible and, thirdly GMROI offers the means by which the performance of alternative merchandise profiles may be evaluated. A fourth benefit is that the additional information is available from existing data: it simply requires gross margin and stock turn data, usually available from the information systems of most retailing businesses. The uses to which GMROI may be put are discussed in Walters and White (1989).

Gearing Ratios

Gearing ratios indicate the relationship between loan capital and equity capital. Loan capital represents funds that are lent to the business solely with a view to earn the lenders sufficient return to compensate their loss of use of their funds. Equity capital is the shareholders' funds. While shareholders 'own' the business and can influence its strategic direction, the subscribers of loan capital do not participate in the company's management: their in-terest is in the interest their loan involvement generates. The relationship between debt and equity capital is important. Regardless of how well the business fares, the commitment to loan interest must always be met. Con-versely the shareholders have no such entitlement: the payment of dividends is at the discretion of the board of directors. A further issue concerning the balance between debt and equity funding is the view taken by investors towards the level of debt. Given that loan interest is an ongoing commit-ment lenders may view an increasing level of debt funding with some con-cern and consequently increase interest rates charged to compensate for what they perceive as an increase in risk (i.e. they express some concern over the ability of the company to continue to meet its interest commitments in the context of current trading conditions or, perhaps, they may have doubts concerning the company's senior management).

Operational gearing measures the sensitivity of changes in the levels of turnover and the resultant change in profitability. It is a function of fixed costs, variable costs and profit. At this point it is worth clarifying the term profit. At a corporate level profit may be generated by a number of activities, some of which may be external to the business (e.g. investments in other companies), as well as that produced by the mainstream activity of the business. We shall exclude external earnings from operating or trading profit. Thus operational gearing is a function of operating/trading profit and the relationship between fixed and variable costs, whilst these too will relate to trading assets (fixed and current assets) used in the mainstream activity. Typically companies with high fixed costs have commensurately lower variable costs. Their operational gearing is high and is very sensitive: if turnover decreases the company with high fixed costs becomes unprofitable sooner than one with a lower level. Conversely an expansion of revenues results in relatively higher profitability. Accurate forecasting is beneficial to high fixed cost companies.

Investment Ratios

These are used by investors when appraising the company as a financial investment. Investment ratios are of particular interest within the context of strategic profitability, the first is the price earnings ratio (PER). The PER is calculated by dividing the share price (the middle market price, the average at which shares can be bought or sold on an investor's behalf: the 'bid' and 'offer' prices) by the earnings per share (EPS); this is accepted as the profit attributable to ordinary shareholders divided by the average number of shares in issue during the year. The PER reflects the market's view of the company's growth potential, the risks involved and its dividend policy. The PER depends upon both the company's performance and that of the industry. The level of the market index also influences the value of PERs. In general a high PER suggests either a dynamic company or that the share is overvalued, while a low value clearly suggests the reverse situation. However the PER must be viewed in relationship to the industry and stock market performances. Dividend policy influences the PER: the need to provide both income and capital gain for investors influences and is influenced by the company's dividend policy. The company must also consider the need for funding growth from retained earnings and this influences dividends actually paid out. Industry 'norms' and current prospects are also influential. *Dividend yield* and *cover* are measures of dividend policy implementation.

The *net asset value* (NAV) is an indication of the book value of assets per ordinary share. Clearly the value given is dependent upon the balance sheet values of assets, but it is suggested that it does give some indication of how much the price of the company's shares depends upon the ability of the company to generate profits and how much it is backed by assets. The net asset value is often used in determining the initial or opening bid in an acquisition. *Market capitalisation* of a company is the market price of a company's ordinary share in issue multiplied by the number of shares issued. It is a useful measure of the relative size of companies.

Investment ratios are important measures of strategic productivity inasmuch as they can be used to make comparisons with competitors within and out with the sector. Comparisons made of competitor companies within the sector gives an objective view (the City's view) of the effectiveness of their strategic direction. Comparisons of companies in other sectors offers a view of the returns and the competitor strengths and weaknesses in potential sectors for diversification.

Liquidity Ratios

Retailing is more of a cash business than most other businesses. The added value process in distribution is typically much simpler and much quicker to effect than it is for manufacturers. Consequently it is useful to be able to monitor the effectiveness with which cash is managed within the retail business. This is important from two aspects. The first concerns the payment of suppliers in order to obtain maximum benefit from settlement terms. The other concerns the use that can be made of suppliers' cash to develop the business: retailers operating with core product areas whose stockturns are high do have a level of 'permanent' negative working capital in their financial structures and the aggressive business will use this to develop the business. There are five measures of liquidity of interest:

The *current ratio* is a broad indication of the short-term financial position. It is a comparison of current assets/current liabilities: a generally accepted value of the ratio is 2.00 but this has, in recent years, become about 1.5. In any event the ratio is influenced by a number of factors and should be considered within the context of their influence. For example, the nature of the company's business is very important: for furniture retailers and jewellers, both of whom require to maintain high levels of stocks and typically have low stock turns and often give generous credit terms, the current ratio requires to be higher than average. A retail business operating with very fast moving items, a cash only business and with much of the stock financed by suppliers' working capital would be expected to have a lower value ratio. It is a measure of the ability of the business to meet its operating costs and of its ability to convert short term (current) assets into cash (an investor or creditors view of the business).

The 'quality' of the assets is important. Any merchandise likely to be marked down significantly will influence a view of the current ratio as would the fact that a large loan due for imminent repayment or other, similar debts. Seasonal activities are also an important consideration, where the level of short term borrowing may increase the average level of borrowing during the year. This together with extended supply chains can have a significant effect on the value of the ratio.

Not all assets are readily convertible to cash should the need arise. For some retailers stock either loses its value rapidly (fashion merchandise) or is slow to realise its cash value (furniture, jewellery and some consumer durables). The *quick ratio* recognises this by excluding stock values from current assets, thus the quick ratio (or acid test) is an indication of what would happen if the business was suddenly required to meet its debts. This ratio is usually seen as being 'one' but again the nature of the business has a strong influence and examples of successful and secure businesses can be found where this ratio is less than 0.5; food retailers are typical in this respect.

Any doubts concerning liquidity should prompt an examination of *cashflow* performance. Holmes and Sugden (1992) suggest two measures of cashflow that indicate performance:

> Gross cashflow = depreciation plus profit (after tax)
> plus increase in deferred tax.
> Net cashflow = gross cashflow minus dividends.

We suggest similar measures but modify them. Gross cashflow we suggest is *strategic cashflow* because the element of property, equipment and vehicles, and for large retailers, systems results in an increase in depreciation. The influence this may have on future cashflow projections and potential future ventures should be identified as it could have a significant influence on the level of funding required. We also suggest that *operating cashflow*, cash generating from trading activities is possibly more useful in retailing as it can be used to measure the effectiveness of the management and use of both company and suppliers' short term cash within the business. In this context a useful additional indicator is the reciprocal value of the working capital turnover ratio i.e. working capital/sales which indicates the increase in working capital requirements (and how this may be funded) if the business is expanded. Thus operating cashflow is defined as:

> Profit (for trading period) after tax plus the increase in total working capital (due to the affect of negative working capital).

Operational Productivity

It is the task of the operating managers (buying and merchandising, operations and distribution) to deploy the resources such that operational productivity performance produces the required operating profit from the capital employed. Clearly we can expect to see some overlap between the ratios used to measure productivity at both the strategic and operational levels.

Both efficiency and operating ratios are the concern of the board and of operating management. Their respective interests will become clear as these ratios are discussed. Return to Figures 13.3 and 13.4.

Efficiency Ratios

It is suggested in Figure 13.3 that two aspects of efficiency are important. Senior management, the board, have concern with resource utilisation as an investment and consider the opportunity cost of investing capital in alternative areas within the business and of investment in other businesses. At an operational level management's concern is to maximise the return on resources committed to the business and do so in more detail. Figure 13.3 suggests that both levels of interest do focus on the same resources however, the interest at board level is a more aggregate view and considers the returns that may be earned in other activities. The operating managers' concern is to implement the strategic decisions made by (and together with) the board and to monitor resource performance in detail.

Figure 13.5 identifies three major resource areas, the productivity performance of which is very important at the operating level. The sales, costs and contribution produced (or expended) per unit of resource input of space, stock and staff (employees) are vital data for both planning and control. For planning purposes the sales and operating costs per unit of space and per full-time equivalent employee are the initial inputs into the process which results in evaluating the viability of an expanded business. These data when considered alongside the additional fixed cost facilities that are required will indicate the likely performance that can be expected. The data may also

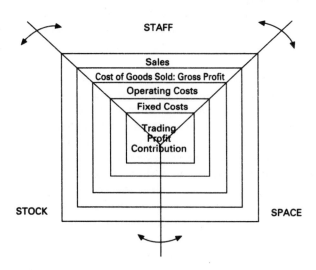

Figure 13.5   Resource utilisation and costs: productivity performance

be very helpful when evaluating repositioning decisions or perhaps entry into an alternative form of retailing. At a corporate level data will be viewed as an aggregate, however the operational management group will seek data in considerable detail.

Space productivity should be considered from a number of aspects. Departmental space performance will differ markedly, sales in core product merchandise will be expected to outperform sales of 'service' merchandise which is held primarily to promote choice and give credibility to the range assortment. The in-store location has a significant impact on space productivity. Stores operating multiple floors usually find wide variations in sales and contribution of space. Typically ground floor space will outperform space on floors above the entry point, furthermore selling space located some distance away from an entry point or an escalator or elevator access will show lower sales and contribution per unit of space. Thus for operational purposes management should be very clear how it intends using space productivity data and from this structure the collection and dissemination of information.

Employee productivity has its own set of problems. The usual method is to measure sales and contribution on a full time equivalent (FTE) basis but this can be misleading because of the range of tasks and remuneration rates that obtain. It is important to identify levels of activity and responsibility among employees and structure productivity measures by role or task. Therefore while we may find an overall sales or contribution per employee figure useful when comparing stores it is not too revealing when activities are substituted for turnover. For example, it is more useful to know cases merchandised per employee hour, or perhaps items scanned per hour, customer enquiries handled per day. Given activity rates together with wage rates a more significant productivity performance profile will emerge and will facilitate more selective decision making when productivity improvements are being sought.

The size of the store and its merchandise mix may influence employee productivity. This can occur in a number of ways and may have positive or negative affects. For example, it is often necessary to use handling equipment in large volume throughput stores and this should enhance employee productivity. Different merchandise ranges may introduce characteristics that facilitate merchandise handling and as a consequence employee productivity would appear to be greater (e.g. a shift of emphasis towards unit packed hardware and aggregates (sand, cement, etc.).

Stockholding is the third resource featured in Figure 13.5. Stockturn is a familiar productivity measure for distribution companies as is its reciprocal – stock cover. The well managed business maintains sufficient stock to meet customer expectations for variety and availability but is cognizant of the penalties of carrying too much stock. Thus with customer satisfaction in mind the task should be to minimise stockholding in order to minimise interest charges, reduce storage space requirements and reduce the mark-downs that result from obsolescent (or obsolete) stock. The performance measures used typically report stockturn, i.e., the sales or cost of goods sold divided by average stock-holding or the stock cover, the number of days stock to meet average sales.

As with employee productivity some refinement of the average value should be considered. For example, stock productivity of core merchandise, which can account for some 40% to 60% of the total revenue and profit, should have specific attention, as should merchandise at the other end of the spectrum. Slow moving 'service' merchandise items, typically in the range to expand the choice offer and give credibility, should be reviewed against dif-ferent criteria. Whereas core merchandise stockturn is monitored to ensure that its levels are optimised within the requirements for customer availability and variety with an emphasis on providing customer satisfaction, 'service' merchandise should be evaluated more upon what it contributes to maintaining customer perceptions. In other words, we should be evaluating 'service' merchandise with a view to assessing its contribution to the customer perception/customer expectation objectives more than its financial performance.

There are other factors which also influence stockholding performance; space is one consideration. Superstore type operations e.g. food and DIY have extensive ranges, some of which are excessive within the context of maximising stockholding productivity. This occurs because of the competitive requirements of choice and to some extent availability. Productivity measures should ideally identify the cost-effectiveness of stockholding between and within merchandise groups. Another factor to be considered is the influence on stockholding of promotional activities. Coordination between promotional event timing and stock availability is essential, particularly when the merchandise offer features manufacturers' brands price marked for a time based offer. Unless the merchandise is available at the appropriate time full benefits of the promotion are missed and result in loss of full margin sales after the event. Often for non-price promotions there is a surplus of stock remaining which lends to reduce the stockturn of the merchandise item or group for such time as it takes to sell through. While the situation can be brought back into balance it can be an expensive disruption.

Operating Ratios
Earlier we considered the importance of ratios that indicate the effectiveness of management in generating returns on sales and investment in the business. These it will be recalled were ROCE (return on capital employed), gross profit (gross margin). While they are considered to be primary indicators of profitability they do suggest much about how the business is managed at an operating level.

Growth in ROCE should be examined for indications of the impact of incremental investment. A well managed business would be expected to show a higher incremental return on additional capital inputs, due to economies of scale effects (discussed in Chapter 6). Failure to do so should raise questions concerning the effectiveness of the company's management. For example, food retailers and DIY operators have expanded the number of outlets at a rapid rate in recent years. Clearly we would expect new outlets to take some time to reach an optimal level of sales, however, if an analysis of incremental ROCE shows no significant effect (or perhaps even shows decline), questions should be asked concerning the potential for growth of the business, the wisdom of the incremental investment, the effectiveness of the management implementing the strategy supporting the investment, or perhaps a review of all three topics.

Profit margin on sales ratios should also be considered within the context of operating profit if this differs from the company's total profit. The total profit may include a number of items outwith the control of the management group responsible for implementing strategy and consequently does not reflect their managerial effectiveness. Both the gross margin and the operating margin are important ratios because when viewed as a trend they indicate a number of important performance aspects of the business. Gross margin indicates the effectiveness of buying from two aspects. One is the effectiveness of the buying/merchandising group in its selection of merchandise: a steady rate of growth with few mark-downs suggests that the group understands its target market and is buying appropriately for their needs. Constant margin performance may also suggest that pricing is relevant to the market place and achieves volume objectives. Constant or increasing gross margin would suggest that range width and depth are balanced and this would be supported by both the level of mark-downs and the stockturn performance. Further indication would be given by the trend in distribution costs and performance. A similar argument may be made for operating margins. Changes would suggest shifts in productivity performance of labour, space, distribution service and stockholding (availability levels).

The ratio of sales turnover to capital employed in trading is another useful operating ratio. An increase in performance is shown by an improvement in the sales/capital employed ratio but the improvement may be attributable to a declining capital base (as would occur if it was not renewed and depreciation steadily devalued the capital). A rapid increase in the value of the ratio may indicate that the company is attempting to do too much business with the capital base it has.

Holmes and Sugden suggest an interesting combination of ratios:

$$\frac{\text{Operating profit}}{\text{Sales}} \times \frac{\text{Sales}}{\substack{\text{Capital Employed} \\ \text{in Trading} \\ \text{Operations}}} = \frac{\text{Operating profit}}{\substack{\text{Capital Employed} \\ \text{in Trading} \\ \text{Operations}}}$$

This is useful in identifying options for management to increase operating profit in relation to capital employed:

- Increasing the first factor, the profit margins by:
  reducing costs, or;
  raising prices.
- Increasing the second factor, higher output per £ capital employed by:
  increasing sales volume
  reducing capital employed.

Another worthwhile ratio to consider which offers another perspective is the operating profit (profit generated by the business) from the trading assets or assets managed (the assets totally deployed within the business). This ratio will identify differences between operating profit/capital employed in trading operations and the assets managed by the business. The advantage this offers is that ROAM (return on assets managed) can be disaggregated and be used as a measure of performance for different parts of the business and at different levels of responsibility within the business.

The board would take a strategic view of these ratios and would look for long term indicators and implications that would influence their decisions to expand, contract or perhaps maintain the investment level in the business. Operating management would take a much shorter term view, they would be concerned with budgeted performance levels and the overall impact of over/under achievement of the planning periods objectives.

Given that the credit card companies and other service companies have reduced the importance of credit financing and bad debts for retailers it remains a cost of doing business. However the collection period should be monitored by retailing companies to measure the effectiveness of credit in generating customer sales and perception responses. The collection period calculation remains the same regardless of who actually collects the customer debts.

Use of credit allowed by suppliers is a useful measure of operating activities. This can be measured by expressing trade creditors as a percentage of sales or by multiplying trade creditors (divided by sales) by 365 to obtain a value in days credit taken. An alternative ratio is to calculate the percentage of trade creditors/stocks to see what proportion of the stocks is financed by suppliers. Again the nature of the business has an important influence. Food retailers may well exceed 100% while jewellers and furniture retailers would be well below the 100% level.

An additional measure to identify the extent of capital used in financing operations may be calculated by the relationship: working capital/sales. Different retailing activities result in different values. Food retailers typically have low, even negative values, with higher values for furniture, durables and jewellers etc. An interesting comparison may be made between this ratio and trading profit to sales to see whether increased sales are generating sufficient extra profit to provide the additional working capital required.

13.3 MARKET AND CUSTOMER PERFORMANCE

Market Performance Ratios

While overall market share is important it is not a particularly meaningful measure for some markets. For example, the apparel markets are highly segmented such that some are completely unrelated to each other and information concerning levels of activity are of interest only and as such do not add very much to effective decision making. It follows that market segment activities are of interest and market data detailing competitors' activities and specifically that giving relative market segment shares and relative growth rates should be sought.

However, even within market segments care should be taken to ensure that detailed, specific data is not overlooked. Returning to the apparel example, it is useful to identify how the information should be collected. For example, product categories may be more important for retailers who have specialist merchandise ranges such as leisure wear or perhaps who concentrate on specific price point segments.

Data that would provide a basis for assessing actual and potential market performance should include:

* Market overall size Growth
* Market segment sizes rates
* Major competitors:
   trends   market $\left\{ \begin{array}{l} \text{Size} \\ \text{shares and} \end{array} \right.$
                  segments
* Margins:
   market   Gross and $\left\{ \begin{array}{l} \text{Market, segment,} \\ \text{Major competitors: trends} \end{array} \right.$
   segments   Operating
* Customer expectations
   and preferences: Market and $\left\{ \begin{array}{l} \text{Primary and} \\ \text{secondary} \\ \text{characteristics} \end{array} \right.$
   relative perceptions market
   of competitive   segments
   'retail offers'.
* Product range   Market and   Major competitors
   coverage   Market segments
* Pricing leadership Price trends
* Seasonality of   Markets and $\left\{ \begin{array}{l} \text{Proportion of annual} \\ \text{turnover occurring} \\ \text{in any one season.} \end{array} \right.$
   business   market segments:
                number of
                seasons.

* Selling space: actual available and distribution: sales and contribution per unit of space; cost of space.	Market and market segments:	{ Major competitors: by location; geographical; shopping location (malls, high street – primary and secondary)
* Supply structure: suppliers/customers	Market and Market segments	{ Numbers and proportion of business supplied.
* Promotional expenditures	Market and Market segments: Major competitors	{ Amounts spent by media type. Promotional spend (below the line)
* Market positioning	Major competitors: Market and Market segments	{ Customer perceptions Supplier perceptions Company perceptions.

Most of this data is collected and used by retailing companies. However some topics may require amplification. *Product range coverage* is of particular interest to a business which is contemplating market entry. It indicates not only the customer expectations but also the nature and extent of the investment required for serious competitors. Similarly with *pricing leadership*: a knowledge of relative prices, volumes and gross and operating margins provides another indication of the nature of competition and performance. *Supply structure* data, when compared with margins generated, provides an indication of the role and influence of suppliers within the overall market and within segments. Information of this nature can be very useful when used in conjunction with data describing customer preferences to identify opportunities for retail brands and labels. Relative *market positioning* as perceived by company management, supplier and customers has obvious benefits. Not only can this information clarify the competitive dimensions of a market segment but it can also identify major strengths and weaknesses as perceived by suppliers and customers. The nature of characteristics by which market segments are defined should be re-emphasised: shopping missions, price sensivity, product categories, end use applications, delivery method may have quite separate importance issues. It is important that this issue is clarified and data collection based upon such characteristics rather than on traditional segmentation dimensions.

13.4 CUSTOMER SATISFACTION PERFORMANCE

Two aspects of customer satisfaction performance were suggested as important in Figure 13.1. These are customers' activities and customers' expectations.

We have discussed customer performance earlier, the chapters devoted to understanding the customer (Chapters 9 and 10) described how shopping mission typology provides a basis for identifying and forecasting customer purchasing activities and their expectations for merchandise, customer service and store environment characteristics. It is useful to consider how the two may be combined, and how the information generated might prove useful.

In the previous chapter we considered how customer purchasing is likely to vary by shopping mission. It will be recalled that average transaction, the number of items and range purchased is likely to vary by shopping mission. Similarly the ratio of browsing/purchasing visits will vary by mission. This information is particularly useful when considering strategy implementation decisions. It has two uses: it can be used to forecast revenues and contribution and it can also be useful in planning the offer characteristics (i.e. merchandise etc.) and the likely operating costs and resulting margins.

Clearly the following relationship obtains for any retailing situation or shopping mission type:

$$\text{Revenue} = f \begin{bmatrix} \text{Total} & \text{Purchasing Visits} & \text{Purchase} \\ \text{number of} & 25\% \text{ of} & \text{characteristics,} \\ \text{customers;} & \text{total visits} & \text{size and value} \end{bmatrix}$$

or

$$\text{Revenue} = \text{Customer Visits} \times \text{Customer Spend}$$

This follows from the earlier discussion concerning shopping missions that total revenue generated is a function of the proportion of total customer visits resulting in a purchase being made and the nature of the purchase (i.e. the items purchased and their value – the average transaction).

It also follows that profitability is a function of the costs of operations required to service the customers' expectations. This can be expressed as:

$$\begin{array}{ccccc}
& & & & \text{Range of} \\
& & & & \text{customer} \\
& & & & \text{services} \\
& & & & \text{offered} \\
& & & & \downarrow \\
\text{Contribution} = f\,[\text{Revenue;} & \text{COGS;} & \text{Occupancy costs;} & \text{Staff costs}] \\
& \uparrow & \uparrow & \\
& \text{Merchandise} & \text{Store Environment} \\
& \text{Characteristics} & \text{Visual merchandising} \\
& \text{and dimensions} & \text{service facilities)}
\end{array}$$

It also follows that revenue and contribution are a function of customer expectations and perceptions. A customer in a distress purchase shopping mission is expecting to find the one or two items required and is unlikely to be concerned or influenced by other factors. Therefore we can be confident in the assumption that revenue and contribution will be primarily a function of customer expectations, and subsequent to the visit their perceptions.

The decisions required by a firm contemplating a market entry (or repositioning) are described by Figure 13.6. Sales generation is clearly a function of customer satisfaction which itself is measured by customer purchasing activities and expectations (and subsequent perceptions). These influence the decisions by management which result in the extent of the differentiation of the business. Each shopping mission will have requirements for elements of both merchandise and service differentiation. The successful business is that which uses its resources to ensure that customer perceptions exceed expectations and this is measured by customer transaction performance and customer perceptions as monitored by tracking studies.

Customer satisfaction performance should therefore be measured by:

Customer purchasing activities:

Number of browsing visits	Average for
Number of purchasing visits	total customer base
Average transaction per visit	Specific data for
Range of items purchased	Target customer groups
Number of items purchased	

Figure 13.6 Customer satisfaction and related decisions

Customer perceptions (extent to which expectations are met)

- Merchandise characteristics
- Merchandise augmentation
- (Merchandise density levels)
- Visual merchandising
- Service augmentation
- Service density
- Service intensity

The expectations of customers should be monitored prior to implementing a decision either to enter a market or to reposition the existing offer. Ongoing performance may be monitored by regular tracking study research.

SUMMARY

This chapter has considered the issues of performance monitoring. It has considered both company and customer performance as productivity issues that are essential inputs into a successful business.

Corporate productivity has been discussed within two dimensions: the need to be strategically perspective as well as managing the current business. A series of inter-related performance measures have been suggested as being useful. Corporate performance also includes market based issues and these were identified and discussed.

Customer satisfaction performance was suggested as a combination of what customers do, their purchasing behaviour and the extent to which their expectations are realised; it is assumed that satisfaction in this dimension is maximised if their perceptions exceed their expectations.

Part III

Managing the Business to Achieve Results

INTRODUCTION

To manage effectively requires a clear understanding of both customer and corporate satisfaction requirements. Part III works on the premise that corporate success is achieved when both customer satisfaction and corporate performance operate at mutually satisfactory levels. To do this requires performance criteria and measures for both customer and corporate performance are the first task.

Changes to strategic direction of a company usually occur because of dissatisfaction with the growth potential offered by current activities. It is not unusual, in fact it has come to be expected, that the character and nature of customer expectations and their store visiting and purchasing behaviour will differ as and when the strategic alternatives change. Thus the shopping missions dominant in one type of business may well be insignificant in another. It follows that the implications for merchandise, store environment, customer service and customer communications decisions will differ and require evaluation prior to resource allocation decisions being made.

Having made necessary decisions to allocate resources their implementation requires a coordinated and integrated management activity. Furthermore the shopping missions may change bringing with them changes in customer expectations. As this occurs there will be a need to review critical success factors. Allocating resources and perhaps considering the changes required to the planned strategy has implications for the implementation activities.

14 Key Decision Areas: Objectives, Strategy Options and the Role of Shopping Missions

INTRODUCTION

In this chapter we consider the interrelationships between corporate objectives, corporate strategy options and customer shopping missions. A company considering a change in its strategic direction usually does so because it is dissatisfied with the growth potential offered by its current activities. However, the expansion of the 1980s and the contraction of the early 1990s suggests that a thorough evaluation of alternatives prior to implementing them may prevent subsequent poor performances.

It is not unusual, in fact it should be expected, to find the character and nature of customer expectations' store visiting and purchasing behaviour to differ as and when the strategic alternatives or opportunities change. Thus the shopping missions which are prevalent in one type of business may be almost insignificant in another. Furthermore, the characteristics of the purchases made may differ considerably. For example, consider two types of businesses, both in food retailing; a superstore multiple and a convenience store multiple. The majority of superstore customers are likely to make regular planned visits or shopping missions, possibly weekly, making large volume purchases. By contrast the convenience store customer will mostly make distress purchasing visits. Purchase volumes will be small in both transaction size and items and more likely than not they will be unplanned (see Table 14.1).

There are some obvious implications for merchandise, store environment, customer service and even communications. We might also expect that the profile of the sales generated to differ between the store types, as will the profile of costs as resource allocation is planned to meet customer expectations. It follows that corporate expectations of performance may require some important re-considerations.

The performance differences may not at first appear too obvious. For example, the cost of handling transactions is unlikely to differ markedly between the multiple superstore and the multiple convenience store. It is likely that both will use scanning linked to automatic cash tills, therefore the labour requirement and throughput of customers (productivity) will be

249

Table 14.1   Shopping missions: typical characteristics

Shopping Mission	Browsing Visit Frequency	Purchasing Visit Frequency	Average Transaction Value	Items Purchased	Range of Items Purchased
Destination Purchase	Low	High	Low/ Medium/ High	Low	Low
Planned Regular Purchasing Visit	Low	High	Low/ Medium/ High	Low/ Medium/ High	Low/ Medium/ High
Planned Comparison Shopping	High	Low	Low	Low	Low
Planned Browsing Visit	High	Low	Low	Low	Low
Impulse Purchase	Low	Low	Low	Low	Low
Distress Purchase	Low	Low	Low	Low/ Medium	Low/ Medium

much the same. But the difference that will occur will be the size of the cash transaction, clearly the number of items processed will have an influence but it is unlikely that the average cost per transaction activity will differ markedly. Thus it should not be surprising for management to find that the revenue, cost and profit profile of the two operations activities may differ considerably, furthermore the number of transactions required to achieve a specific level of profit will clearly differ considerably.

There will be other differences to be reconciled. Research has shown that the identification with a retailing business by management and employees is much stronger for companies with a high profile, up-market positioning which satisfies their status and self-image aspirations. As a result there is more visual effort and enthusiasm which supports the promotional effort of a business by management and employees who are pleased to be seen using the store and its merchandise. It follows that there is far less association between staff of less attractive businesses. Both may be profitable businesses and meeting planned objectives but the identification with the business does not occur. This could prove to be an important motivational issue for new businesses which involve positioning responses with which staff have little or no empathy.

There is also the issue of critical success factors. Earlier when these were discussed in Chapter 1, it was suggested that critical success factors were characteristics that were seen as essential to successful operations. They may be effective merchandise/buying activities capable of meeting customer preferences for variety and exclusivity, e.g. quick response distribution systems with a cost-effective facility for maintaining high levels of availability of selected merchandise ranges. What is to be considered during the evaluation of business development alternatives is the requirement that may evolve for investment in facilities offering quite different capabilities and capacities. These may involve organisational functions as well as operations and operational effectiveness. Both merchandise and service differentiation may be given significantly different emphasis in an alternative development direction.

It will be recalled that in Chapter 1 we suggested that before a decision was taken concerning implementation a series of questions concerning 'fit' were considered. It will be useful to return to these and examine their relevance as the topics within this chapter are discussed. This chapter continues by considering the implications for sales generation, gross margins, operating (trading) margins, operating and strategic cashflow and for profitability.

14.1 ISSUES FOR SALES GENERATION DECISIONS

Chapter 2 introduced a wide range of topics relating to the alternative methods of creating sales revenue. We assume here that these apply in the process of implementing strategies or changing strategic direction. However we are now interested in considering these more from the impact that they may have on shopping mission activities and expectations. For example, a strategy which results in a range of shopping missions within which browsing and comparison shopping are dominant has implications for the way in which the response is characterised by strong visual merchandising which 'demonstrates' the merchandise effectively. This suggests that prior to deciding upon which strategy to pursue, the shopping missions which will dominate should be identified and the implications considered for the positioning response and its attributes.

There are some businesses which are characterised by high customer throughput but with low average rates of transactions. Often this is the reality of that type of business and a new entrant may find it difficult (and expensive) to attempt to influence customer behaviour such that they spend more time in the store and consequently more money. The strategy that is more likely to be successful is one which identifies related purchase items that have similar customer appeal and which would be purchased on impulse. An example may be the distress shopping mission for staple food items, where other staple items (also likely to have been forgotten) are included in the assortment. Low value impulse items not necessarily distress items, may prove successful, particularly gift or treat merchandise categories.

Sales Volume and Shopping Missions

It follows that a knowledge of the range of customers' shopping missions, and which is the most dominant, is helpful in deciding the composition of sales revenue. It is a useful input for planning and controlling an existing business, but is essential when evaluating alternative sectors. Table 14.2 suggests characteristics of typical shopping missions together with the implications for attributes within the positioning response.

The characteristics of average transaction values, items and ranges purchased will clearly vary by type of offer. Destination purchases for specialist merchandise could clearly be for low value items, but may be very frequent. By contrast a destination purchase for a consumer durable will be much higher value but with a very much lower visit frequency. Merchandise augmentation may expand the range of purchases and the transaction value for both. Similarly for planned regular purchasing visits, a regular weekly food shopping visit will vary with family size, but probably vary little by visit once established as a 'planned regular' shopping mission. Distress purchases, by definition, will be characterised by low visit frequencies. The purchase value will vary with the nature of the distress. An emergency during meal preparation may involve a transaction valued below one pound. A DIY emergency requiring extra supplies of decorating materials could be a much higher value.

Table 14.2 Shopping missions: issues for sales volumes generation

Shopping Mission	Browsing Visit Frequency	Purchasing Visit Frequency	Average Transaction Value	Items Purchased	Range of Items Purchased	Attributes which may Improve Sales Volume
Destination Purchase	Low	High	Low/ Medium/ High	Low	Low	Merchandise: Availability and Augmentation Service: Information
Planned Regular Purchasing Visit	Low	High	Low/ Medium/ High	Low/ Medium/ High	Low/ Medium/ High	Merchandise: Core range availability
Planned Comparison Shopping	High	Low	Low	Low	Low	Merchandise: Choice, Availability and Augmentation Visual Merchandising
Planned Browsing Visit	High	Low	Low	Low	Low	Customer Communications Service Facilities: Childcare, etc.
Impulse Purchase	Low	Low	Low	Low	Low	Visual Merchandising Merchandise: Choice and Availability
Distress Purchase	Low	Low	Low	Low/ Medium	Low/ Medium	Merchandise: Core range availability Service: Extended hours.

Sales increases can be obtained by increasing the number of outlets, i.e. growth through replication. However, there are some potential problems. While an apparent sales increase often occurs, the real value may be reduced by a number of factors. The increase may be accompanied by decreases from nearby stores, achieved only at increased costs of promotion and possibly infrastructure costs (longer opening hours, etc.) or perhaps only results in a redistribution of sales.

The importance of core merchandise groups should not be overlooked. They can be an important consideration in creating credibility among customers, who may reject the 'offer' if merchandise they consider essential is not featured. Competitive advantage may be realised by the creative introduction of innovative merchandise. This usually implies an element of exclusivity which further implies high price premiums and requires high sell through rates. Competitive advantage may also be established by identifying 'segment peripherals', customers who would become regular purchasers if small adjustments were made to the range. This may prove to be relatively simple and inexpensive to achieve such as offering more choice or perhaps addressing the need for greater convenience or possibly augmentation within some elements of the range.

The combined roles of customer database management and customer communications are often overlooked. The increasing sophistication of both activities has led to an increased success of 'off the page' sales and the 'specialogue'. Both have benefited from the improved profiling of customer purchasing behaviour; catchment location and analysis and buying patterns, research to identify merchandise and service preferences. Companies with experience in this market are achieving an increasingly higher sell through rate, higher margin performance and notable growth.

Consumers' attitudes to pricing can differ considerably between segments and between shopping missions. It is not surprising to learn that price sensitivity is low for distress purchasing shopping missions but can be very high for comparison shopping missions. Furthermore there is research (see Styler and Walters, 1991) suggesting that low prices are not necessarily essential, rather there is a price band within which the consumer is satisfied that value (price/quantity, price/quality, etc.) is obtained.

Local marketing (or assortment ranging to meet local demand characteristics) has implications for both sales and margin management. Clearly the more representative to local demand requirements the merchandise range can be made, the greater the sales response will be. However, there are a number of factors to be considered. The first concerns information. To be able to meet the local characteristics requires initial research to determine what the assortment should contain and the specific characteristics concerning choice, availability, quality etc. Once in place it then requires close and frequent monitoring because if the local demand varies considerably and if local marketing is an essential feature of the new strategy the costs of stockholding and distribution servicing may prove to be considerably higher.

A second consideration is that of management style. To be effective local marketing requires devolved responsibility. Local management should be able to adjust replenishment orders (not simply volumes but additions and deletions) if the strategy is to be effective in terms of customer satisfaction and profitability. The information base is available to both 'automate' and 'inform'. It has to be used to 'empower'. It follows that accountability and responsibility should be linked to motivate performance through an appropriate incentive scheme. This requires management to undertake a very thorough review of management structure and style.

14.2 GROSS MARGIN DECISIONS AND MANAGEMENT

Consistently high gross margins are attractive and very often are a dominant factor in the decision to enter a new market. However a number of issues characterise margin mix performance and possibly it is the intimate knowledge of customer preferences and expectations, together with that of their relative importances between merchandise characteristics and areas where compromise can occur. It follows that the margins currently being achieved within a market may not be easily realised, they are achieved only after considerable expertise has been established together with the assimilation of a considerable amount of customer data.

However, low overall margins do not necessarily suggest a segment or sector norm. It could indicate the reverse, that an opportunity exists for a competitor who is able and prepared to profile customer expectations and to provide an offer which meets these needs. It may also be that customer expectations for choice and availability will differ across the assortment: core range merchandise differing from 'service' items. Clearly some elements of an assortment can be rationalised and improve margin performance without diluting customer satisfaction.

The most important issue for gross margin management concerns the margin mix and the control that can be exercised in maximising its value. For example, many merchandise ranges are too wide. It may be (mistakenly) considered that either customer service or range credibility are dependent upon an extensive range of variety whereas one or other are more a function of immediate availability of a core range of items. The range of colours in paint in DIY stores is an example. It was once a feature of the offers of small and large stores alike that a wide range of colours, sizes and paint finishes was seen as essential. The DIY multiples soon identified those which accounted for the bulk of their sales and adjusted their assortment such that the margins were increased by improved availability of core items and reduced stockholding (and therefore costs) of 'service' colours and sizes.

More recently the ability to blend colours on site has increased the choice to the customer, reduced stock-holding costs and increased the margin yield.

Store (retailer) brands have been important in increasing gross margin performance. They have three main characteristics. Typically they are used as same quality/lower price products within merchandise groups where consumers are found to have no strong loyalty towards manufacturer brands or where the product is a 'commodity' item. They also have an important role in differentiating the assortment and the retail business, and in this role they may have no direct competition from manufacturer brands (for example, the Marks & Spencer recipe convenience food range) and thereby offer the retailer more freedom on pricing. A third characteristic, one which is becoming increasingly less important, is to provide lower priced versions of high volume items. Consumer purchasing expectations have shifted towards quality and away from quantity in recent years due largely to the efforts of the major multiples. However, it is interesting to observe the increased activity of continental food discount operations in the United Kingdom (1992–93). This may be due to a shift in consumer expectations brought about by prolonged effects of a recessionary climate.

The relationship between target and realised margins and pricing is an interesting issue to be evaluated before deciding upon a specific strategy to penetrate a new sector. Many sectors, such as ladieswear, have much lower 'sell through' rates than other sectors, food being an obvious example. As a result many operate a progressive mark-down policy whereby prices are reduced regularly the longer the item (garment) remains unsold. Consequently they plan for this and expect a range of margin performance across the assortment based upon experience of previous sales patterns. In these situations it is also important to accept that after a period of time it is unlikely that the item will sell as regular merchandise and should be disposed of through channels handling these types of merchandise: anonymity is essential.

Concessions are an alternative which many retail companies use to offer customer variety *and* to optimise margins. Typically products which require both width and depth to give customers choice and availability (and fashion or style) will have high stockholding costs and low stockturns. The concession company has a different costs profile to the 'store buy'. Stockholding can be centralised such that very slow moving merchandise may be transferred quickly to meet a sale but more importantly the volume/margin equation is very much different. Whereas the store buy is often a very low order value, the specialist can purchase at much more attractive terms. It follows that if well managed, concessions can benefit concessionaire, host retailer and the customer.

Supplier relationships are important in a discussion concerning margin performance. By optimising the number of suppliers the overall margins achieved across the assortment can be improved. (This was discussed in

Chapter 3.) Here we are considering the topic from the point of view of a potential entrant into a new sector and the first question to be asked should concern why there is the actual number of suppliers active within the product group. Clearly margin performance can always be improved by reducing the number of suppliers but this may have the effect of reducing customer satisfaction. It is quite possible that the reason for what at first seems to be an excessive number of suppliers may well be to do with sourcing specialisation to achieve exclusivity and variety. An over-zealous new entrant may overlook these vital components of customer expectations, rationalise the number of suppliers and reduce the sales and gross profit because of the impact on customer satisfaction.

The use of information within the supply chain is becoming a favoured means by which stock levels may be controlled in aggregate terms and for local availability effectiveness. A new entrant should look for opportunity to use information effectively in this way and thereby create competitive advantage. For example, EPOS output shared with suppliers can reduce production and distribution costs by ensuring *relevant* quantities and varieties throughout the retailers branches: costs and customer satisfaction may in this way both be improved.

It has been found that working with suppliers such that their strengths are developed and their weaknesses eliminated is an effective strategy. It follows that prior to implementing growth repositioning or diversification strategies the potential for vertical coordination (as opposed to vertical integration should be investigated). It also follows that this approach to supplier/distributor relationships should be an integral part of any existing buying/merchandising activity if gross margins are to be maximised. The need to establish mutually acceptable 'controls' for suppliers' merchandise and distribution service should not need to be discussed; however it has been the case on many occasions that gross margin performance has been improved considerably by introducing essential controls to manage the consistency of quality, reliability and availability of supplier distribution services.

Finally there is the issue of product augmentation. Not only can the overall value of a customer transaction be increased by including related merchandise items in product group merchandise ranges and visual merchandising but so too can the overall gross margins. Often the margins on 'accessories' are higher than those of the primary product group and the selling effort required to increase the size of the purchase often by a proportionally small amount, is not major. Clearly research should be considered to determine the extent to which customers' own budgets, and therefore, purchasing elasticities are expandable at the time of purchase. Essentially we are considering the addition of an element of impulse purchasing to a destination or planned purchase shopping mission, which by definition may have a budget constraint.

Gross Margins and Shopping Missions

Shopping missions clearly have an impact on gross margin performance levels. Table 14.3 suggests some possibilities for increasing gross margins.

Destination purchases are unlikely to be influenced by price once the decision to purchase has been made. If gross margins are to be increased it is likely that this will only occur if a related purchase is suggested to the customer. The use of visual merchandising to propose additional expenditure on accessories (and other products and product-services) may achieve this. Regular purchasing shopping missions typically have average transaction values and consequently margins can be expected to be close to those planned. Examples of planned regular purchasing missions would include the weekly bulk food purchasing visit to a superstore and perhaps the beginning of term visit to buy school clothes. Price is usually not the most important feature, convenience and availability usually rank above price with perhaps choice also important and of more importance than price depending much upon the merchandise.

Improvements to the margin mix may be achieved by introducing new products and new ranges, thereby encouraging innovatary spending among the target customer group. The convenience motive may be extended into the products purchased by including convenience based products which add value for the customer and increase the gross margins of the product group. Concessions may prove cost-effective as will 'local marketing' based ranges. Planned comparison and browsing shopping missions typically include an element of price comparison which inevitably implies price competition. To this end it is hardly surprising to find that customers will, having identified the product they require, extend the exercise into price comparison. Both missions may find that gross margins may be enhanced by product and service augmentation which offer added value and perhaps an increase in range width to offer more choice to the customers pursuing these shopping missions.

Impulse purchasing shopping missions should achieve planned gross margins. By definition these purchases are not influenced by a range of criteria but rather occur because of the attraction of the merchandise. It is likely that margin targets may be enhanced by expanding the range of items offered. However, care should be exercised in this respect because of the low probability of impulse purchases compared with the higher probabilities seen with planned purchasing. Distress purchases may be argued in a similar manner. Price insensitivity may be extended on some essential items, thereby achieving higher gross margins. Some product augmentation, particularly in DIY product ranges may increase both transaction values and gross margins.

Table 14.3 Shopping missions: issues for gross margin management

	Average Transaction Value	Items Purchased	Range of Items Purchased	Realised Gross Margin Performance	Attributes which may Improve Gross Margins
Destination Purchase	Low/Medium	Low	Low	Planned Gross Margin	Visual merchandising: Product Augmentation
Planned Regular Purchasing Visit	Low/Medium/High	Low/Medium/High	Low/Medium/High	Planned Gross Margin	Product development: New products and New Ranges
Planned Comparison Shopping	Low	Low	Low	Lower than Target Gross Margin	Product Augmentation and Service Augmentation to provide Added Value
Planned Browsing Visit	Low	Low	Low	Lower than Target Gross Margin	As above plus emphasis on assortment width where appropriate
Impulse Purchase	Low	Low	Low	Planned Gross Margin	Extend impulse item focus on children and others in group
Distress Purchase	Low	Low/Medium	Low/Medium	Planned Gross Margin	Extend price insensitivity and product range

14.3   MANAGING OPERATING (TRADING) MARGINS

There has been a tendency over recent years to use the benefits of point of sale data capture to manage the retail business more closely from the centre. The extent to which this is effective is being questioned. Clearly the view that the branch operation is a tightly controlled cost centre has attraction when overall margins are small and stringent cost controls are seen as one (often the only) method of ensuring rigid operational control of an organisation comprising well over 200 branches. However, some businesses do not respond to this approach, requiring branch managers to be creative or entrepreneurial in their roles simply because the merchandise has a fashion element or perhaps requires a strong local appeal both of which may only be effective at a local level.

An attractive opportunity in a new market sector may require considerable analysis for a business whose philosophy is one in which they have been very successful either pursuing the cost centre management approach (or have viewed branches as profit centres). It is possible that the culture of the organisation may be such that it cannot cope with the two philosophies operating together, worse still it may attempt to impose one management style across the business. Acquisitions or business startups in new sectors may well be subjected to an inappropriate style of management, only to find subsequently that the business suffers either because it lacks flexibility of response and cannot pursue profitable local opportunities or has too much flexibility and over-responds. Either way it is certain that the margin performance will be less than optimal. It follows that at the evaluation stage, prior to implementation, consistency and capability are two features of the organisation structure and of management style that are essential precursors to the implementation of a growth or diversification strategy.

An issue often overlooked by retailers when deciding to expand their branch operations is the availability, at acceptable hourly rates, of staff who are suitable in terms of number and also quality. Often sites that appear to be 'ideal' from a market potential view often, during the development stage (by which time the commitment has been made) do have cost problems as it discovered that sufficient staff are unavailable at the budgeted labour rate. A number of companies are now incorporating a search for suitable staff within the evaluation of the catchment market potential analysis. With operating margins very low the leverage exerted by only marginally high wage rates can result in a loss situation. CACI's ACORN service has been adapted by a number of multiple retailing companies to profile both potential customers and staff.

The importance of information for planning and control purposes has been raised on a number of occasions in this text. Typically information is used to 'automate' the business (to manage stock levels and staff scheduling).

An increasing number of companies are using data to develop a database of corporate and customer performance: to 'inform'. Information can be useful in a strategic role such that we have planning control and delegation. In this role we suggest that information is used to 'empower'; to enable effective decision making to be made by all levels of senior and middle management. At a senior level performance data may be used to profile revenues and costs necessary for evaluating the impact of expansion upon the infrastructure (e.g. distribution and systems). At a middle management level the decisions may be responses to local market opportunities. Thus we may expect to see aggregated POS data being used to evaluate store alternatives and to examine alternative space allocation and visual merchandising formats.

Visual merchandising is also a factor to be considered within a discussion on operating margins. Visual merchandising, together with merchandise density are two aspects of space allocation which influence browsing/purchasing shopping missions and the value and composition of customer purchases. Effective visual merchandising can be 'expensive' in the use of space, often using more space than the operations management are happy to admit to. However, the opportunity to increase the transaction value by the use of coordinated merchandise displays, suggesting uses and applications, has been evaluated by many companies who have been very satisfied with the results. By contrast high levels of merchandise density enable retailers to combine storage and sales display activities. In so doing they sacrifice many of the benefits offered by visual merchandising preferring to rely on the extent of the merchandise offer, and often a price offer, for effect. There is an interesting aspect to be considered. Research suggests that product range credibility is an objective that many retailers attempt to achieve. How this is done depends very much upon the sector in which they operate: fashion retailers are likely to do so with exclusive and innovative merchandise featured in creative displays. DIY retailing often looks to the extent of its ranges to demonstrate such a claim. Clearly this is an important issue to be resolved by new entrants. An obvious task for any new business is to gain both customer credibility and market share. Credibility eventually can lead to a role in which market standards can be influenced together with other important issues such as choice, quality and price points.

Operating hours have a large influence over operating margins. Often the problem for labour scheduling is one of intensity rather than the length of time the outlet is open. Many city centre locations find the day is characterised by peaks and troughs of activity due to the fact that many customers are working locally and use the time before and after work and lunch periods for shopping purposes. As a result labour requirements during intensive activity may not be able to be met while at other times during the period there may be an excess of staff. This can have implications for personnel policies and for customer service. A consistent level of customer service will be difficult to maintain if activity levels fluctuate to any great extent suggesting that those companies who identify the service features that are essential will be moving towards a position of competitive advantage.

There is another aspect to consider. Extended shopping hours are for some retailing situations accompanied by changing patterns of merchandise demand. This will undoubtedly involve higher distribution costs. Convenience store operators have found that they may have three or four distinct patterns of demand throughout the day requiring additional service visits or alternatively they carry excess stocks, thereby not optimising the use of space. Again this is another factor for consideration when evaluating alternative strategies.

The role of customer service within the retail offer is appearing to be increasingly important. There are a number of facets for consideration. The first concerns the purpose or objective of customer service. Earlier it was suggested that service may be seen as a vehicle by which the business differentiates itself and creates added value for customers via a service offer. An alternative view considers customer service to be a support facility which is essential if customers and potential customers are to consider the store as a competitive option. Clearly the implications are significant for the use of space, staff, merchandise and consequently for costs and margins. We can use service intensity to measure the extent of the use of staff to provide advice information and transactions service. Service augmentation (services), the proportion of total 'retailing' area dedicated to service facilities, information centres, childcare and crèche facilities, changing rooms etc. The new entrant will need to know customer expectations and competitive responses to be able to determine the nature of the service offer that will create competitive advantage within a sector. Given this information some judgment will be required to estimate how the consumer will respond.

Given that the objective may be to encourage the customer to spend more time in the store (and therefore more money) decisions to expand those facilities which encourage both should be considered. The provision of childcare facilities and supervised crèche areas have been successful in furniture and durables retailing. Facilities for male partners, comfortable seating, newspapers and coffee have been successful in exclusive ladieswear retailing. Given answers to these topics the new entrant is better equipped to evaluate opportunities. However, often not all of the costs are identified. For example, the sales density will vary by type of offer and often a more useful performance measure is the average customer transaction value rather than the sales per square foot or sales per employee. The average transaction when considered alongside customer purchasing visit rate can be a more significant statistic as it profiles activity levels as well as basic returns. Opportunity costs should also be considered because quite different returns can be expected from different retail formats. Furthermore, the costs of store fitting maintenance are important: the use of bright, light colours and floor coverings will require more frequent cleaning and replacement.

Alternative delivery formats should be considered prior to making a decision to implement strategy. It is at this point in the decision making that most flexibility exists. Alternative formats are becoming increasingly viable due primarily to the increasing sophistication of information technology. For example, catalogue operations and off the page sales are considerably more cost-effective in the early 1990s than they were in the mid–1980s, due primarily to the ability to profile media readership and combine accurate catchment profile data.

Finally the need to monitor operations activities such that relevant rather than average data is provided for decision making is essential. A company stockturn or sales per employee statistic is quite meaningless for a large company comprising 20 000 Stock-keeping units (SKUs) allocated across a large number of product groups and sold through a large number of stores with wide ranging size and location differences. Both the existing business and the new entrant should aim to identify characteristics of the business which are the key to the overall performance. These may be core product groups, key areas of space in the store, the perceptions of customers across a range of key competitive issues. For both businesses, the existing business and the new entrant, average performance data may not make management aware of critical performance variances soon enough.

Operating (Trading) Margins and Shopping Missions

Having discussed some of the issues that concern management when making implementation decisions we consider the implications of shopping missions on operating (trading) margins. (See Table 14.4.)

Destination purchases are unlikely not to realize their target margins for the reasons discussed earlier. However, management should attempt to increase the operating margin by ensuring that adequate information and advice is available during the purchase (service augmentation) and that merchandise items that may augment the sale are displayed and are in stock. It should not be assumed that a destination purchase cannot be lost, nor should it be assumed that its value is constrained by the fact that the decision to purchase has already been reached. Often the customer has not been aware of the range of (or perhaps the utility offered by) the accessories and service alternatives offered.

Planned regular purchasing missions should result in the realisation of operating margin targets. Provided the planned availability levels across the merchandise range are maintained it follows that there should be no loss of sales. Given the topics discussed earlier (gross margin management and shopping missions) it also follows that close attention to visual merchandising and merchandise density may result in some improvements in both gross and operating margins. Operating margins may be improved by looking

264

Table 14.4 Shopping missions: issues for managing operating (trading) margins

	Average Transaction Value	Items Purchased	Range of Items Purchased	Realised Operating Performance	Attributes which may Improve Operating Margins
Destination Purchase	Low/ Medium/ High	Low	Low	Planned Operating Margin	Product and Service Augmentation
Planned Regular Purchasing Visit	Low/ Medium/ High	Low/ Medium/ High	Low/ Medium/ High	Planned Operating Margin	Visual merchandising and/or Merchandising density
Planned Comparison Shopping	Low	Low	Low	Lower than Target Operating Margin	Product and Service Augmentation Service Intensity
Planned Browsing Visit	Low	Low	Low	Lower than Target Operating Margin	Service Density
Impulse Purchase	Low	Low	Low	Planned Operating Margin	Ensure cost-effective use of space. Availability.
Distress Purchase	Low	Low/ Medium	Low/ Medium	Planned Operating Margin	Monitor use of staff and trading hours. Extend to cover 'distress' times. Rationalise other times.

for opportunities to display related merchandise items for which there is evidence to show that sales of both items may increase (and therefore so too will the margins) if they are displayed together. The management of merchandise density is less obvious. There are clearly areas of the merchandise assortment that are replenishment items, replenishment occurring on a frequent and regular basis. Very little, if any at all, comparison shopping is considered and customers pass through sales areas oblivious of the amount of stock held in the sales area space. For such items it is not unreasonable to consider operating economies that might be available if the merchandise density is increased and the store becomes a little more crowded than average. Provided the level of sales is not reduced it is possible that operating margins may be improved.

For planned comparison and browsing shopping missions the arguments are similar to earlier topics raised for gross margin management and for operating margins during destination purchases. We can add the importance of both service intensity and service facilities. The level of service intensity (the number of dedicated service staff) may influence the comparison shopper or the browser either to purchase immediately or establish very favourable perceptions such that the store is clearly preferred, as and when a purchase is made. Similarly larger than average (and more flexible) service areas such as childcare areas, etc. may well create similar perceptions.

Impulse purchasing will only occur at maximum margins if availability is constantly monitored. They may be improved by closely monitoring the effective use of space (both sales and margins) to ensure that what is often prime space is actually producing a maximum return.

Distress purchase shopping missions may be improved by closely monitoring staff numbers and trading hours. Often both sales and margins may be improved by matching trading hours with the times that 'distress purchasing' may occur. For example, Sunday mornings are well known for car DIY activities, the spring public holidays are similarly well known for home decorating. Knowledge of these times may enable the retailer to schedule trading times such that they respond to customer needs.

14.4   A LOOK AT THE IMPORTANCE OF OPERATING CASHFLOW

Positive cashflows from trading operations are an essential consideration for any management decision. Both existing and potential strategy decisions should consider cashflow implications prior to their implementation. One obvious area for evaluation is the assortment profile. Two characteristics that often are not given sufficient attention are assortment variety and assortment availability. While customer choice can be very important a number of aspects can be overlooked. Firstly it is not necessarily the case that the same amount of choice is required across the assortment, indeed it is very easy to assume that customer choice expectations are the same for all of their purchases. This clearly may not be so and the dimensions of variety should be carefully researched with this in mind. It is quite unusual for ladieswear offers to make the same choice available across outerwear, underwear, hosiery and outdoor/weather wear. Careful research can identify those product groups for which choice is a primary expectation and stockholding may be concentrated in those areas. A similar approach may be taken for availability where customers' expect immediate availability for core product merchandise items and usually across the entire range of a distress purchasing range of merchandise. Another consideration in this discussion concerns the range of both choice and availability by price point. For a majority of planned purchases the consumer has a price range in mind, furthermore they have a good idea of price ranges offered by the stores they usually purchase from. It follows that for both choice and availability there should be concern to ensure that both are maximised between the lower and upper price bands of relevance to customers' price expectations because this is where their purchasing activities are likely to take place.

Terms of trade should be evaluated on the basis of margins likely to be realised and on stockturn. Margins should be evaluated with the objective of ensuring that they are adequate to offer recompense for the length of period the merchandise will be carried in stock and, therefore, to cover the interest charge (real or opportunity cost) that will be involved. A similar view should be taken for stockturn but in addition to the rate at which stock can be turned into cash opportunities to use suppliers working capital (without unduly penalising the business) should be sought. Negative working capital can be an extremely useful source of cash (discussed in Chapter 5) and every opportunity to use it without damaging the business (either by losing out on settlement terms or possibly damaging supplier relationships) should be taken. There is an obvious link with gross margin management, 'sell through' rates and stockturn performance. Terms of trade negotiated should reflect the 'sell through' performance (where this is relevant) by agreeing a margin that compensates for interest or stock carrying costs and also for the subsequent loss and interest charges on very slow moving merchandise items.

While bearing the discussion of the previous chapters in mind management should consider the revenue and profit increases that may occur through customer responses to increasing such characteristics as variety, availability, exclusivity and quality. Where the increase is found to be significant the incremental increase on working capital commitment may be minimal and as such prove to be very cost-effective. Often it is well worthwhile evaluating the effects of adjusting the characteristics of the existing merchandise offer prior to expanding the assortment with additional product groups. This has two major benefits; one is an increase in 'presence' within the existing product group and with it increased credibility with the customer; the other is a smaller commitment of cash (or working capital) because the additional stockholding is a marginal cost rather than a much larger investment in new range.

An examination of the existing or proposed supply chain can provide an opportunity to reduce the working capital cycle and with it the need for operating cashflow to be committed to stockholding. Many of the benefits accruing from such an analysis are also available to eliminate concerns about margin management: efficiencies in supply chain management can improve gross margins by optimising the number of suppliers and operating margins by locating stock at strategically significant locations such that customer satisfaction is increased (or maintained at an acceptable level) while the supply chain costs are minimised. Clearly some of the issues require close examination and trade offs between 'costs and satisfaction' may be required. For example a 'quick response system' for the fast moving core product range may require higher service costs than the average service replenishment system. Viewed from the perspective of customer service and customer response, however, the increases may be seen as essential and the response may require the allocation of additional stockholding resource to meet the objective. In such instances the increase in working capital commitment can be justified by the increase in customer sales and the cash that may be generated.

This all suggests that while assortment policy should be customer-led the issues and implications for working capital decisions do require to be considered. This is particularly important for new ventures where research into matching the customer expectations for merchandise characteristics will establish working capital requirements and the cost of maintaining working capital to sustain availability choice etc. An essential input into the calculation of working capital will be the differential values of availability and choice by price points.

14.5 CONSIDERATIONS FOR STRATEGIC CASHFLOW

If a business is to expand it will require both profits and cash. It is obviously less expensive for a business to fund its expansion from its own resources, consequently any business planning should consider the implications of its decision making on cash availability, cost of capital and funding sources.

The Boston Consulting Group matrix approach to planning has had widespread coverage and is but the method of viewing planning. It will be recalled that this employed a matrix identifying market share (volume achieved) and growth rate of the business (or product) on its two axes.

This concept is a useful start for the evaluation of the existing business (to identify the self funding potential) and of proposed businesses (to identify the short term need for cash and their long term potential to generate cash for future expansion). It is preferable for any business to be self funding because this avoids the serious debt levels that have created problems for a number of companies in recent years (for example, Laura Ashley, The Burton Group, Next to name but a few). The concept also encourages the business to plan a portfolio approach for its development and to manage the portfolio to ensure that strategic cashflow objectives are met.

The Boston Market Growth/Market Share matrix may be reinforced with the Directional Policy Matrix. In this approach both the environment and the business' capabilities and capacities are considered when evaluating opportunities. The importance of having strong strategic cashflow can be considered by the directional policy matrix as it can be considered within the context of market attractiveness (i.e. does the prospective market offer an opportunity to develop strong cashflows?) and cash can also be considered as a competence factor (i.e. does the business already have strong cashflows?). The 'wildcats' and 'stars' within the Boston matrix may need substantial support while the 'cashcows' offer an existing source of cashflow. The analysis would identify cash surpluses and cash requirements.

As with operational cashflow incremental expansion, based upon an existing competence, should first be explored. It can provide the growth requirements sought by the business and, at the same time, improve credibility, continuity capability, capacity utilisation and competitive advantage (all ideal features of a strategy) without imposing strains on the capital requirement of the business or increasing the size and nature of its overhead structure.

14.6   CONTRIBUTION

The level of contribution offered by existing and potential strategies should be evaluated to ensure that adequate cover of overhead is provided. Strong positive contribution ensures funds both for expanding the existing business and for new ventures. A record of positive contribution from business operations and control over the overhead activities, particularly if the business is diversified, facilitates raising funds at low interest rates as and when they are required.

14.7   THE IMPORTANCE OF PROFITABILITY

There is a tendency among many retailing companies to trade-off short term profitability for volume growth, the theory being that profitability is easily 'engineered' from volume due to the benefits of economies of scale and the amortisation of overheads over volume sales. The reality appears to be that in pursuit of growth the overhead continues to expand as the fixed asset infrastructure of space and distribution facilities increases, often out of control, and typically to a level that is higher than that required. As a result the period of 'ploughback' is projected further into the future and profit is a long term feature of the venture. But the benefits of short term profitability should not be overlooked. Short term profits ensure an ongoing return to the shareholder and help maintain a healthy EPS (earnings per share) and consequently a high profile in the 'City'. Long term profit growth is essential if the aspirations for growth of shareholders, management and employees are to be met. Long term growth also impresses suppliers who are more amenable and flexible towards low risk customers than they may be to those considered as having 'risk profiles'. Finance sources take a similar view.

With the new experience provided by the recession of the early 1990s another reason for strong short and long term profitability has emerged. Possibly for the first time ever (certainly in the history of most retailing businesses) property values have declined. Whereas regular property revaluation was a regular exercise by which financial directors enhanced the book value of their companies, they are now considering the realities of declining property values and are beginning to record these in the company's annual financial statement. It follows that strong profit trends in both the short term and the long term should be essential features of current and future strategy decisions in order that these problems may be avoided.

SUMMARY

We have reviewed the major areas in which planning and control decisions are important to the successful implementation of retailing strategy and management. The chapter has considered a number of issues that create and maintain high levels of sales volume, the argument having been made that without a high level of sales revenue the business may not be viable. It is interesting to observe that the Kingfisher view in this respect is that high levels of sales volume is: 'Get the volume right and there's no reason why net profit and earnings should suffer. In fact they should improve' (Geoff Mulcahy, reported by Patience Wheatcroft, *Retail Week*, 6 November 1992).

Gross margin management is essential. Some companies are finding that the days of increasing gross margins have ended. Consumer price awareness (and increasing price sensitivity) have prevented price increases and supplier margins are such that realistic buyers in retailing companies are looking not to negotiate even further on margin but seeking areas where suppliers and retailers may mutually benefit: the exchange of information in integrated supply chain management systems is one such area.

Operating (trading) margins were discussed in detail. The role of information management in both control and planning decisions was identified as an important issue. Two other issues of significance discussed in the chapter concern the role of operations management as profit managers rather than simply as cost controllers and the need to monitor alternative systems of customer satisfaction in an attempt to identify alternative delivery options.

Cashflow is an important feature of successful retailing management. Profitable businesses that either cannot meet operating costs or have cash available for expansion are at a disadvantage. If they cannot meet their operating costs they are not going to be around in the medium or long term. Without strategic cashflow they may well be unable to take advantage of the opportunities that arise.

Positive contribution and profitability are obvious requirements from any strategy. Contribution will ensure that overheads are recovered and control maintained. Profitability throughout the lifespan of a venture is seen as an indication of a sound approach to management and lowers the risk perceptions of potential investors. Strong contribution and profitability will ensure high EPS values and consequently will ensure high share prices and capital gains for the shareholders.

15 Managing the Implementation Process

INTRODUCTION

Essentially management is concerned with two basic decision types: strategic decisions concern the long term application of resources and will involve further decisions concerning the raising of funds, while the short term is concerned with operational decisions and these typically concern the adjustment or redeployment of in-use resources. This chapter considers the issues and activities involved in the implementation process. Of particular interest is the use of shopping missions and customer purchasing behaviour for developing a focus for the implementation activity.

Other considerations to be explored are the interrelationships that develop between decision areas, for example the implications that merchandise decisions may have for and upon customer service, store environment and customer communications. The impact of the decisions are likely to extend into support infrastructure areas such as distribution and information.

Finally we look at ways and means by which we may consider costs and revenues. A simple model is developed which provides a method by which the impact of the activities discussed throughout the text may be integrated during the evaluation activity prior to implementing decisions.

15.1 THE STRATEGY MODEL REVISITED

Throughout this book a distinction has been made between strategic and operational decisions. In Chapter 1, Figure 1.2 presented a retail strategy model developed by the author in a previous text (see Knee and Walters [1985]). Research and observation suggest that some small changes to the model are required. Figure 15.1 illustrates these changes. It can be seen that in the revised model repositioning has two roles: operational repositioning and strategic repositioning.

Revised Operational and Strategic Options

Operational repositioning occurs in the short term as and when management considers it necessary to respond to changes in the existing customer base which require small adjustments to the offer attributes. The refocusing of merchandise characteristics to reflect the importance of convenience has led to the development of a wide range of prepared meals which have also

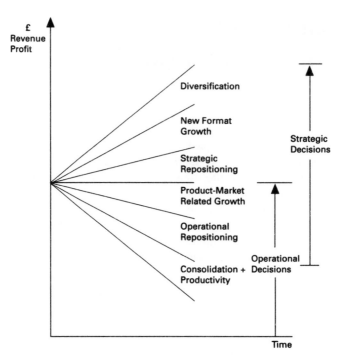

Figure 15.1   Strategic and operational decisions

reflected the consumers' broadening tastes (the reference to J. Sainsbury earlier is an example). The incremental increase in customer services is another example of operational repositioning. The objectives of operational repositioning are to maintain close contact with the customer base, adjusting the offer sufficiently to maintain customer loyalty. It is not aimed at creating entirely new customers or penetrating new segments, that is much more the role of strategic repositioning.

Strategic repositioning is a response to the requirements of a new or additional segment. Often it does not require a complete shift by the business but rather an overt statement by the business that it has recognised the customer opportunity and the response is an offer which meets the customer needs identified. The Tesco Metro stores and the Boots store grouping are examples of strategic repositioning as was the recognition by British Shoe in 1988–9 that consumer fashion, exclusivity and quality expectations were relevant to footwear as well as apparel merchandise. The resurrection and rejuvenation of old fascias as brands reflecting these customer attitudes were the company's response. Regrettably the recession intervened and the strategy programme was not fully implemented.

Product market related growth, is the development of the business within its areas of expertise. This was the early Ansoff strategy model (1970).

Product-development is aimed at extending, widening or deepening the existing merchandise assortment so that customer transactions are increased. Thus the inclusion of pharmacy departments, flowers etc. by the large food multiples has this together with margin enhancement as its purpose. Marks & Spencer's moves into numerous merchandise groups and into financial services is another example.

Market-development, the geographical expansion of an existing successful format, has other different sets of objectives. Market development strategies rely largely upon economies of replication for their effectiveness. By expanding the number of outlets offering the same merchandise, service and store environment numerous benefits accrue. The increased sales volume has an impact on buying terms thereby improving gross margins. There are economies of scale in operations and distribution (together with the facility to use slack fixed asset capacity) thereby improving operating margins. Add to this the benefits of promotional economies and the improved overhead recovery rate and the incremental profitability created by market development may be quite large.

New format growth, the development of new offers which are based upon an existing format, is another change in the strategy model. Typically these occur as specialist offers, successful within a larger format, are expanded and extended to become multiple activities in their own right. The Boots photographic service is an example, so too, is the optican service both of which have moved out of the larger branches and into multiple operations. Formats may also undergo some changes in response to changes within the market place. Argos has introduced both a large and smaller version of its original format. The 'Superstore' offer has a larger range of merchandise and customer inspection facilities while the small 'Best Sellers' branches offer an edited range of merchandise based upon the lower volume opportunities of smaller catchment areas. Factory shops or discount club operations, are an emerging format in UK retailing in the early 1990s. Branded merchandise, mostly apparel, is increasingly sold in off-centre locations in which store environment characteristics are less capital intensive than the conventional high street outlets for both apparel and footwear. Price differentials are significantly lower and their growth rate is impressive. While these are considered as competitive to the high street and shopping centre located multiples there is some evidence to suggest that an opportunity in this format may be seen for more effectively increasing 'sell through' margins. Hitherto, slow selling items are progressively reduced in price until they are sold or until they are sold during a sale. The off-centre factory shop offers a more rapid stockturn at what may be a lower margin. However, if all of the costs involved in slow moving merchandise are considered (including opportunity costs) then it is likely that the out turn will be more favourable.

Diversification, activities include both acquisition and organic expansion of the business into related and unrelated areas. The apparent drive for growth through acquisition prominent in the latter half of the 1980s was followed by a period of entrenchment in the early 1990s. It was also a period noticeable for strategic rationalisation. Many of the acquisitions of the 1980s resulted in some less than ideal 'fits'. As a result the 1990s saw Sears disposing of its menswear activities and Storehouse disposing of Richards and Habitat (and at the time of writing attempting to dispose of Blazer). This suggests that the experiences of the 1980s have produced some lessons well learned and clearly the implementation criteria discussed in Chapter 1 have been adopted in some measure. The rationalisation moves of Sears and Storehouse suggest that consistency and consonance are important issues. It follows that capacity utilisation and credibility are also important: the Storehouse action of moving towards two businesses, BhS and Mothercare would suggest that they are considering the huge managerial economies of scale that would result from centralising operations and distribution. The Kingfisher/Darty combination is an interesting development within the context of the Single Market. Such a combination offers benefits through procurement economies as well as managerial economies. The Storehouse move towards a 'consistent' business suggests that conglomerate activities do need some common denominator factor otherwise the synergy of large business combination may not be as profitable as it may have appeared. By contrast conglomerate retailing has been successful for Kingfisher. Possible reasons for this may be the strong cash producing aspect of B & Q, together with a portfolio effect of a mixed range of businesses which can lower risk in recessionary periods.

Consolidation and Productivity

Consolidation and productivity remains as it was described in Chapter 1, essentially an operational decision making area concerning the productivity of resources but clearly the implications of rationalisation should be well thought through for long term implications. An outlet that is closed and an adjustment to the assortment should be evaluated against the opportunity the action offers competitors. Finally the diversification into supply and service areas should be considered. Events over recent years suggests that backward vertical integration is not particularly profitable whereas vertical coordination has less risk and clearly no capital commitment. Laura Ashley is probably the most notable move out of manufacturing to focus management skills on managing the retailing aspects of the business. Asda also retreated from manufacturing, releasing both capital and managerial capacity for the retailing aspect of the business by disposing of a meat processing and packing plant. By contrast the vertical coordination philosophy of Marks & Spencer has produced better results. Product specification and quality control are two obvious benefits, but possibly more important in times of recession is not having the problem of underutilised production capacity and unnecessary overheads and fixed costs.

Clearly there is overlap between strategic and operational decisions. Figure 15.1 suggests that the strategic implications of decisions may extend well into the operational decision making area, the longer term issues of competitive reaction to branch closures and range rationalisation were mentioned in the previous paragraph and situations can be thought of whereby operational repositioning decisions may have long term aspects (and vice versa; the decision to pursue strategic repositioning may result in serious short term implications). An example of such a situation probably occurred in BhS in the late 1970s, early 1980s when it took the decision to move closer towards Marks & Spencer and redesigned its store interiors (the Harlow exercise) using Conran Associates to review the merchandise ranges and the overall offer. The subsequent shift in positioning almost certainly resulted in some loyal BhS customers transferring their loyalties and spending elsewhere, probably to Littlewoods.

15.2 SHOPPING MISSIONS AS A FOCUS FOR STRATEGIC AND OPERATIONAL DECISIONS

Shopping missions offer a means of implementing decisions. During the discussion on shopping missions and the examples illustrating how they may be used in Chapters 10 and 11 it was suggested that shopping missions do vary for the same individual and the suggestion was also made that location will have a strong influence over the dominant mission type. For example, an off-centre convenience store is likely to receive more distress purchase missions than planned, regular visits during which large transactions occur.

There are also other reasons for missions to change. For example, competition may result in the commercial need to change elements of the offer. The steady expansion of food discount multiple operations, Aldi and Netto, clearly is creating (potentially) short and medium term problems for Kwik Save, Asda and Gateway initially and possibly Sainsbury, Safeway and Tesco in the longer term. One possible influence this may have, once there is a 'national' coverage of outlets and their impact on consumer shopping behaviour has a significant impact is for planned regular shopping missions to be split. The manufacturer brand loyal consumer may find that the lower prices offered on those items offered by the discounters is sufficient incentive to purchase such items from a local discounter and follow this with a visit to a full range superstore to purchase items not available from the discounters. See Figure 15.2.

The shopping missions may remain as they have been for some time. They may be essentially the same but show evidence of changes in customer preferences, for example a distress mission continues to be just that but the

276

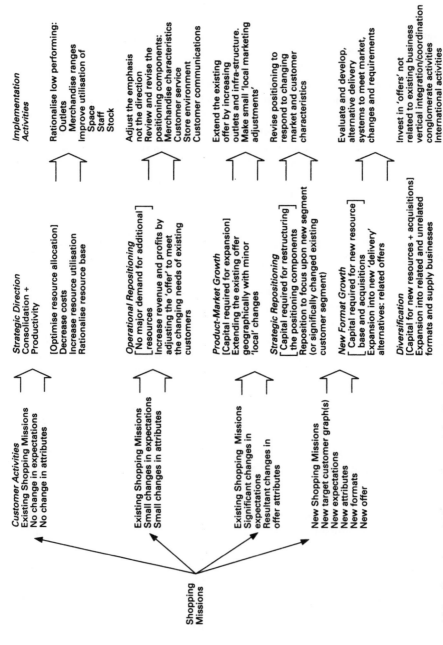

Figure 15.2   Shopping missions and strategic direction options: implementation issues

customer begins to look for different types of merchandise, the forgotten ingredient for an 'international' dish rather than one for a basic meal. Other influences operate. In this example travel and an increased interest in food and food preparation, has had a large impact. However, it suggests that the mission purpose remains unchanged (it remains a distress purchase but the merchandise requirements have changed).

Clearly some missions may show potential for growth without changes to the characteristics of the mission. Franchised businesses are examples, the offer has growth potential essentially through territorial expansion but may be adjusted to meet local needs. There may be entirely new opportunities, created by combining products and services, for example the Mail box franchise has been created by combining the packaging, postal and communication needs of both consumers and small businesses around a convenience based theme. There may be opportunities to expand an existing offer in which the expertise developed in domestic markets can be used to satisfy shopping missions for which no local offer exists, or perhaps is not expanding at a sufficiently rapid rate, for example Mothercare, IKEA and Early Learning Centre are concepts with elements of specialising and appeal that have been transferred internationally, each responds to specialist shopping mission requirements.

An analysis of shopping missions can indicate the probable impact that may be expected on performance. It will also provide information concerning the requirements for resources and of the risk because the company will be able to review projected performance; the likely customer response in terms of sales and contribution compared with the resources required. Perhaps a greater benefit is the facility to monitor consumer behaviour trends and identify the changes that are occurring in overall trends, and particularly those relevant to the dominant shopping mission types that are serviced by the company. This offers the means by which strategic directional changes are occurring in the context of shopping missions. Figure 15.2 suggests how shopping missions may evolve over time and the impact these changes may have on strategic direction. The changes that occur within the missions and the characteristics of new emergent shopping missions will suggest alternative strategic direction opportunities, or changes that are necessary to the existing direction. This in turn will identify changes to the implementation activities, examples of these are given in Figure 15.2 where the managerial tasks are identified.

The emphasis of Figure 15.2 is on the need for management to consider both the shopping mission characteristics and the strategic direction of the business. By focusing upon both, the effectiveness of resource allocation can be improved. For example if sales and profitability are demonstrating a satisfactory growth performance it would suggest there to be evidence that customer satisfaction is being achieved and no major changes to the offer made are necessary. However, a situation in which customer research shows customer satisfaction at an acceptable level but margin performance is declining suggests that the strategic direction should focus upon consolidation and productivity issues. The implementation activities should include a review of low performing outlets and merchandise ranges (and items within ranges), which would suggest areas of the offer which could be adjusted (consolidated) provided that no major changes are made to the characteristics of the offer that are shown to be important to customer satisfaction. For other activities productivity increases may be sought. Here the activities should focus upon maintaining the important elements of the offer but seeking ways in which the costs of maintaining the offer may be reduced: in other words we are seeking to improve resource productivity.

New shopping missions offer a different challenge. Possibly the growth of home shopping will provide examples for consideration in the very near future. The use of IT to facilitate customer store and product selection processes and the use of customer response information via database management to focus merchandise selection and customer targeting by retailers offers the retailer the means by which technology may be used both to influence and to respond to shopping missions. The implications for implementation are equally interesting. Information technology can be just as effective in the 'delivery' process as development of financial services illustrates. The Midland Bank's Direct service is an example of the use of IT to manage the entire process. Other examples include Kay's development of catalogue shopping through Prestel and a less IT intensive application of teleshopping by the direct sales music companies.

Other interesting developments are the response by retailers to customer preferences for quality and convenience. Quality in furniture retailing has been improved by reducing the handling of products by coordinating deliveries from suppliers' stockholding rather than holding stock at the point of sale or in the retailers' warehousing systems. Thus vertical coordination of the distribution activity not only reduces costs (less handling occasions and lower stock levels) but also improves quality by reducing potential damage due to handling frequencies.

Shopping mission analysis clearly provides an input into strategy formulation. The benefit it offers is that it is customer based. As the examples have suggested changes identified in customer responses are very useful indicators as to what resources are required and how they should be allocated. This, it is suggested, is preferable to the allocation of resources in order that an assumed performance response may be achieved simply by selecting a strategy option without prior detailed consumer/customer analysis. There is emerging evidence which suggests that the recession of the early 1990s has resulted in long term changes to customer expectations. This may be seen in the comparison shopping missions whereby an emphasis on quality and 'durability' are strong features. This is emerging in apparel markets also, where the consumer preferences for durable, classic styles favours that

for contemporary fashion. Shopping missions may change, less impulse purchasing, more planned purchases with classic styling and design longevity
together with quality as important merchandise characteristics. Consumer
durable purchases are likely to be less 'fashion' items and more functional
purchases; hence quality, durability and after sales care will become important characteristics.

15.3 SHOPPING MISSIONS, POSITIONING AND CRITICAL SUCCESS FACTORS

Shopping missions should also be used to identify changing requirements
for critical success factors. Figure 15.3 suggests that shopping missions may
also be used to identify the attributes and positioning characteristics that
are essential features of the offer to be made to the customer.

In Figure 15.3 an approach is shown in which attributes (derived from

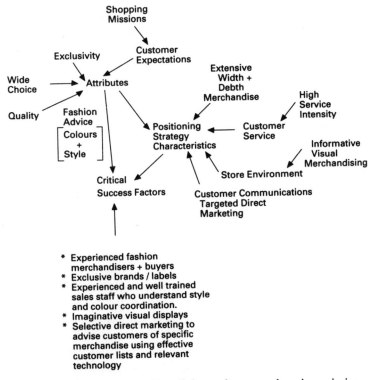

Figure 15.3 Identifying the working linkages between shopping missions,
customer expectations, attributes, positioning and critical success factors

shopping missions) are matched with positioning strategy characteristics. Both are then used to identify those features (the critical success factors) essential to successful implementation of decisions. Figure 15.3 presents an hypothetical example. The example describes a situation in which, having researched customer expectations (and having explored the trade-off issues) the important attributes to emerge were, exclusivity, wide choice, quality and advice.

The positioning response by the company should provide extensive width and depth in the assortment; customer service will be based around experienced, knowledgeable (and well trained) staff whose experience is in selling to equally knowledgeable (in the sense of knowing what they want) customers. The store environment should through its visual merchandising activity reflect the fashion advice (styles, colours, etc.) required by the target customer group. Customer communications should be targeted and relevant to meet customer needs. The critical success factors essential for the response to be implemented can then be evolved. As Figure 15.3 suggests they relate to buying and selling staff (and the organisational) issues of recruitment and training. They are also concerned with the information and advice role that the visual merchandising activity should undertake. The communications issues concern accurate and detailed customer mailing lists supported by an effective information management system. This gives us an outline of what it is that is necessary to develop a framework for decision implementation. We now look at some of the issues that may arise during the process.

15.4 MANAGING STRATEGIC AND OPERATIONAL DECISIONS AND THEIR INTERRELATIONSHIPS

Implementing both strategic and operational decisions involves choices between options because resources are usually scarce: it also involves management in thinking through the interrelationships between the positioning characteristics. For example, a decision to expand the merchandise offer by an additional range will raise issues concerning customer services, the store environment and probably customer communications together with implications for distribution and operations activities. The range of decisions confronting management is clearly very large, much too large to be dealt with in this text. Accordingly we shall consider the types of decisions and offer these as examples as approaches as to how decisions may be approached.

A broad and initial classification of decisions is to differentiate between strategic and operational decisions. Strategic decisions are those requiring a commitment of resources for an extended time horizon. Typically these are decisions concerning diversification, strategic repositioning and growth from new formats. Each will comprise a series of interrelated decisions in-

Figure 15.4   Developing added value and a positioning statement

volving merchandise, customer service, store environment and customer communications. The required outcome will be a series of integrated decisions with which a coordinated positioning statement is made. Figure 15.4 illustrates this.

Operational decisions are more likely to be adjustments to the positioning characteristics during which the overall positioning stance will be maintained while small adjustments to merchandise, customer service, store environment and customer communications are made. The result will be an operational repositioning which results in a more cost-effective use of the resources involved. Other operational decisions may be adjustments to achieve increases in customer activities that will increase operational performance.

Strategic Decisions

An example of strategic decision issues is given in Figure 15.5 in which the type of decisions involved in merchandise assortment development are considered. Based upon customer shopping mission characteristics a series of merchandise objectives is developed (together with a forecast of expected sales revenue, margins, contribution and cashflow) which in turn identify the decision areas around which management will develop a merchandise strategy. In Figure 15.5 the important features suggested are those which contribute to customer satisfaction and which identify areas of significant costs. Merchandise assortment characteristics are the assortment response

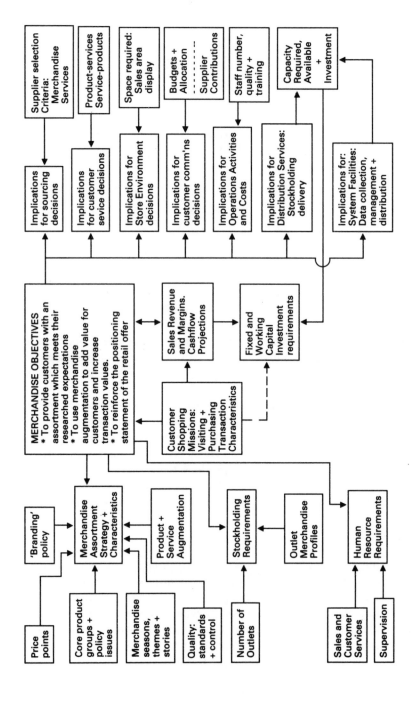

Figure 15.5 Merchandise decisions: strategic perspectives

features identified by research activities. These are basic features concerned with range dimensions of core products, width and depths price points, retail brands and the number of merchandise seasons, themes and stories required. An important feature, one which will have some significance for space requirements and stock investment is product augmentation, the specification of accessories for each range within the assortment.

Stockholding requirements results from determining the merchandise coverage for outlet categories and the number of branches and is influenced by the overall dimensions determined by the assortment characteristics.

Staff requirements are influenced by merchandise decisions. There are a number of issues. The nature of the product will have an influence on both number and quality of staff, products requiring demonstration and information support are likely to increase the number of staff (service intensity) as will products requiring installation and after sales service. Supervision and staff training are other aspects to be considered as are seasonal merchandise offers and those with specialist applications.

Merchandise strategy decisions clearly have implications for other functions and may be responsible for increasing costs in these areas. This raises more issues to be resolved, some of which are suggested in Figure 15.5. Obvious areas are sourcing, customer service, store environment, customer communications and the operations and support (or infrastructure) activities. For each of these activities or functions the impact of changes of volume throughput, the characteristics of the merchandise etc. will influence the nature of the tasks to be conducted, activity levels and costs. Some of the factors to be considered are included in the diagram but it is likely that others will exist. Other considerations will emerge. For example, the impact of changes of volumes will influence operating economies and may require the company to reconsider its investment programmes. Substantial volume shifts over the foreseeable future may influence managements' distribution investment policies: it certainly will bring their attention to the issues.

Given information on volumes, capacity requirements (and capacity availability) together with sales revenue and contribution forecasts it is now possible to consider fixed and working capital requirements. Before these are finalised the sensitivity of customer response should be tested. The initial customer research will have identified customer purchasing characteristics: their purchasing frequencies and average purchasing transaction values. Wide variations in either purchasing frequencies or average transactions (either low or high) should suggest the need for a closer evaluation so as to avoid situations of over or under capacity occurring. Under capacity situations are likely to result in poor customer service while over capacity will raise costs if the capital investment is to achieve forecast returns.

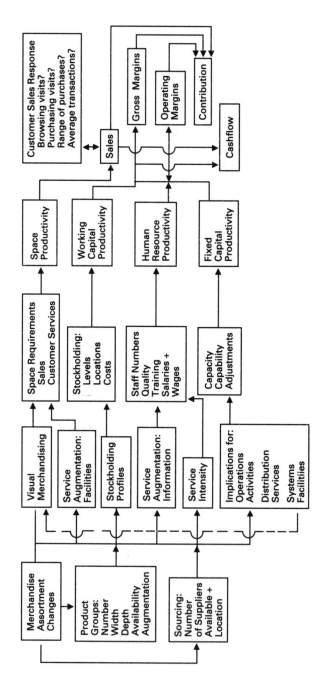

Figure 15.6 Merchandise decisions: operational perspectives

Operational Decisions

Operational decisions are, by definition, short term in their nature and influence. Consequently we are not concerned with investment decisions but clearly are concerned about the productivity of fixed assets. An example of a merchandise related operational decision is featured in Figure 15.6 in which the decision components surrounding an initial decision to make an adjustment to the merchandise offer are identified.

The merchandise changes typically relate to the characteristics of one or more product groups such as range width, depth, availability or possibly augmentation. These are issues which would influence the operational positioning of the firm and are likely to be responses either to competitor activities or identified by ongoing customer research. These decisions are likely to involve sourcing factors either being brought about by a change in the sourcing base or requiring changes in it. A number of attributes are likely to be influenced by changes decided upon and those in turn will cause changes in resource requirements and/or performance levels.

In addition to having an influence on the direct resources of space, stockholding and staff there are inevitably considerations to be made for the supporting infrastructure functions. As with the strategic decisions example concern is with the impact of volume changes upon capacity and capability characteristics of operations, distribution and systems facilities. However, unlike the previous example the concern is more immediate and capacity increases will be sought from outside the capability of the business (unless it is known that excess capacity exists). Distribution service capacity is available from 'third party' companies, so too (at least to a limited extent) is computer systems capacity. Service adjustments are typically made by increasing the number of part-time staff at appropriate times.

The performance issues that arise concern the responses that the changes bring about. Figure 15.6 suggests that operational decisions are brought about because the changes suggested will result in an increase in customers' sales response such that sales, margins and contribution will more than cover the additional costs involved in effecting the changes. To ensure this occurs the productivity increases should be evaluated both on an incremental basis and on the overall increases achieved. There are similar decisions required in the functional areas of customer service, store environment and customer communications. Space prevents a detailed treatment of each of these.

15.5 AN IMPLEMENTATION MODEL

Having discussed some of the problems and issues that surround implementing managerial decisions it is now necessary to develop a method by which decisions may be implemented. Prior to committing resources a question should

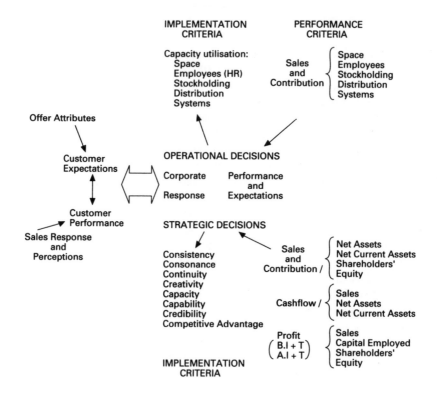

Figure 15.7   Decision criteria for 'fit': strategic and operational decisions

be raised concerning 'fit'. 'Fit' is a measure of how well a decision can be integrated into the ongoing strategic and operational activities. Figure 15.7 identifies the issues. It re-introduces the strategic implementation criteria and suggests criteria that should be applied to operational decisions. Customer criteria must initially be based upon forecasts. Offer attributes will have been identified by research and the sales response levels are objective forecasts of revenues and profits based upon the assumption that customer response will meet these levels provided the attributes meet customer expectations. At an implementation stage management can only accept these forecasts after having satisfied itself on the viability of the forecasts and the underlying logic.

The sales volume forecasts will have been based upon a projection of customer purchasing activities (i.e. their browsing and purchasing visit frequencies, average size of purchase transactions and the range and items purchased) for the dominant shopping mission(s). Customer expectations of attribute features together with the knowledge of the selection on and purchasing decision processes that accompany the shopping missions will have been considered during the decisions that have been made concerning the merchandise and service components comprising the offer format and positioning characteristics. This will be useful when considering physical features of the store environment when management experience can determine viable values for the basic performance characteristics of sales/space, sales/employee and the related measures for merchandise density, service intensity and other relevant attributes. These will be valuable parameters with which to work during the implementation of the plan. Given the projected, quantitative, values for both customer purchasing activities and for the attributes, the management responsible for the implementation task have explicit targets against which they may make initial assessments on operational viability. For example, doubts concerning achieving overall sales expectations will be signalled early by overall (and detailed) sales and merchandise density performance projections. At such a juncture modifications may be considered.

Having satisfied itself on fit the process of implementation can be initiated. Figure 15.8 develops the initial proposal into a 'working option'. Before capital is allocated the proposal should be examined to ascertain both viability and sensitivity. A number of issues are important. Many proposals for investment are made based on the assumption that minimum activity levels will be achieved. In retailing this is essential because both gross and operating margins are dependent upon volume throughput. It follows that an initial task is to ensure that the firm can finance the number of outlets (and the infrastructure) that are required if the profit objective is to be achieved.

Implementation and evaluation are not discreet activities. Thus the 'what if?' activity should continue during the implementation process. This approach is particularly useful when the project is specialist in its nature and the shopping missions defined suggest that while the 'offer' may be attractive and exclusive, the size of transactions may be low, thereby requiring a large number of purchasing visits if profit forecasts are to be achieved. In such a situation the options are few. Many specialist retailers attempt to widen their merchandise assortment with the objective of increasing choice and, it is hoped, average transaction per customer. However, the result often is that the offer loses its focus and direction. The problems raised are numerous. The merchandise selection task is not easy and the criteria of consistency, consonance and continuity should be applied to the merchandise selection just as it should be applied to the overall project. These criteria apply to quality, style continuity and price. Often it is very difficult to match these criteria across an extending merchandise range.

Another aspect of this part of the implementation process also is concerned with volume and viability. The optimum number of stores for critical mass is, typically, quantitatively based. It assumes that the projected number of stores can be acquired without compromising the store selection criteria. Often the qualitative issues are more significant and compromises on site, situation and size are made, with the result that the volume forecast

Shopping Missions [Dominant Types] ↔ **Customer Responses by Shopping Mission(s):** Browsing visits / Purchasing visits / Average transactions Per visit / Purchase characteristics

Customer Expectations

Customer Selection and Purchasing Processes

Optimum Number of Stores for Critical Mass

Merchandise Considerations

Customer Service Considerations

Gross Margin Profiles

Merchandise Selection

Financial Considerations

Supply Characteristics

Offer Format and Positioning Characteristics

Operating Margin Profiles

Branch Development

Branch Operations

Distribution Operations

Field Management Activities

Operations Management Structure and Tasks

Merchandise Planning

Customer Service Planning

Store Environment Planning

Customer Communications Planning

Distribution Support Service Requirements

Range Plan: Core merchandise 'Service' Merchandise Seasons Price points Features mix

'Qualifying' and Determining Service Facilities

Ambiance Display Design

Information + Persuasion Personal + Non personal

Systems Support Requirements

Merchandise Stock Holding Requirements

Human Resource Requirements

Aggregate Space Requirements

Stockholding Costs Cycle Stocks Safety Stocks Stores and Distribution Centres

Operating Costs Occupancy Staff and Supervision Maintenance. Advertising and Promotion

Capital Costs Development Building Fixtures fillings Infra-structure

Forecast Capacity Current Capacity

Incremental Capacity Required

Total capital Requirements for Investment

Total Operating Budgets

Total Capital Budgets

Sales + Margin Forecasts

Contribution and Cashflows

NPV

Cashflow Generated

Performance Expectations

Sales Volumes Growth	Gross Margins Markdowns	Operating Margins	Contribution	Cash flows

| Space | / | Stock | / | Staff | Capital | Employed |

Resource Productivity Measures

Return as Investment

15.8 A decision implementation model

cannot be achieved. Alternatively, the projected operating margin profiles may be compromised because of operational and distribution service difficulties which result in increased costs, and management must then decide whether the prescribed levels of service are necessary.

Having considered these issues in some depth the process continues and begins to deal with the implementation of the merchandise, service, store environment and communications proposals. While these are firm (having been based upon customer/consumer research and subsequently evaluated from a costing point of view) the planning of resource allocation now moves into detail. By this stage of the activity the proposed number and location of stores is known and the process of implementing the actual plan can be undertaken and firm budgets for investment and operations be determined.

The Merchandise Plan

The merchandise plan has six components:

- Merchandise strategy profile
- Range planning
- Sourcing and the buying plan
- Merchandise allocation
- The merchandise sales plan.

The *merchandise strategy profile* identifies the key merchandise groups that are essential to create credibility with the customer group. Decisions at this stage of planning concern the role of national and international suppliers and of retail brands; concessions; width, depth and availability; price points; merchandise seasons, and; margin and stockturn targets.

Range planning develops the merchandise strategy into more quantitative areas. Given the 'policy issues' that have been established by the merchandise strategy profile, range planning specifies core product groups and the basic stock within each core product group together with the model stock list which expands the product group and gives it authority. Basic stocks are the staple or commodity items that are expected to be in stock at all times. The model stock items usually have a lower availability and add variety of choice to the range. At this point in the planning process a sales forecast for each product group together with overall stockholding requirements (based on width, depth and availability characteristics) are developed.

Sourcing has a number of activities. First of all sources of merchandise that will meet the criteria prescribed (volumes, quality, exclusivity, production flexibility, distribution service, ordering systems and adequate terms of trade) must be identified. In addition to these factors there are the qualitative issues of supplier/distributor relationships covering product development and exchange of data etc. which are equally important. The *buying plan* details or schedules the purchasing (and payment) activities over a prescribed budget cycle. Many retailing companies operate open-to-buy budgets which once established are aimed at controlling buying activities in order to maintain a relatively tight control over cashflow.

Merchandise allocation may be a component of range planning. Large multiples, operate a range of stores of different sizes, locations and sales potentials within a range of different catchment areas. Consequently branch stock decisions are based upon branch categories and branch sizes and the stores will be allocated merchandise ranges (and volumes within the ranges) on the basis of: size and sales potential, location and sales potential, company presence and catchment share, and current and potential competitive activities. Once the branch allocation has been decided upon the stockholding requirements and sales forecasts can then be completed in detail.

The merchandise sales plan identifies the sales to be achieved and the stock levels to be held in the stores and distribution facilities throughout the company. Typically it has two components:

For stores (and regions):
• Basic and model stock lists
• Sales expectations (including sell through rates and markdowns)
• Stockholding levels
• Stockturn expectations
• Cashflow expectations
• Target return on assets managed.

For distribution facilities:
• Merchandise volume throughput and stockholding by:
    total company
    region/regional distribution centre
    store
• Distribution performance requirements:
    Availability
    Delivery frequency
    Delivery reliability

Capacity utilisation and budgets for planned capacity levels for the warehouse and transport activities.

The merchandise planning activity has five purposes:
• It details the merchandise requirements for the buyers:

By:	By:	By:	By:
Sales seasons	Product Group	Price points	Stocking profile
Regions	classification	and Stock	and Availability
Stores		Allocation	

- It details financial requirements by identifying lead-times and consequently short falls and surpluses in the cash budget.
- It can be used to identify capacity requirements necessary to produce distribution service performance levels at branches.
- It can be used to plan space allocation at branches.
- It provides information for manpower planning in branches and distribution centres.

Customer Service Planning

Customer service planning has five components:

- Determining the service objectives to achieve competitive advantage *and* increased corporate performance.
- Establish an appropriate strategy for service design, delivery and evaluation.
- Organisation structures for delivery.
- Intra-company considerations.
- Inter-company considerations.

Determining the service objectives is an activity with a twofold purpose. Clearly it has a basic purpose of improving sales and profit performance by increasing customer visit frequencies and transactions. To do this requires customer service to create added value for the customer. These objectives are mutually supportive in that unless the customer recognises the added value benefits of the service offer they are unlikely to increase both visits and spend within the store.

Customer service design, delivery and evaluation is the next step. It involves identifying the levels and content of the service offer that differentiates qualifying services from determining services (i.e. the level and context of service required to persuade customers to consider the store as a 'first choice' store). This is essentially a task whereby product-services, personal services and service facilities are identified and performance criteria established and resource requirements and investment implications determined. The delivery issues concern the structures and systems necessary if the services are to be provided. Evaluation measures concern:

Availability ⎫	Qualifying Services ⎫	Competitive
Quality ⎬	Determining ⎬	Advantage
Reliability ⎭	Services ⎭	

the purpose being to use evaluation to modify both the services offered and the delivery methods used.

Organisation for service delivery may follow a number of alternatives. The most effective is that which suits the company's culture and style. What is essential is that the commitment to service should be total; it should be an explicit statement that prescribes service objectives and the role of all company employees. The tasks of all levels of management, the resources required and the performance expectations are part of the organisation process. *Intra-company considerations* will arise because of the integrated nature of the retail offer. Furthermore the complexity of the offer components (e.g. the technology of products within the merchandise ranges) requires supporting services to advise on use, manage installation and offer after-sales services and maintenance. Information may be offered through visual merchandising display and customer information centres. Service facilities occupy selling area, their location should be decided such that they are effective but at the same time the opportunity cost (the impact onsales) is not excessive.

Inter-company considerations are an issue because suppliers may be more cost-effective in providing some aspects of customer service. Effective cooperation should be sought such that both the company and the supplier benefit from an initiative. The delivery of furniture and consumer durables from suppliers' central distribution facilities is cost-effective in reducing damage and reducing stockholding costs of both supplier and retailer. An instore presence of suppliers sales and service personnel (or rapid access to them through an IT link) is another form that cooperation may take. As many products become more complex and product-uses expand across application situations, so too does the need to offer a wide range of service and advice to customers.

The customer service plan offers:

- A means by which the company's offer may be enhanced by adding value through service.
- Service plans for specific branch category requirements.
- A means by which selected customer groups may be identified and offered selective service packages.
- A customer service budget detailing customer service cost/benefit features.

Store Environment Planning

The store environment plan has six factors:

- The specification of the 'ideal' store; its location, its size and shape, and the number of locations required and feasible (i.e. match the specification for successful trading).
- Store ambience themes and the role of visual merchandising.
- Customer handling systems.
- Customer service facilities.
- Intra-company considerations.
- Inter-company considerations.

Specification and identification of store profile and locations is an important issue. A detailed analysis of available data (census of population, regional data on employment, incomes and expenditure) together with commissioned research (customer surveys, catchment profiling by service companies (C.A.C.I., Mosaic, etc.) and a review of local authority planning intentions provides information on suitability and availability of locations. To this should be added the input from merchandise planning activities which will provide a lead in determining the size and shape of the 'ideal' location. Merchandise planning can also indicate the ideal number of stores for achieving volume predictions and gross margin targets. There should also be some attention given to the areas of compromise that are acceptable in the specification. These should be categorised as such and be supported by statements identifying how performance will differ from that planned if compromises are made.

Store ambience themes and visual merchandising are the means by which the offer is presented to the customer. This may only involve store design but is increasingly being applied to supporting media, such as catalogues, used to extend the appeal of the offer. Ambience has two levels. There is the overall 'atmosphere' in which the company's philosophy concerning quality, choice, exclusivity, service and customer care is presented. In addition there is the operational aspect which reflects the merchandise requirements and integrates with merchandise seasons, assortment profiles and service facilities. Visual merchandising is the implementation vehicle. Visual merchandising has the tasks of: making a positioning statement, arousing interest, encouraging comparison and moving customers towards a purchase; it should inform the customer group of the benefits of the coordinated offer the company is making and of the added value that is available. Effectively designed ambience and visual merchandising management will: increase sales revenue (by increasing purchasing visits, range of purchases and, therefore, average transaction values); increase gross margins (by directing customers towards higher margin merchandise and influencing coordinated purchasing); contain costs (by using visual merchandising as part of the customers' purchasing decision process, thereby reducing the number of staff required); improving productivity (by converting browsing visits into purchasing visits) thus increasing sales and contribution per unit of selling area and per employee), and add value to the customers' purchases (by offering advice on style and colour coordination, product application and problem resolution) through the visual merchandising activity.

Customer handling system are important from two aspects. Given a positioning offer specification the method by which customer transactions (and purchasing advice is given) should reflect the positioning. However, wages and salaries may well prove to be excessive and often cost-effective compromises for customer handling must be identified. These should be consonant with the customer service strategy but at the same time affordable. The location of customer handling systems is an important store design consideration. The installations should be clearly identifiable but not obtrusive, furthermore they, together with the staff, should reflect the customer service theme. It should be remembered that customer service does not end once the decision to purchase has been made.

Customer service facilities in the context of what and how these facilities are offered should be reflected in the store environment design by integrating them into the store environment. The facilities themselves should reflect the level of service implied by the 'offer' being made. For example, a high service, exclusive ladieswear retailer should ensure that this is extended into changing room areas, waiting areas for customers' partners (refreshments, newspapers, etc.) and even crèche areas if appropriate to the target customer group.

Intra-company considerations raise similar issues to those raised by customer service. Merchandise characteristics are often accompanied by store design requirements, or can benefit (by increasing sales) from specific treatment by visual merchandising. Examples include: consumer durables (where kitchen installations and demonstration areas are effective); furniture (room settings are more effective than solus isolated product displays or even worse, like with like items) and sports equipment (where displays of related products or perhaps video films of sporting activities) add atmosphere and excitement. To be effective these applications require coordination and liaison across a number of functions and decision areas.

Inter-company considerations again have similar issues as those raised earlier. Some suppliers, anxious to preserve their own positioning continuity, will meet all or a significant proportion of the costs of design and fixtures for selling areas devoted to their products. While this has obvious attractions it does have disadvantages in that some discontinuity may appear in the store environment design, the visual merchandising and ambiance themes.

The store environment plan offers management:

- The means by which total space requirements can be derived together with the means for evaluating alternative uses of space and the implications for sales and contribution per unit of space.
- A means by which space utilisation can be evaluated within the context of sales and margin enhancement.
- Another alternative for adding value to the offer by the information content of visual merchandising.
- A space allocation and budgeting activity which is deductive but which derives the optimal space allocation plan and, at the same time, a costing process.

Customer Communications Planning

A customer communications plan considers five issues:

- A clear statement of communications objectives.
- A strategy which identifies communications options and resource requirements.
- The deployment of resources to support the merchandise programme.
- Other intra-company considerations.
- Inter-company considerations.

Communications objectives have a number of purposes. They may be: to create an awareness of a need by the customer; to identify alternative solutions capable of satisfying the need; to persuade the customer that one particular solution (the company's) is the most suitable; to persuade the company to make a decision to purchase; to demonstrate alternative product uses, and to develop a strong relationship with customers by influencing and developing favourable perceptions of the overall offer of the company. This task presents varying difficulties. The 'single brand' company, e.g. Sainsbury and Laura Ashley can achieve the communication task by a skilful blending of merchandise, visual merchandising and customer services. However the department stores, who may have customers with a range of shopping missions have to consider those when deciding upon a communications programme which recognises that not only do the shopping missions differ among and between customers but that individual customer's shopping missions may vary during the one visit to the store as different departments are shopped.

The communications strategy identifies media and resource requirements. The strategy selected should identify with the store selection and purchasing decision processes of customers and be structured to take the customer group through the cycle commencing with developing favourable perceptions towards the company, moving through the evaluation and comparison stages to purchasing decisions. For this to be completed effectively it requires a thorough evaluation of external and internal communications media. This entails a review of personal and non-personal media and an evaluation in cost-effectiveness terms of the alternatives available. Use of sales personnel for effective communications may require considerable training and in company support. The increasing effectiveness of data base technology (and the decreasing capital and operating costs) makes direct marketing a serious contender among conventional advertising and public relations options.

Deployment of resources, or the final selection of media, should also consider the merchandise programme, particularly the merchandise seasons and promotional themes. Thought should also be given to the need to educate customers in reasons for purchasing as well as for the use of products. The expanding ranges of produce items, both fruit and vegetables, often requires supporting information for both use occasions and preparation methods. Some of the promotional expenditure of the larger food multiples is deployed for this purpose. The output of this element of the planning activity should be a media schedule detailing the type of media to be used, when and at what cost. Clear indication of how it is to be integrated with other activities (e.g. merchandise promotions and introductions, customer service developments and new store openings) is also an output.

Other intra-company considerations include the unexpected problems that may occur when faults are found in products. The ability to notify customers of the problem, quickly but without creating alarm, is an important feature of a communications facility. To do this efficiently does have a positive impact on how attitudes towards the company are formed and maintained. It should be remembered that these and other communications activities (many of which are only indirectly related with the mainstream of the business) are seen and assessed by investors, suppliers and other stakeholders whose attitudes may be important to the company.

Inter-company considerations of concern are possibilities of joint programmes which share expenditure with suppliers. Clearly the issues raised earlier, the control and direction of such joint ventures requires careful consideration. A large financial input or contribution towards the communications budget while it is attractive can be dysfunctional by creating 'noise' that distorts the positioning statement created by the merchandise, service and store environment decisions.

From the communications plan we aim to develop:

- A detailed programme for informing and educating customers which identifies with their information needs and their decision making processes by shopping missions.
- A detailed schedule identifying activities with the required resources, their deployment and their costs by both merchandise group and location.
- A clear view of the relationships that are expected between sales volumes and the communications, expenditures required to achieve sales and profit objectives.

The Operating and Capital Expenditure Budgets and Investment Appraisal Schedule

The result of the planning activity is to provide an aggregate of resource requirements but detailed sufficiently for their acquisition to be commenced. Thus we have schedules for merchandise and buying management from which merchandise budgets can be developed by product group, by region and by retail outlets. From this information augmented by sales forecasts the cycle stocks and safety stocks can be expressed as both merchandise sales activity and cashflow projections at store level and in distribution systems.

The planning detail also identifies the human resource requirements and when the store planning data is combined with this data an operating cost budget may be projected which details occupancy costs, staff and supervision costs. This is completed by details from the customer communications plan with an advertising and promotional cost schedule for the merchandise seasons and outlets.

Possibly more important is the capital cost budget which is developed from the store planning activity and from which the entry costs can be finalised. This budget details the investment in property, equipment and fixtures for the branch network, distribution and the systems support structure. An important feature of the process should be an assessment of the capacity utilisation changes that are likely to occur. Assuming that the investment decision is an addition to the existing business it follows that existing sales and distribution capacity should also be reviewed. This will result in minimising any additional investment that is required. It should not lead to the use of property equipment or any other facilities that are inappropriate, rather it serves as an audit of the capital requirements (and availability) of the business prior to making unnecessary capital expenditures. It may lead to the opportunity for the disposal of facilities that are no longer large enough or perhaps in the wrong location. There is also the possibility that the total costs of the business may be reduced by consolidating distribution and operations facilities.

The budgeting process is completed by using the sales forecasts, operating and capital budgets to verify the initial return on investment. Clearly the proposal would not have reached the planning stage if the initial investment appraisal had shown a doubtful return. However, it is useful to repeat the appraisal when more detailed and accurate costings have become available. As we can see from the planning process it is likely that a number of variations from the estimates will occur and a review prior to initiating the implementation is valuable.

Operations Management Resources and Tasks

Operations Management activities are specific to the task to be performed. Consequently reference that is made here can only refer in broad terms to structure and tasks. For most retail businesses operations resources include store locations, merchandise, data processing equipment, human resources and of course the customer base. The operations division is responsible for: manpower planning, updating the in-store systems, maintaining documentation/procedures manuals; maintaining all work studies, organisation and methods, new operational methods, etc., and maintaining an ongoing review of standards and times for working tasks.

At an area (or regional) management level tasks are delegated such that the managers at this level are responsible for managing all store operations and activities in the area; ensuring that prescribed performance standards are achieved ensuring that training programmes are conducted undertaking necessary audits of store activities and initiate appropriate actions liaising with service support personnel, undertaking regular territory and store visits, and ensuring that appraisals are made of field and store personnel.

A number of operations performance measures are usually made. These typically measure; costs to sales ratios; stock losses actual/planned (%); actual hours worked/budgeted hours; items handled per man hour labour costs per items handled; stock item count/computer reported levels; customer complaints incidence; store contribution percentage; store net profit percentage (after full cost allocation); stock availability percentage; promotional schedules met on time; training completed as scheduled; sales per square foot; sales per £1 stock held; sales per £1 labour cost; sales per 1 rent, and a regular comparison between original 'project' viability and actual performance as a return on investment, net present value or internal rate of return.

Distribution Management Resources and Tasks

As with operations management so too with distribution activities. The tasks undertaken and resources are company specific. Typically distribution resources comprise warehousing (own account and third party), computer systems, vehicles (owned and/or leased) and human resources. The distribution organisation is responsible for: defining, updating and changing the distribution strategy of the company; providing data for distribution centre work load planning; reviewing system efficiency and maintaining an on-going review of distribution equipment suppliers that may improve system efficiency, and take the initiative in the design, specification, building and equipping of all new distribution facilities.

Within the distribution system, distribution centre managers have a number of delegated responsibilities. These usually include: all intake to the distribution centre; all stock movements; all replenishment order processing; all transport activities to and from the branches as scheduled by operational necessity; deliveries of excess stocks and damaged items (including warranty returns) to suppliers; all day-to-day disciplinary and industrial relations issues, and maintaining staff levels and training.

Distribution performance measures typically include: managing activity performance within budgeted levels; meeting productivity standards and costs per unit in the following areas, goods inwards handling, inspection, internal transport activities, order picking activities, returns of damaged stock, returns of good stock, vehicle cube utilisation, transport costs per mile and transport costs per delivery. In addition, replenishment requests (numbers) should not exceed a pre-determined level, time limits should exist for the exposure of high risk stock (prior to delivery to branches, tachograph readings should be within legally required limits, delivery delays within prescribed limits, picking up errors within prescribed limits, stock availability requirements by product group and, vehicle maintenance as per schedules.

Systems Support Requirements

While the systems needs for operational and strategic planning differ in many respects there is a link between them. Operational decisions will require systems that are capable of identifying and classifying customer shopping behaviour (frequency of visits, transaction values, etc.) features. These systems are used for inventory control and replenishment. Data from these sources may be used in CAD (computer aided design) systems to evaluate the impact of changes in the retail offer element (and indeed in the reverse direction: to evaluate the impact that changes in shopping missions imply for the retail format). Longer term issues arise from customer purchasing data. Trend analysis may identify shifts in shopping missions that have long-term implications for both store location decisions, current and future format decisions.

External data is essential for decision implementation activities. While internal systems will provide customer and sales data flows, and to a degree will provide information concerning the success (or otherwise) of the project it may be insufficient. Often management requires qualitative data which reports customer attitudes and perceptions. This data may be obtained from tracking studies (discussed in Chapter 10) but often data emerging from focus group activities is more revealing, providing information that is descriptive but which when compared with quantitative data and together with company performance can be very helpful.

Other external data, such as catchment profiling, has been described earlier (see Chapter 10). Its usefulness in the planning and implementation stages is in identifying potential markets and when several sources of data are combined, e.g., catchment profiles, consumer spending, home and car ownership, together with competitive profiles and activities, performance expectations may be adjusted and merchandise and service offers revised.

Systems support systems may be seen as having a number of facets. While they are used to automate decision making concerning stock levels and labour scheduling they may also be used to 'empower', to devolve decision making to a level where specific decisions are made more effectively.

There are a number of issues to be considered and it is incumbent on management to identify how decision making can be made more effective during the implementation of a project and afterwards during the operational management of the venture.

Sensitivity Analysis

Part of the final review of the implementation process, prior to making commitments, is a sensitivity analysis. As part of the review management should be encouraged to examine the forecast cost structures. Earlier, in Chapter 9, operational gearing was discussed and specifically the impact of high levels of operational gearing on contribution as volume fluctuates. As the project is now much closer to being operational it is good management practice to check the initial assumptions upon which the forecasts of both revenues and costs were made. Changes that may increase operational risks and lead to a lower level of contribution performance through the cost structure of the business should be reviewed together with opportunities to make changes to the operating gearing (by changing the fixed cost/variable cost relationship).

The financial model of the business introduced in Chapter 9 (Figure 9.1) may be used to investigate sensitivity areas. Figure 15.9 has been developed from McCammon (1970). It permits the examination of the impact of the cost changes on the overall return on assets and also offers the facility to examine the 'trade-off' possibilities that exist on an intra-company basis and an inter-company basis.

Intra-company cost topics that may be explored include the operational gearing issue among others. Fixed costs may be increased by the introduction of an EPOS data capture system but this will reduce the variable costs of stockholding and staff levels in branches. Another intra-company issue concerns the rationalisation of low performing outlets and merchandise ranges, both of which will have implications on the return on assets. The nature and extent of the impact can only be determined after the operational gearing effect (fixed costs: variable costs) and the change in contribution to overhead (overhead cost allocation) has been explored. Changes in attributes may also be investigated. For example, a change in the level of service offered by the addition (or reduction) of staff will have obvious implications for operating margins. However, the improvement that should be experienced in sale revenue should offset these increases. The inter-company options facing management can be similarly explored. For example the impact on margins of a smaller supplier base or perhaps of using third party distribution services may be investigated.

The model offers a useful aid for both the initial planning activity and the implementation of plans because at any stage the model may be asked a number of inter-related 'What if?' questions. The result will be a more effective result as and when the project is operating. We can extend the model to examine the implications of changes in financial management structure and, as a consequence, the cost of capital. Figure 15.10 adds a financial gearing element to the model which can be used to demonstrate the impact of more or less gearing on the return to the shareholders. In Figure 15.10 the shareholders' investment is considered to be the ordinary share capital

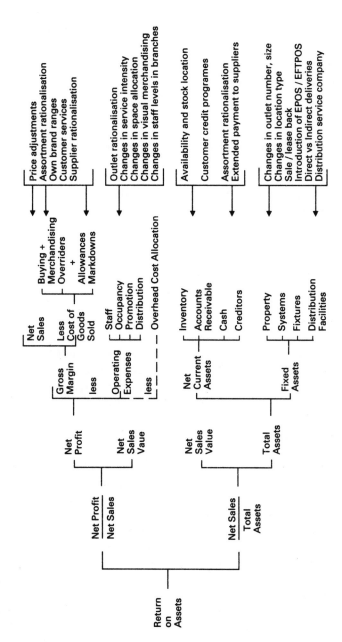

Figure 15.9 The strategic profit model: adapted to show the impact of retail management decisions

Figure 15.10   The strategic profit model adapted to show the impact of financial gearing

plus retained earnings, thus long term liabilities are omitted. If we assume that Net Assets = Capital Employed then:

$$\frac{\text{Net Assets}}{\substack{\text{Return on}\\\text{Shareholders'}\\\text{Investment}}}$$

is a measure of the gearing in the business. We also assume that Net Assets = Trading Assets. This is a useful extension of the model because it introduces the funding option. It follows that if money can be borrowed, long term, at a pre-tax interest charge of 12% and invested in assets that return 24% the shareholders' earnings will be larger if expansion is financed by borrowed funds than if financed by equity funds.

Performance Expectations

Performance criteria were discussed in detail in Chapters 12 and 13 and they have been discussed in the context of operations and distribution management in this Chapter. The specific needs of companies varies with the type of business sector in which they operate and the management systems and organisation structure used to implement and manage decisions. The suggestion that is implicit in Figure 15.8 is that as a project evolves, through the planning stages and into the implementation activity the precise performance criteria, their reporting frequencies and their dissemination will be determined. Chapter 13 presented a range of measurement criteria based upon the premise that performance should be measured at a strategic level as well as at the operational level. The argument made in the latter part of Chapter 12 is that the activity based management analysis will result in establishing performance measures based upon activities that contribute towards customer satisfaction. This does not in any way minimise the importance of resource productivity measurement: they continue to be basic indicators of productivity as the performance measurements applied to the operations and distribution functions suggested.

SUMMARY

This chapter has served to synthesise the concepts, issues and discussion of the earlier chapters. It revisited the strategy model used by the author in previous work and introduced in Chapter 1. The revisions made to the model were suggested by events in the retail business environment.

The use of shopping missions to focus decision in both strategic and operational planning was established and examples of how they may be used effectively were made. The chapter used shopping missions to identify changes that may become necessary to the critical success factors and positioning of the business. The point made in Part III has been that a group of well defined critical success factors are essential if an effective response is to be made to an opportunity.

The necessity to consider the interrelationships between decisions and functions was discussed at length. The basic point to be made from this discussion is simply that unless the planning activities are conducted with these cross-functional issues in mind problems may subsequently occur because of an unnecessary use of resources (resulting in excessive costs, a poor customer offer, or both). These considerations are necessary at both the strategic and the operational levels of decision making.

The remainder of the chapter was devoted to developing a model for use when implementing decisions. It used the materials developed throughout the text and explored the issues confronting the manager when planning the detailed implementation of strategic and operational decisions.

Part IV

Retail Decision Making in Action: Examples from the Retail Sector

INTRODUCTION

Part IV reviews the recent management responses of major retailing companies. Desk research from company reports and observers comments in the financial press has resulted in a review of managerial strategic and operational decisions within major UK and Continental European businesses over the 1992–3 period. The decisions are examined within the context of the framework of the model used throughout the text.

This review is followed by a case study prompted by observing the development of a format by a retailing business. The revenues and costs are close estimates to the actual amounts but because of this the case is presented as an anonymous business. It illustrates how research and format test marketing may be used to evaluate a format concept using the concepts and techniques developed or reviewed in this text. The reader is encouraged to consider both the decisions taken and the opportunities facing the company.

16 Implementing Retailing Management Decisions: Recent Examples

INTRODUCTION

The recession period since 1989 has led to significant changes in consumer attitudes towards their expenditure patterns. Whether these will change over time and revert back to the patterns of the 1980s is arguable. A Mintel Report (1993) report suggested significant differences among European consumers. Some of the topics reported upon were clearly established trends, such as the population and demographic trends and the socio-demographic trends in divorce. However, what is of interest are the expenditure comparisons of the UK and other European countries on food, leisure and clothing and footwear. On each UK spending is below other major European countries with the exceptions of food (where the Netherlands' spend per household is the lowest) and leisure (for which the Belgians spend least). UK average expenditure on food, drink and tobacco is 16.6% of household budget; on leisure 10% and clothing and footwear 5.6% and this typically is spent on low priced products imported from Asia. Consumer credit levels fell during 1991–2. Mortgage applications reached a hitherto unknown low level. House prices decreased steadily such that by 1992 they were in some areas they reached 60% of the values enjoyed in the mid-1980s.

The issue confronting retailing management is to identify consumers' expectations for the short and medium term. The general view was well expressed by Ben Laurance in the *Guardian* (May 20, 1993): 'Just about every retailer one asks says that, in the nineties, consumers will pay greater attention to "value". Kingfisher is particularly vocal (although by no means alone) in promoting the idea that higher profits will come from generating higher turnover with slimmer mark-ups. Even Marks & Spencer felt it right last year to cut prices in order to stimulate demand. And in food retailing, the huge expansion by discounters – trying to snatch custom from the superstore operators who have hitherto put emphasis on quality, convenience and choice – illustrates a new-found nineties interest in thrift'.

The remainder of this chapter examines retailing decisions within the context of this environment.

16.1   EXAMPLES OF RETAIL MANAGEMENT DECISION MAKING

Introduction

As the introduction to the chapter suggested there have been considerable pressures put upon retailing managers in the past five years. Despite these pressures, which have come from the impact of the worst retailing recession for 60 years, there has been growth of sales and profits by many companies. The remainder of this chapter considers the strategic and operational decisions that have been implemented by major companies across a range of product sectors. To examine these activities the model developed in Chapter 1 and used throughout will once again form the basis of the analysis.

Each of the companies' activities is considered in the context of generating sales, gross margin management, operating margin management and contribution to overhead and profit. Figure 16.1 indicates the particular activity influenced by the Company's decision. Thus a decision which will influence operating margins taken by Asda will be indicated thus:

Operating   Asda (2,7)
Margin
Management

The bracketed numbers are the notes in the text referring to the specific decisions.

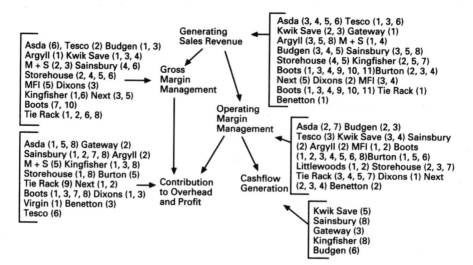

Figure 16.1   Plotting retailing decisions

Asda Stores

During recent years Asda has been under considerable competitive pressures and, at the same time, was experiencing funding difficulties. Their new chief executive implemented some major policy changes in both the strategy and operations of the business.

A substantial reduction in overhead structure and costs was implemented (1) together with a decrease in operating costs through a wage freeze (2). New formats have been introduced (3). Dales is a discount based offer, aimed at competing for an expanding segment of the food market while Renewal was seen as a repositioning exercise to reinforce a move back towards the price led offer that the company once relied upon. This action was accompanied by a focusing on assortment variety while maintaining price competitiveness (4). Produce ranges have been expanded to compete with high street specialists (5); non-food participation was also a concern with notable expansion taking place in recorded music, specifically CD products. The company, clearly concerned with space productivity and utilisation, undertook a number of range rationalisation activities (7); for example a review of the pack varieties of brown sauce revealed 19 different bottles. These were considerably reduced. For the year 1992–3 the return to the 'Asda value' strategy of the 1980s, together with a greater emphasis on fresh foods (where it has lagged behind Tesco, Sainsbury and Safeway) and the implementation of the cost reduction programme resulted in a 13% improvement in profitability.

Tesco PLC

An extensive store opening programme together with a strong merchandise development programme were major features of the Tesco activity. The financial press did comment on the extent of the capital programme and to the fact that the new store openings accounted for a large proportion of sales growth. A general view was that this contribution was perhaps too large. It was also noticed that sales productivity was continuing to increase, but doing so at a decreased rate. Price promotion was a response to decreasing average transaction values (1) together with joint promotions with Acorn (computer vouchers for schools on purchase values of £25). Local pricing (2) has been implemented as a means by which local price competitive situations may be resolved, 'Multibuys' have also been a response to decreasing transaction values.

The store opening programme included large superstores and an expansion of the smaller 'metro' stores in busy urban/commercial areas (3)(5). The large stores were significant in the company's move towards generating larger operating economies, and thereby resulted in an increase in operating margins. The smaller stores increased market penetration in urban areas and could be seen as an element in the customer service programme by providing seven day extended hours service to residents of inner city areas.

Organisational changes were made in which branch management structures were revised: functional management replaced product management and considerable savings in costs were the result.

The acquisition of Catteau (6), a French food retailer with a diverse range of outlet types, will provide Tesco with a number of benefits. For example there will be the expertise gained in operating a subsidiary at the some distance from the main centre of the business, there will be the expertise gained in operating a more diverse range of stores, the facility of an added dimension to merchandise development and, of course, the potential to improve upon buying margins through the effect of increased volumes.

Kwik Save

Kwik Save has enjoyed relatively uninterrupted growth for a number of years as it expanded in areas typically 'under shopped' for good outlets. As we have seen the competition within the discount sector of the food market has intensified and Kwik Save has not been slow to respond. An own brand programme (1) has been launched across the range clearly with the intention of enhancing gross margins. A large expansion programme, 100 additional outlets throughout Scotland is planned for 1994 (2).

Both gross margins, and sales volume are in mind with the use of concessions for produce sales in the stores. Clearly the company is also conscious of the impact these will have on transaction values (3). It is also very likely that the produce concessions will enhance operating margins: Kwik Save have the sales benefits (albeit at a discount) but not the costs of preparation, storage, distribution and waste.

The use of information technology to manage stock levels and space allocation has been accompanied by range extensions (4). This will provide Kwik Save with a dual benefit: they will be able to increase average customer transaction values (and customer satisfaction) and they will also increase gross margin yield. It could also be added that their operating margins should benefit through improved stock and space management (and by inference) labour productivity. The company can be seen to be using information to ensure that cash generation as well as profit is achieved (5).

Sainsbury

The strong growth and profit record of Sainsbury is due to many ways to the resolute focus on its main core business (1). The Company has avoided high risk diversification opportunities by joint venture programmes with partners who provide the expertise Sainsbury lacks. The focus of the company's development has been in investment in existing stores to improve operating efficiency (2)(3). The expansion would appear to be planned to optimise economies of scale in operations, distribution and promotion. Sales growth and gross margin management have been reinforced by investment in product development (4): during 1992–3 the company introduced 1400 new items and 1000 were reformulated.

An awareness of the business environment, its changes and its opportunities, through a marketing research programme ensures that Sainsbury can respond with appropriate location and merchandise decisions (5). An example of the coordinated marketing research/marketing decision process working well for the company is the success achieved by exploiting the own brand detergent Novon (6), a decision resulting in a doubling of Sainsbury's market share in that sector. The effective implementation of the corporate financial structure is reflected in the way in which the proven format is maintained and is managed to promote profitability and cash generation through high sales intensity, lower costs and smaller price increases (7)(8).

Gateway

Gateway has been a store group that has experienced financial problems. Generally thought to be over-geared the company's senior management has spent much of its time with its financiers restructuring its debt. Burdened with this debt Gateway has struggled to meet interest payments most of which (if not all) have absorbed the profit that has been generated. Following the lack of any significant success with Somerfield, Gateway turned to Food Giant (1) a price led offer to promote the sales volume clearly needed if it was to generate a contribution to profit, overhead and the interest payments. Food Giant was based upon a format which comprised 10/12 000 square feet selling area, a 'basic' store environment in off-centre locations. Prices were some 10–15% below average prices set by competitors across volume selling manufacturers' brands. The concept is to be expanded to 100 stores.

Debt restructuring continues to be a problem for Gateway and its parent Isosceles (2) and it has been suggested that further disposals of selected stores to raise cash is a possibility (3).

Budgen

Budgen has also had its problems. Essentially a small but specialist retailer it has focused on a specific segment of the food market. Lacking the benefit of volume to generate acceptable margins profitability performance has been disappointing. The involvement of the company in a buying consortium with Londis and G rele K (1) will go some way towards rectifying the gross margin problem while the introduction of IT merchandise systems (2) should contribute to improved operating margins. These are likely to be further enhanced by the improved operating efficiencies developed in distribution (3).

Local pricing (4) is an important feature of the Budgen offer. By pursuing a specialist formal price flexibility improves margin management. The offer relies heavily on exclusivity and choice together with a visual merchandising treatment that reinforces a 'quality' positioning. One of the problems of such an offer is that merchandise density is typically low and may result in low customer transaction values; values which are much lower than the superstore competitors operating large stores, out-of-town, with considerable car parking facilities. The company recently (July 1993) announced an experimental format. Penny Market is a low priced offer competing in an expanding segment of the food sector.

Argyll/Safeway

The Argyll Group has been very active in building responses to both the recession and the European opportunity (1). By following an aggressive store opening programme for Safeway the company has built volume and hence margins approaching those of its competitors, Sainsbury and Tesco. This has also enabled the company to develop cost-effective operations and to maintain operating margins at an optimum level (2). As a major partner in the European Retail Alliance (refer back to Chapter 8) Argyll has taken a long term view concerning its operations (2). By maintaining its Lo Cost and Presto brands Argyll remains competitive in the expanding discount sector (3).

Mixed and Non-Food Retailing

Marks & Spencer

Marks & Spencer have been aware of the problems caused by the recession. A pricing strategy was introduced to shift the product mix towards lower price points (1). Prices of the more staple clothing and food items were also reduced to achieve volume objectives (for example, the popular selling ranges of jeans were reduced from £22.50 to £19.50). Furniture prices have also been adjusted (4).

However, conscious of sales volume, transaction size value and gross margin achievement the company has introduced merchandise augmentation characteristics where possible. The availability of wedding list services, butchery, self-service produce and store-to-car service are a few of the examples of merchandise augmentation and customer service introductions made recently (2). The wedding list service is all-embracing. It offers a catalogue selection, and a store wide computer listing of wedding gifts already purchased in each of the 35 participating stores.

Merchandise development has continued to expand both the departments and the ranges within departments (3). The planned store development activity emphasises expansion of the existing format in the UK and on the Continent with concentration on large stores and food only satellites. The company reports numerous requests from overseas for Marks & Spencer involvement (5). While the company suggests that it may expand the format internationally, the Far East being one possible area, it does not foresee any further acquisitions. However, in its 1992–3 report the acquisitions which were performing at a disappointingly low level are beginning to contribute.

Storehouse

During the Spring/Summer of 1992 Storehouse rationalised the business by disposing of (or announcing the intention to dispose of) those components it saw as lacking 'fit' (compatibility) with the core business (1). At the same time four layers of management were dismantled together with a significant reduction in store employees. Some 800 full time staff were replaced by 2000 'keytimers' who work between 12 and 20 hours per week (2). Service departments, such as architecture, were closed and quite radical developments such as Mothercare eventually 'putting out' its IT and information management activities to a service company were encouraged (3).

Within the rationalised business, BhS and Mothercare, visual merchandising has been introduced with the objectives of advising customers of product coordination possibilities (service augmentation: information) and to build transaction values (4). A store loyalty card has been introduced with the object of encouraging repeat visits (BhS and Mothercare become destination purchase stores) increasing gross margin benefits and larger average transac-tions from price insensitive customers (5).

Supplier rationalisation has been implemented with improved gross margins and more flexibility as the objectives (6). Space productivity will be improved due to the 'increase' of space by some 30% by replacing floor standing wardrobes with wall fixtures (7). As space increases visual merchandising and merchandise density are likely to be used more effectively in the drive to increase sales volume. Once Blazer has been sold the BhS/Mothercare business will be expanded by replication (8). Further acquisitions are not seen as a profitable method of growth.

Kingfisher

Kingfisher, by contrast to Storehouse, has expanded its conglomerate activities with considerable success (1). A joint venture with Staples has established the company in an additional product-market and the Darty acquisition has expanded sales and profits. Darty enables the company to improve buying margins in Comet. One commentator suggested 'It (Darty) earns some of the best margins in the world'. Furthermore, Darty's expertise in manufacturer branded product sales will benefit cash margins through higher selling prices (8). In addition to the impact on earnings Kingfisher will gain from the expertise Darty has developed over recent years in customer service. It is in areas of merchandise and service augmentation that competitive advantage can be built. If this can be done cost-effectively (in other words with the benefit of very large international volumes) the impact on gross margin (cost additions) can be minimised. Darty provides Kingfisher with this opportunity.

Future growth of the business is seen to lie in 'growing markets' (3). Kingfisher describes these as markets which '. . . mirror demographic and lifestyle changes of the times . . . an older and better off consumer, at ease with technology and may be working from home. Someone with active brain-working pastimes'.

The Darty acquisition also suggests that the Company is cognizant of the importance of purchasing volumes in a European context. Large retailing businesses will be 'indispensable to any manufacturer supplying the European market.' Clearly by expanding the reformatted Comet together with Darty (planned to expand from 130 stores to between 180–200 by the end of the decade) Kingfisher will be a significant retailer in the consumer durables product-market (6). Such expansion would appear to be more effective than that achieved by a domestic acquisition (such as Dixons). Growth can be managed and to a degree is accompanied with less risk.

Dixons

Despite the impact of the recession Dixons has managed to maintain creditable sales volume and profit margins. Some rationalisation of its business has contributed towards this (1). In its US activity it is rebuilding management, procedures, systems, and service. Curry's is being repositioned into an off-centre superstore centre (2) as is Silo. Silo has run up losses of £58.6 million, closures will leave 185 stores. Two new formats are being tested. They will specialise in brown goods (emphasising computers and home office equipment). They do not stock white goods. (Silo was sold in 1993.)

The company, due to its extensive overseas sourcing, expects an adverse effect from the 1992 devaluation of sterling forecasting possible price increases in the region of 5–20%. In a price competitive market (one which forced the electricity boards' retailing activities to consider their future seriously and from which the London Electricity Board retreated) this could cause Dixons some problems.

Operating profits for 1992–3 increased. This comprised a £200 000 contribution from PC World, an increase in market share and the increased number of Currys out of town superstores (18 were opened) bring the total to 133, all of which operate at lower costs and higher margins.

Littlewoods

A somewhat secretive company. However, the move out of food and the concession agreement with Iceland (1) suggests that volumes were insufficient to earn satisfactory margins from their high street locations. A reduction of staff in the mail order operation suggests further problems (2).

Tie Rack

Tie Rack can be seen as the most successful of the specialist retailing formats. Having experienced some difficulties the company has begun to make profits. It has developed a merchandise strategy which is based on a focused range of ties and scarves together with some related products such as waistcoats and shirts. The strategy requires frequent design changes thereby maintaining a fashion interest in the range and maintaining customer awareness and a high visit frequency. This strategy is likely to establish Tie Rack as a destination purchase shopping mission (1). A competitive view of pricing

(6) is another component of the merchandise strategy together with a product development activity looking at own brands and corporate neckwear both of which will offer the opportunity to improve the gross margins of the merchandise assortment.

A concurrent rationalisation programme has been implemented. The relationship with suppliers has been improved resulting in improved buying terms through bulk purchasing discounts (2). The US operations costs have been reduced by closing a warehouse (4). The introduction of an EPOS system at a cost of £3 million is aimed at improving cost control and operating margins (3). Further rationalisation has been achieved by closing loss making stores (5). While the company has reduced its number of outlets and reduced its franchised operations (7) it has improved overall performance (8). Further expansion will be sought in the UK and on the Continent.

Burton

Burton has been a casualty of the recession of the early 1990s. Like many other apparel retailers it has experienced the sharp reduction in consumer spending. In response Burton undertook both cost reduction action and at the same time took action to increase the sales productivity of its outlets. A number of staff restructuring activities aimed at decreasing full-time staff and replacing them with flexible part-time employees (1). A standardisation of employment terms, equal pay, the reduction or removal of 'benefits' was implemented with the objective of simplifying management and administration (2).

Merchandise ranges were reviewed. Low volume ranges (and those lacking 'fit') were rationalised resulting in (on average) 30% fewer items per branch. This has resulted in more selling space for the remaining ranges and enabling the availability of sizes and styles to be increased (3). An increase in selling area was also achieved by revising layout and replacing fixtures (4). As a result a more effective visual merchandising programme has been possible. It has more impact at a lower cost. The company has also implemented a programme in which fascia brands are being focused on their customer segments, for example Top Shop is being returned to an offer characterised by low prices (5).

MFI

Furniture retailing has had similar difficulties. Much of MFI's management decisions have been directed towards increasing operating efficiencies and sales productivity. An investment in systems (1) has resulted in improved operations with lower staff numbers in stores. Stock control systems and distribution efficiencies have reduced warehouse space requirements (2). Improved store layouts and visual merchandising has increased sales by approximately 6.5% (3) and Sunday opening (4) has also helped improve sales volumes. Further economies have been achieved by implementing a programme of backward vertical integration. This has considerable impact, a 1% increase in sales results in the addition of £2 million to profit (5).

Next

Next faced serious problems at the end of the 1980s and early 1990s. Having expanded by increasing selling area and increasing the fascia brands it found a confused and disenchanted customer who, because of restricted disposable incomes (high levels of personal debt, redundancy and an increasing lack of confidence) no longer gave Next the support it enjoyed in the early and mid-1980s.

The company's response has been effective. It rationalised the fascia brands (1) and returned the business to the format that had accounted for its huge success. The merchandise strategy focused on style and finish offering the style/quality/price combination successful in the early 1980s (1). Ranges are now restructured to appeal to the same target market. Choice has increased and development of the merchandise offer is based upon the existing assortment (3).

A store rationalisation programme reduced the number of stores (from 361 to just over 300). Sales in 1992 increased by 20% while space decreased by 13% (2). The resulting productivity has been apparent in the improved performance. Productivity improvements continue, enhanced by improved information management which ensures replenishment of fast selling items – a problem in the past (3).

Visual merchandising has been made more effective. Both instore and window displays are changed more frequently: the coordinated merchandise displays once again improving transaction values and providing customers with coordination advice (service augmentation). Next is returning to its 'destination purchase' shopping mission status (5).

Boots

Boots have made some major changes to their retail organisation which have resulted in significant increases in performance. Buying and merchandising have been reorganised into business centres based upon product groups (1) which has enabled the buyers/merchandisers to develop greater knowledge and expertise within merchandise groups rather than across a number of unrelated areas (2). Store operations have also undergone changes. Operations management has been reorganised into large and small stores groups: it was found that the problems were quite different and more effective management was possible by this change (3). Space productivity has been improved by the effective use of Spaceman for merchandise ranging and space allocation (4).

Operating efficiency has also been improved through EPOS installations which has been completed throughout the chain of 1100 stores (5). This is expected to result in stock reductions of some 20% over 1993–4, some £50–£60 million less in working capital. The EPOS facility is also expected to improve staff scheduling such that it will be easier to meet the pattern of demand in the stores. A change in the balance between full-time/part-time staff is envisaged. A 1% reduction in staff costs results in a saving of £270 million (6).

Improved gross margin performance has resulted from a revised product mix. Direct product productivity (DPP) control of 42 000 lines has increased gross margins (7). DPP has facilitated range decisions by store location and store size. The sophistication of the information system provides information on price sensitivity, particularly important for own label products. Sales of seasonal lines are tracked and prices adjusted to ensure the 'sell through' at optimal margins through price adjustments. The information system provides for rapid replacement of fast moving items. Customer transactions are increased by cross promotions (e.g. films and sun tan oil), another feature of the information system. The development of a loyalty scheme, based upon 5 million customer medical records is also a service provided by the informa-tion system (8).

Developments in the merchandise areas have parallelled store operations changes and these have supported the development of specialist retailing activities e.g. Health and Beauty, Opticians and Photographic Processing (9). An expansion of the Health and Beauty store portfolio has been extended by an agreement with Sainsbury to open concessions in Sainsbury superstores offering the Health and Beauty format from 100–200 square metres instore outlets (10). The Company has been innovative and ready to experiment. A sandwich outlet was experimented in London in 1992. (11)

Benetton
Benetton is a company that has caused comment for a number of reasons. Benetton, well known for its vertical integration has focused on manufacturing costs and improved its contribution margins by some 38.1% to 39.2%. (This in the context of a vertically integrated business has significant implications for overall profitability). A new production facility has reduced the number of employees from 800 to 280, energy costs have been reduced by some 30% and packaging costs have been reduced by 40% by the introduction of a new packaging system (1). Sales are expected to rise following list price reductions of 4.8% for 1994, reinforced by the lira's devaluation (2). In some markets this will mean a 20% price reduction.

Despite the recession Benetton forecasts a 10% increase in profits and sales in 1993–4 (3). Corporate diversification (sports equipment) is planned to continue and to develop 10 world leading brands!

SUMMARY

This chapter has identified examples of retail decisions by a number of companies operating in different sectors of the retail market and in different segments within the sectors. The analysis suggests that they share the view that margin management at both gross margin and operating margin levels is an essential feature of current retailing practice. However, the analysis also presents evidence that a large majority of the companies do actively seek growth opportunities. As can be seen a number of them have managed their businesses effectively over a difficult period whilst some have managed for recovery not simply for survival.

The examples reviewed have also illustrated many of the principles discussed in earlier chapters. The final chapter is a case study which uses the principles extensively in implementing a decision to reposition the company.

Bibliography

The research for this chapter has been undertaken over an extended period. It was a process by which the companies identified were 'tracked' by monitoring published sources of information. The publications utilised were:

Company reports
Mintel (various reports)
Verdict (various reports)
Marketing Week
The *Financial Times*
The *Guardian*
The *Independent*
The *Sunday Times*
The *Independent on Sunday*
The *Evening Standard*
Retail Week.

17 Implementing Retailing Management Decisions: Fleetwood Ltd

This chapter is based on observation of a retailer undergoing a repositioning exercise. Fleetwood does not exist as a company but the case study is based on a company which has just recently successfully adjusted its market positioning. The process described follows the decision making process likely to have been followed by the company. A business plan is agreed and implemented. The reader is encouraged to consider what actions should be taken after twelve months successful trading.

17.1 FLEETWOOD LTD

Introduction

Fleetwood commenced business in South London in the 1880s. John Fleetwood opened a single small store selling household products including cookware, cast iron utensils, galvanised buckets, cleaning materials and other items that were necessities in Victorian households.

Over the years the Company expanded but remained a family business. The product range reflected changes in consumer needs and requirements. During the 1960s and 1970s the range was predominantly household products but the range expanded to include some of the newer products that accompanied the increasing interest in cooking as a leisure activity rather than simply as a household chore. This expansion included a number of accessories, such as containers in glass and ceramics.

As the business grew its philosophy shifted. It began to see itself as a destination purchase store for customers seeking more practical gifts for weddings and other occasions. By this time, and by now we are in the early 1980s, the Company operated some fifty stores. The merchandise range began to reflect the consumer preference for quality and some exclusivity and Continental cookware and utensils were introduced very successfully. The portfolio of stores had also changed. While the number showed no major increase or decrease, it was between 60 or 70 stores at this time, the size and location characteristics varied considerably. As a consequence it was not surprising to find substantial performance differences across the stores and the merchandise ranges.

By the late 1980s the Directors began to think about the shape of Fleetwood for the 1990s. A profit and loss account and balance sheet for 1988–9 provides information on the financial position of the Company. They had commissioned some research which suggested to them that consumer attitudes towards their homes had changed over the past 15 to 20 years. The introduction of design into household products by Conran and the growth of the Habitat store group during the 1970s had clearly made an impact on consumer preferences. The research had found that customers were conscious of design as well as functional properties of kitchen and dining room products. The research showed quite clearly that for a viable number of potential customers there was an opportunity to develop an 'offer' which was based upon both style and functional efficiency in these two well used areas of the home.

In essence the research findings suggested that among the AB, C1 socio-economic groups (who were typically ACORN Is and Js), aged between late 20s and mid-40s there was an opportunity for a multiple retailing activity which offered ranges of quality merchandise not found in other stores, at affordable prices. Fleetwood considered the research to be helpful in that it offered some focus to the direction that it had been moving during the past five years or so. However, being cautious, they felt that should first explore the concept. They were aware of the fact that Habitat had, during the 1980s lost its way and they were not in a position financially to take risks. It was decided that three store types would be used to evaluate the concept which was described as: 'A store for the person who is concerned both with style and function in the products they purchase and who consider that both style and function are attributes that may be combined effectively in areas of the home that usually are seen in a utilitarian context.' The implementation of the concept requires an understanding of form and function, colour and design and an ability to identify merchandise that conforms with this concept in kitchen and tableware, in glass and ceramics, in furniture, lighting and textiles.

The stores selected for the concept development and testing were selected on the criteria of:

Size: it was considered essential to future operations to evaluate the concept across a range of typical Fleetwood stores. In so doing it would identify 'ideal' store sizes and would also give an indication as to the suitability (or otherwise) of the existing stores should it subsequently be decided to 'roll-out' the format.

Performance: it was decided to use stores whose sales of merchandise items which would be included in the format (or similar) were above average. It was considered that this would indicate suitability of both merchandise and location, as again, the Company was concerned that it had, by now, some 80 stores.

17.2   THE FLEETWOOD CONCEPT STORE

By this time (1988–9) the store portfolio comprised: 10 stores of 5000 square feet 15 stores of 3500 square feet 57 stores of 2000 square feet The concept store format was aimed to provide the customer with a wide choice of merchandise items for the kitchen and dining room. The complete range would offer: cookware, tableware, ovenware, cutlery, glassware, furniture, lighting, textiles and a range of natural accessories. The management's thinking behind the assortment strategy was to provide a wide range of choice in each assortment category but with the emphasis on the medium to higher range price points. In order that the transaction value be maximised a range of accessories was planned to augment the merchandise.

It was clear that store environment was to be a critical feature of the concept. Fleetwood had as a company always demonstrated design flair in their merchandise displays but they considered that a more professional approach was required and for the concept test they sought the services of a design consultant.

Another obvious feature of the concept was service and in the test stores it was decided to offer gift wrapping and a style/design service. A wedding list service was considered but not introduced as it was seen as a commitment to their customers which would not be continued if the decision was made not to proceed and roll-out the concept.

17.3   THE CONCEPT TEST

To establish a viable 'spend' and to obtain some results of significance the store sample was structured as follows: 2 – 5000 square feet (L) Large; 3 – 3500 square feet (M) Medium; and, 12 – 2000 square feet (S) Small. Their locations were largely similar: high street locations in suburban shopping centres or provincial towns with population numbering approximately 150 000. Each store had demonstrated an above average performance in the merchandise categories that were to be included in the concept format.

To build anonymity into the concept test the name Crosby was used and the locations were subjected to a cost-effective design exercise which was simple and which had as a principle the thought that the merchandise would be the focal point in a simply designed format. The cost of the change was achieved for £30 per square foot.

The stores were traded for a twelve month period and the results were as shown in Table 17.1.

It was clear from the performance that there were difficulties with the small category stores. It became clear that 2000 square feet was insufficient to display effectively the full range of the new assortment. Initially the Company's response was to reduce the width of each merchandise group and

Table 17.1 Test store performances

Store Category	Sales per sq.ft. per year	Average Customer Transaction	GM Target	GM Achieved	Stock-turn	Operating Cost as % Sales
A (5000 sq.ft.)	£135	£22.50	55	50	8	23
B (3500 sq.ft.)	£110	£20.00	55	50	8	23
C (2000 sq.ft.)	£75	£12.50	55	45	10	25

Table 17.2 Existing Fleetwood Stores' performance

Store Category	Sales per sq.ft. per year	Average Customer Transaction	GM Target	GM Achieved	Stock-turn	Operating Cost as % Sales
A (5000 sq.ft.)	£100	£17.50	45	43	8	25
B (3500 sq.ft.)	£85	£15.30	45	41	10	26
C (2000 sq.ft.)	£60	£10.75	45	40	12	27

evaluate the result. The transaction values did not increase, nor did the margin performance. In other stores the Company decided to restrict the number of ranges offered. Furniture and the basketware together with the rugs were withdrawn. This did nothing to improve the performance to any degree.

Customer research was used to monitor perceptions of features of the offer. (Table 17.1 and Figure 17.1 shows the responses.) Again the small stores indicated some serious problems that were clearly related to their size. The very poor responses to store environment characteristics presented the Company with an obvious conclusion: the concept was clearly not viable in stores of this size. However, the remaining results were encouraging and when compared with the financial performance the results of stores from the existing Fleetwood format were considerably better, as shown in Table 17.2.

Consequently at a board meeting it was decided to implement the Crosby format in the 5000 square feet and 3500 square feet stores.

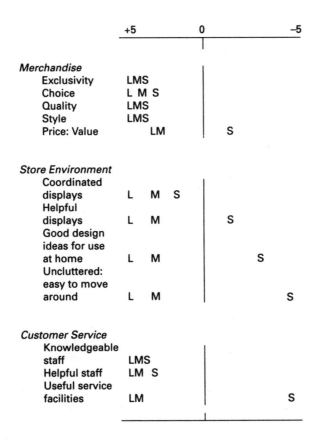

Figure 17.1 Customer perceptions of the Crosby offer characteristics

17.4 IMPLEMENTING CROSBY: SOME PLANNING ISSUES

Following the board meeting at which the decision to implement Crosby had been taken management set some objectives for the exercise. There were a number of decisions required and these were:

- What is the role of Crosby within the Fleetwood organisation: is it to be a subsidiary or is it to be developed such that it will replace the Fleetwood offer?
- What is the mission or purpose of Crosby? How will the customer see that Crosby is different?
- How many outlets are to be developed and over what time period?
- What is the merchandise strategy to which the buying/merchandising has to work? Within the strategy what is the role of merchandise augmentation? What are the differentiation characteristics?
- What is the customer service strategy direction? How will customer services differentiate the Crosby offer with service facilities and augmentation and staff characteristics and number?
- What will be the role of visual merchandising in Crosby with regard to information and persuasion?
- Information management with respect to the Crosby operations needs *and* to customer activities, responses and purchasing is another important decision.
- Distribution management will require clear direction if choice and availability are to be maintained and particularly so if sourcing is from non-domestic suppliers.

In response to these considerations a business plan for the introduction of Crosby was developed.

17.5 THE CROSBY BUSINESS PLAN

Introduction

Following the successful concept testing of the Crosby concept it is now our intention to expand Crosby into a substantial business. Initially Crosby and the existing Fleetwood business will be maintained separately for marketing and financial management purposes. However, a number of options are being considered once the Crosby format is trading successfully. These are:

- To divest the Fleetwood activity and focus management effort on Crosby.
- To maintain the two businesses as separate entities.
- To 'franchise' successful Fleetwood stores to the existing Fleetwood store managers but maintaining a procurement, merchandising and distribution

activity to service the 'franchisee's' needs.
- To franchise the Crosby concept in order to expand the business more rapidly than may be done so with existing resources.
- To consider borrowing (debt funding) to expand Crosby.

The current Fleetwood financial position is shown by the profit and loss account and balance sheet.

17.6 MISSION, OBJECTIVES AND STRATEGIC DIRECTION

Mission: Crosby will provide customers with an opportunity to add functional style and design to their homes at affordable prices.

Objectives: Crosby will provide the following sales and contribution amounts (financial) within its first two years of operations:

	£m.	
	Year 1	Year 2
Sales	£23.75	£34.14
Contribution	£2.97	£5.12

The intention is to operate twenty 5000 square feet (A) type outlets and twenty 3500 square feet (B) type outlets in the first year. In Year Two the intention is to add five more stores in both categories.

Objectives: Crosby marketing activities will return the following customer (marketing) performance:

- Customers will see Crosby as both a destination purchase store and a planned browsing shopping visit store.
- Customer transactions showed average:
  'A' category stores £27.50
  'B' category stores £22.50.
  Sales per square foot:
  'A' category stores £150.00
  'B' category stores £120.00
- Gross margin targets for both stores will be 55% but in the first year of trading we anticipate 50%–52.5%.
- Stockturn target is to be 10 times per year.
- Target customer perceptions are to see Crosby as:
  A store with exclusive quality kitchen and dining room products (and accessories) at prices which, while a little more than prices for products fulfilling similar functions, clearly can be seen to offer added value through their aesthetic appeal.

- A store whose service to customers is always helpful and considerate.
- A store whose service facilities add value and are not expensive and trivial afterthoughts.
- Visual merchandising will primarily help customers by demonstrating product use and style coordination.

Positioning: Crosby's market positioning will be based upon kitchen and dining room products that are both functional and aesthetic in their appeal. The merchandise offer will be supported by a very high level of personal attention offered by knowledgeable sales staff together with service facilities offering a 'wedding list' service, gift suggestion and gift wrapping. Close customer liaison will be maintained through a customer database.

Target Customer Profile: The Crosby customer is likely to be aged between thirty and fifty, in the AB and aspirant C1 socio-economic group. More important is an attitude towards style: they are interested in style and product function in equal proportions and seek well styled as well as functional products for their homes.

17.7 CROSBY MERCHANDISE STRATEGY

Merchandise assortment is planned to include:

Cookware: A range of applications and finishes comprising enamelled (coloured) pans, stainless steel, aluminium and glass. The applications will be extensive: saucepans, rice cookers, omelette pans, sauté pans, stock and sauce pots, vegetable and fish steamers; with a range of speciality applications, fondue, wok and crêpe pans. Roast and bakeware included casseroles and bake pans.

Merchandise augmentation will include a range of accessories; cook's knives, chopping boards, tools and gadgets, a complete range of storage jars and boxes.

Brands include: Calphalon, Concerto, Brilliant, Traditions, Dualit, Waring, Frabosk, Taylor + Ng. Crosby brands will be introduced where and when possible.

Tableware: A collection of hand-painted pottery and stoneware from well known international sources forms the core range of this merchandise group. It is supported by a range of inexpensive glassware from Spain and glass from Mexico, France and Poland. The tableware group includes jugs, bowls and containers with a range of design appeals, from nostalgic 'fifties' to contemporary styles. Coffee makers; filter, cafetières and percolators are important elements of the range. Oven-to-table ware in terracotta together with a heat and shock resistant white porcelain alternative completes the range.

Merchandise augmentation will include cutlery (five ranges), placemats, napkins and rings, pepper and salt mills.

Brands include: Celina, Bodum, Peter Piper mills, Nancy glassware, Casada-Rainha. Again own brand ranges are to be developed.

Furniture: The purpose of the furniture range is essentially to be a support merchandise range. It is aimed at enhancing the cookware and tableware ranges and in this respect fulfils a visual merchandising role. The three basic materials of pine, handwoven rattan and resin reflect the style and design theme established in the tableware and cookware ranges. By selecting bookcases, tables and other storage type products we can add ambiance to the store format very cost-effectively. The wood range is manufactured to order thereby giving the customer an opportunity to specify dimensions: this strategy is workable due to the fact that the Company commitment is to buy production capacity rather than finished products.

Rattan furniture being sourced from overseas, cannot be flexible in this way. The range is limited to chairs and 2 tables.

The resin based furniture is a range of outdoor tables, stacking chairs, recliners and parasols. This range will be available April/August only and space made available when withdrawn used for wood and rattan.

Merchandise augmentation will be achieved by tableware merchandise augmentation (wood furniture) and by bright cushions and textiles for the summer patio furniture.

Interiors: Many of the items in this range may be considered to be augmentation items for the three other ranges. However, to ensure it has attention by the buying/merchandising group and, more importantly, by customers it is seen as a merchandise group. Comprising rugs, cushions, large basketware, picture frames, table lamps and clocks, pots, vases and planters, paper and dried flowers and seed pods the purpose of interiors is to offer customers ideas for being creative in their own homes and to enhance the visual merchandising in-store.

Homecare: Customers who clearly care about their homes are concerned about maintaining the condition of items in them. Homecare is a range of cleaning and care materials offered with these requirements in mind. Other items included in the product group are a range of plastic bowls, bins, drainers and sink accessories exclusive to Crosby and available in a range of compatible colours. Aprons and other textiles complete the range.

Stock allocation: price points

Low/Medium	15% of stock allocation
Medium/High	65% of stock allocation
High	20% of stock allocation
	100%

17.8   CROSBY CUSTOMER SERVICE STRATEGY

Customer service strategy is planned around:

Service augmentation: facilities. The research suggested that three service offer components would give customer added value and competitive advantage to Crosby. These were identified as:

- Design advice: trained instore consultants that can advise customers on shape and colour coordination during their purchases.
- Wedding list coordination: managing the budget/wedding gift problem together with advising bride and groom as to what their initial requirements are likely to be and using the design advice service to build an ideal assortment within the likely budget constraint. Selections will be 'logged' on computer file and the information will be made available to all Crosby stores.
- Gift wrapping and presentation service: a service that goes beyond a simple gift wrap offer by advising on suitable gifts and gift presentation methods and 'packaging' for specific occasions.

Service augmentation: information. To ensure that customers are given as much information as possible, point-of-sale ticketing includes information concerning:

- product description and application and usage details;
- product required to complete purchase;
- product specification and materials;
- product maintenance instructions;
- product complements and accessories;
- product alternatives (finishes, materials, etc.);
- product delivery details;
- product price.

In addition visual merchandising will offer a style, colour and coordination service (more detail below).

Service intensity. The human resource issues that the customer service strategy imposes concerns the number of staff, their quality and their training programmes. The number of staff will be increased per outlet and emphasis will be placed on ensuring that at least two members of personnel will have some experience and/or training in design related topics.

Staff will undergo regular training in customer care, design and colour coordination, and product knowledge and application.

Customer Service Performance Requirements

Store Category	Staff/Store FTE	Sales/Store Staff 000	Staff Costs % Sales
A	6	£125	13.0
B	4	£109	12.0

17.9   STORE ENVIRONMENT STRATEGY

The store environment strategy is to be structured around:
Visual merchandising: Visual merchandising will have three roles:

- *Customer information and advice*: within which visual merchandising techniques will be used to offer advice to customers concerning the coordination of colours, shapes and textures.
- *Create an ambiance* of style and function within an atmosphere of comfortable, pressure-free helpfulness. It should reflect the store's mood, character, quality, tone and atmosphere to the target customer.
- *Encourage customer purchasing*: by persuading customers to visit all parts of the store, by creating assortment groups that are logically related and in so doing will encourage customers to make purchases of coordinated merchandise items.

By giving visual merchandising these three important responsibilities its use of space should be secondary (within limits) to the effectiveness achieved in creating sales and expanding the transaction value per customer.

Store environment decisions include the location of, and space allocated to, customer service facilities. Space allocated to service facilities is space not available for selling merchandise. Accordingly the overall sales productivity of the store is to be enhanced by the addition of customer service facilities.

Additional locations for Crosby were identified and developed. The criteria for site selection were:

- 'commuter' or provincial town of 100 000/150 000 population.
- Above average Is and Js (ACORN). Ideally one competitor in one or more of the merchandise or service areas.
- High Street location.
- 5000 square feet preferably.
- 3500 square feet minimum.

17.10 CUSTOMER COMMUNICATIONS STRATEGY

The customer communications strategy comprises:

Instore brochures: for each merchandise group and for each customer service facility a four-colour brochure was produced. For the merchandise groups contributions towards the cost of printing brochures were obtained from suppliers.

Instore point-of-sale information: as part of the service augmentation programme detailed point-of-sale ticketing will give a considerable amount of information to customers on product specification and construction, product application and uses alternative finishes, product accessories etc.

Crosby's brochure: a comprehensive brochure describing the Crosby offer is produced and will be distributed in selected parts of the catchment area surrounding each store (the Is and Js).

Showhouse programme: where possible and when mutually acceptable terms could be agreed Crosby merchandise appeared in showhomes in housing developments matching the consumer profile.

A budget for these activities was set at: Year 1 – £250 000 and Year 2 – 200 000 (assumes that Year 1 will bear production costs and that the production material will be used in Year 2.

Customer database: customers and visitors to Crosby stores will be encouraged to give their names and addresses from which a database is to be constructed. The Fleetwood customer database has been reviewed and suitable I and J customers are to be mailed as each Crosby format store opened. They will be added to the Crosby database *only* if they give their names and addresses during a visit to the store.

Crosby Home Shopping Catalogue: Once trading patterns are established a catalogue will be developed featuring merchandise that has established a sales history and can therefore be offered on a continuous basis. The catalogue will also be seen as a means of obtaining customer visits but will be used selectively. More planning is required.

Customer Communications Performance

The effectiveness of the communications programme will be measured by:

- Customer visits
- Customer purchasing visits
- Customer transaction values
- Customer purchasing patterns;
    items purchased
    services used
- Customer awareness of the Crosby format
- Customer perceptions of merchandise and services offers (tracking study programme).

17.11   CROSBY IMPLEMENTATION: SUPPORTING ACTIVITIES

Operations Management

Crosby will have two field operations managers and these will report to the Fleetwood operations director. At the end of year two it is expected that a Crosby operating board will be established. Decisions concerning this development will be made at a later date. The budget for Crosby operations will be included in the overhead budget.

Distribution Services

Existing warehouse facilities will require expansion regardless of Crosby activities. It is intended to use a distribution service company for Crosby storage and transportation. Year one and year two distribution is budgeted at 4.5% of sales for A category stores and 5.5% of sales for B category stores.

Systems Support

In order to maintain high levels of availability and acceptable levels of stock holding an inventory/point of sale system is to be installed. Particular problems with maintaining stock levels have been experienced with product groups largely sourced from overseas. Choice and availability are main sales features of the Crosby merchandise offer and accurate and prompt sales data is required. It is anticipated that a suitable system for Crosby needs in terms of merchandise management and future growth will cost something in the region of £3 to £4.5 million. Clearly this capital investment cannot be made until Crosby has been validated and operated for at least two years. During this period stock levels on fast and medium selling items will be increased to ensure that choice and availability are offered and maintained.

17.12   CROSBY: THE FUTURE (TWELVE MONTHS LATER)

Having operated the Crosby format for twelve months it has proved to be successful thus far and sales and margins targets have been achieved. The question facing Fleetwood are what should it do with the Crosby concept in terms of its future development.

Customer research (see Figure 17.2) suggests that some adjustments could be made but essentially the concept is sound.

Fleetwood consider that Crosby could be expanded to 120 outlets. The returns would improve due to economies of scale, improved buying margins (although these are high at present but a volume effect could have a

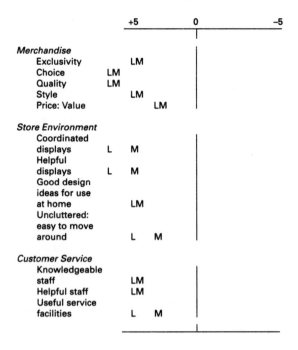

Figure 17.2 Customer perceptions of the Crosby offer characteristics, end of year 2

Table 17.3 Merchandise performance requirements

Merchandise Group	Gross % Margin		Stock-turn	Sales % Participation
	Year 1	Year 2		
Cookware	45	47.5	10	40
Tableware	45	47.5	10	30
Furniture	60	70	6	15
Interiors	42.5	47.5	12	10
Homecare	40	42.5	12	5
Store Type Sales				
	Year 1	Year 2		
A stores	£750 000	£862 500		
	20	25		
B stores	£437 500	£503 125		
	20	25		

large impact on gross profit) and promotional economies. However considerable investment is required. Estimates vary but £20 million, assuming no major property freeholds are purchased, appears to be an average of the estimates.

CROSBY FORECAST SALES, COSTS AND CONTRIBUTION

Year 1

	5000 ft. store		3500 ft. store	
Sales	£750 000		£437 500	
COGS	412 500	GM 45%	251 550	GM 42.5%
Staff	97 500	13% Sales	52 500	12%
Occupancy	112 500	15%	54 700	12.5%
Distribution	33 750	4.5%	24 050	55%
	656 250		382 800	
Contribution per store	93 750		54 700	
Contribution all stores	1875 000 (20)		1094 000 (20)	
Sales Crosby		£23 750 000		
Contribution Crosby		£2 969 000 (12.5%)		

Year 2 (15% growth)

Sales	£862 500		£503 125	
COGS	452 800	GM 47.5%	276 720	GM 45%
Staff	112 125	13% sales	60 375	12%
Occupancy	129 375	15%	62 900	12.5%
Distribution	38 820	4.5%	27 670	5.5%
	733 120		427 665	
Contribution per store	129 380		75 460	
Contribution all stores	3 234 500 (25)		1886 500 (25)	
Sales Crosby		£34 140 625		
Contribution Crosby		£5 121 000 (15%)		

Balance Sheet as at March 31, 1989 (£000)

Fixed Assets

Property	6250	
Equipment	2880	
Vehicles	460	
Less accumulated depreciation	(950)	
		8910

Current Assets
    Stocks   2537
    Debtors   1350
    Cash and liquid   1575
      resources   5642
Current Liabilities
    Creditors   1060
    Bank overdraft   550
    Tax payable   650
    Directors payments due   250   2510

Net working capital   3132
Net assets   12 042
Financed by
    Shareholders investment
        Ordinary capital   7500
        Reserves   4042
      Long term liabilities
        Debenture   500
Capital employed   12 042

Table 17.4   Store environment performance

Store Category	Sales Area	Facilities Area	Merchandise Density	Sales/ sq.ft. p.a.	Occupancy 15% sales p.a.
A	4750	250	£18.75	£150	£22.5 sq.ft.
B	3300	200	£15.8	£125	12% of sales £15.52 sq.ft.

Bibliography

Chapter 1: Understanding How the Business Makes Decisions

COON, D. and WALTERS, D., *Retail Marketing* (Prentice-Hall, 1991).
GILBERT, X. and STREBEL, P., 'Developing Competitive Advantage', in Quinn *et al.*, op. cit. (1988).
HOFER, C.W. and SCHENDEL, D.E., *Strategy Formulation: Analytical Concepts.* (West Publishing Company, 1978).
KOTLER, P., *Marketing Management: Analysis, Planning and Control* (5th edn). Prentice-Hall, 1984).
LEIDECKER, J.K. and BRUNO, A.V., 'Identifying and Using Critical Success Factors', in *Long Range Planning*, 17, 1 (1984).
RUMELT, R., 'The Evaluation of Business Strategy', in Quinn, J.B., Mintzberg, H. and James, R.M. *The Strategy Process: Concepts, Contexts and Cases* (Prentice-Hall, 1988).
WATERMAN, R.H., PETERS, T.J. and PHILLIPS, J.R., 'The 7-S Framework', in Quinn *et al.*, op. cit. (1988).

Chapter 6: Strategic and Operating Economics of the Business

BAUMOL, W.J., PANZAR, J.C. and WILLIY, R.D., *Contestable Markets and the Theory of Industry Structure* (New York, Harcourt, Brace, Jovanovich, 1982).
DAVIES, H., *Managerial Economics* (Pitman, 1991).
LIEBENSTEIN, H., 'Allocative Efficiency Vs X-Efficiency', in *American Economic Review* (1966).
STIGLER, G.J., 'The Economies of Scale', in *Journal of Law and Economics* (1958).

Chapter 7: The Retail Business as a Component in the Supply Chain

COOPER, J., BROWNE, M. and PETERS, M., *European Logistics: Markets, Managements and Strategy* (Blackwell, 1991).
CHRISTOPHER, M., *The Strategy of Distribution Management* (Heinemann, 1989).
FORBES, M., '"Just in Time" Distribution', in *Logistics and Distribution Planning* (1991).
JACK, S., 'Sourcing Under Scrutiny', in *Retail Week* (16 April 1993).
MARTIN, A.J., *Distribution Resource Planning* (Oliver Wright Publications/Prentice-Hall, 1983).
MULLER, E.J., 'Pipeline to Profits', in *Distribution* (September, 1990).
O'MICKY, J.R., *Materials Requirements Planning* (McGraw-Hill, 1975).

Chapter 8: The Retail Business as an International Business

CUNDIFF, E.M. and HILGER, M.T., *Marketing in the International Environment* (Prentice-Hall International Inc., 1988).
JEANNET, J. and HENNESSY, H., *Global Marketing Strategies* (2nd edn) (Houghton Mifflin Co., 1992).
LEVITT, T., 'The Globalisation of Markets', in *Harvard Business Review*, May/June (1983).

MURDOCK, G.P., 'The Common Denominator of Cultures', in Linton, R. (ed), *The Science of Man in the World Crises* (Columbia University Press, 1945).

REYNOLDS, J.I., 'Developing Policy Responses to Cultural Differences', in *Business Horizons*, August (1978).

SALMON, W. and TORDJMAN, A., 'The Internationalisation of Retailing', *International Journal of Retailing*, 4, 2 (1989).

TREADGOLD, A., 'The Emerging Internationalisation of Retailing: Present Status and Future Challenges', in *Irish Marketing Review*, 5, 2 (1991).

WILLIAMS, D.E., 'Motives for Retailer Internationalisation: Their Impact, Structure and Implications', in *Journal of Marketing Management*, 8 (1992).

Chapter 9: An Integrated Approach for Management Decision Making

CYERT, R. and MARCH, J., *Behavioural Theories of the Firm* (Prentice-Hall, 1963).

MAISTER, D.H., 'Centralisation of Inventories and the "Square Root Law"', in *International Journal of Physical Distribution and Materials Management*, 6, 3 (1975).

MYDDLETON, D.R., *Accounting and Financial Decisions* (Longman, 1992).

Chapter 10: Deriving Target Customer Group Characteristics

BUCKLIN, L.P., 'Retail Strategy and the Classification of Consumer Goods', in *Journal of Marketing*, January (1963).

ENGEL, J.F., BLACKWELL, R.D. and MINIARD, P.W., *Consumer Behaviour* (5th edn). (Dryden Press, 1986).

KOTLER, P., op. cit. (1984).

Chapter 11: Interpreting Customer Expectations

URBAN, G.L. and HAUSER, J.R., *Designing and Marketing of New Products* (Prentice-Hall, 1980).

Chapter 12: Allocating Resources to Meet Customer Expectations and Create Added Value for the Customer

BRIMSON, J., 'The Basics of Activity-Based Management', in Drury *et al.*, *Management Accounting Handbook* (Butterworth Heinemann, 1992).

BROMWICH, M., 'Strategic Management Accounting', in Drury *et al.*, op. cit. (1992).

COOPER, R. and KAPLAN, R., *The Design of Cost Management Systems* (Prentice-Hall International, 1991).

DRURY, C., *Management Accounting Handbook* (Butterworth Heinemann, 1992).

HIROMOTO, T., 'Another Hidden Edge – Japanese Management Accounting', in *Harvard Business Review*, July/August (1988).

HOFER, V.W. and SCHENDEL, D., op. cit. (1978).

INNES, J. and MITCHELL, F., 'Activity Based Costing Research', in *Management Accounting (UK)*, May (1990).

KOTLER, P., op. cit. (1984).

LANCASTER, K.J., *Variety, Equity and Efficiency: Product Variety in an Industrial Society* (Columbia University Press, 1979).

LEIDECKER and BRUNO, op. cit. (1984).

PORTER, M., *Competitive Strategy* (Free Press, 1985).

WALKER, M., 'ABC Using Product Attributes', in *Management Accounting (UK)*, October (1991).

WALTERS, D. and WHITE, D., *Retailing Marketing Management* (Macmillan, 1989).

WARD, K., *Strategic Management Accounting* (Butterworth Heinemann, 1992).

WATKINS, A., see BROMWICH M., 'The Case for Strategic Management Accounting; The Role of Accounting Information for Strategy in Competitive Markets' (London School of Economics Working Paper, 1989).

Chapter 13: Customer and Corporate Productivity: Measuring Customer Satisfaction and Corporate Performance

BRINKERHOFF, R.O. and DRESSLER, D.E., 'Productivity Measurement', in *Applied Social Research Methods Series*, vol. 19 (Sage Publications Inc., 1990).

DALRYMPLE, D.J., 'Merchandising Decision Models for Department Stores' (Bureau of Economics and Business Research, Graduate School of Business Administration, Michigan State University, East Lansing, 1966).

DOODY, A.F. and MCCAMMON, B.C., 'High Yield management in the Department Store Field', Parts I and II, in *Department Store Management*, February, April (1969).

HOLMES, G. and SUGDEN, A., *Interpreting Company Reports and Accounts*. (Woodhead Faulkner, 1992).

SWEENY, D.J., 'Improving the Profitability of Retail Merchandise Decisions', in *Journal of Marketing*, January (1973).

Chapter 14: Key Decision Areas: Objectives, Strategy Improving and the Role of Shopping Missions

STYLER, A. and WALTERS, D., *Retailing in a Recession* (unpublished report) (CACI, London, 1991).

Chapter 15: Managing the Implementation Process

ANSOFF, I., *Corporate Strategy* (Penguin, 1970).

KNEE, D. and WALTERS, D., *Strategy in Retailing* (Phillip Allan, 1985).

MCCAMMAN, B.C. and HANMER, W.C., 'A Frame of Reference for Improving Productivity in Distribution', in *Atlanta Economic Review*, September/October (1974).

Index